HOW TO REBUILD THE SMALL-BLOCK MOPAR

WILLIAM BURT

CarTech®

Copyright © 2007 by William Burt

All rights reserved. All text and photographs in this publication are the property of the author, unless otherwise noted or credited. It is unlawful to reproduce – or copy in any way – resell, or redistribute this information without the express written permission of the publisher.

All text, photographs, drawings, and other artwork (hereafter referred to as information) contained in this publication is sold without any warranty as to its usability or performance. In all cases, original manufacturer's recommendations, procedures, and instructions supersede and take precedence over descriptions herein. Specific component design and mechanical procedures – and the qualifications of individual readers – are beyond the control of the publisher, therefore the publisher disclaims all liability, either expressed or implied, for use of the information in this publication. All risk for its use is entirely assumed by the purchaser/user. In no event will CarTech®, Inc., or the author, be liable for any indirect, special, or consequential damages, including but not limited to personal injury or any other damages, arising out of the use or misuse of any information in this publication.

This book is an independent publication, and the author(s) and/or publisher thereof are not in any way associated with, and are not authorized to act on behalf of, any of the manufacturers included in this book. All registered trademarks are the property of their owners. The publisher reserves the right to revise this publication or change its content from time to time without obligation to notify any persons of such revisions or changes.

Edited by: Travis Thompson

SA143P
ISBN-13 978-1-61325-058-7

Printed in USA

CarTech®

6118 Main Street
North Branch, MN 55056
Telephone (651) 277-1200 • (800) 551-4754 • Fax: (651) 277-1203
www.cartechbooks.com

TABLE OF CONTENTS

Acknowledgments		5
Preface		7
Introduction	**What is a Workbench Book?**	8
Chapter 1	**Preparations and Engine Removal**	11
	Manuals and Information	13
	Workspace	14
	Tools	15
	Performance	20
	Pulling the Engine	21
	Unbolting the Bolt-ons	23
Chapter 2	**Disassembly**	29
	Drain Fluids	29
	Remaining Bolt-On Parts	30
	Cylinder-Head Removal	31
	The Bottom End	36
	Disassemble Cylinder Heads	45
Chapter 3	**Cleaning and Inspection**	49
	Media Blasting	49
	Cleaning	50
	Inspecting Each Part	52
Chapter 4	**Machining and Choosing Parts**	69
	Decisions	69
	Choosing a Machine Shop	69
	Block Machining	70
	Crankshaft	76
	Connecting Rods	77
	Balancing	78
	Cylinder-Head Machining	81
	The Right Parts	86

TABLE OF CONTENTS

Chapter 5	**Assembly**	92
	Cam Bearings	93
	Pistons and Pins	95
	Pistons, Rods, and Rings	101
	Freeze Plugs	107
	Screw-In Plugs	109
	Oil-Shaft Bushing	110
	Camshaft	111
	Timing Gear	112
	Oil Pump	113
	Assemble Cylinder Heads	117
	Mounting Cylinder Heads	120
	Head Pins	120
	The Valvetrain	123
	Flat-Tappet Lifters	123
	Lifter Retainers and Guideplates	123
	Pushrods	124
	Rocker Arms	125
	Front Engine Cover	127
	Harmonic Balancer	128
	Oil Pan	129
	Oil-Filter Fitting	131
	Oil-Pump Shaft	131
	Valvecovers	132
	Exhaust Manifolds	132
Chapter 6	**Start-up and Break-in**	134
	Adding Fluids	136
	Fuel System	137
	First Crank	137
	Flat-Tappet Lifter Engines	137
	Roller-Lifter Engines	138
	Ignition Timing	138
	Problems	138
Appendix A	**Source Guide**	139
Appendix B	**Tolerances**	141
Appendix C	**Workbench Worksheets**	142

ACKNOWLEDGMENTS AND PREFACE

I love cars and boats and I have been fortunate in my life that various people have helped me along with my love of the mechanical. The maintenance and massaging of cars, motorcycles, and boats has brought days of joy, hours of frustration, and minutes of true mechanical Zen enlightenment. I have bought one new car in my life (a black 1988 5.0 Mustang GT). I loved and abused the little car. While the purchase brought enjoyment, it paled in comparison with the satisfaction of keeping one of my many jalopies puttering down the road. There is such satisfaction in fixing, building, or modifying something—making it your trusty steed. The following people have taken time over the years and patiently given me free lessons, advice, and knowledge with no hope of ever getting anything out of it (and for the most part they haven't). While much can be learned from reading manuals, without the following people passing on their automotive and marine experience I would be much less the mechanic. So a special thanks to Mack Burt, Lee Thompson, David Magouyrk, Waylon Magouyrk, Danny Peek, Charles Peek, John Swift, Al Harris, Danny Rodriguez, Chris Richards, David Richards, Lou Thurber, and Robby Muth (who didn't really show me anything about cars or boats, but when I was 19 years old he did give me, for free, a Suzuki TS 250 that ran like a top, and that will get your name in a book every time).

Magouyrk Machining and Automotive

While I handled the camera and was the one chained to the computer writing while everyone else was out having fun, this book would not have been possible without the willing assistance of David Magouyrk and the sometimes willing assistance of his brother Waylon. While I am a fair shade-tree mechanic, a book of this scope must be based on the methods of the experienced. David and Waylon were those kids who had taken apart the lawn mower engine (and put it back together) before they started first grade. They made their way through the mechanics of mini-bikes, go-carts, and motorcycles as they grew. Then they graduated to cars. Both decided on machining as a career choice and now, decades later, their machining background is vast. David has worked in everything from precision mold making on conventional mills to running large complex machining centers. Waylon's experience is similar, and he now also teaches machining at our nation's main facility for rebuilding M1 Abrams tanks and other military vehicles. Between them they own and operate Magouyrk Machining and Automotive located in picturesque Ohatchee, Alabama. Here they machine or rebuild just about anything you bring them. On the day we took this picture David was messing around with our little Dodge engine while Waylon was finishing up a build on a large diesel. Beside it is one of the many Magouyrk Racing Engines that leaves the shop. Where building and machining are concerned, the Magouyrks have been there and done that. But that does not stop

ACKNOWLEDGMENTS AND PREFACE

them from keeping their minds open and always looking for better methods. In the racing game, standing still is the same as going backwards. The advice given in this book is based on their years of machining and engine building. That doesn't mean it's the only way, it's just their way, and their way has put many a racecar in victory lane.

Birmingham Piston Warehouse

On more than one occasion in the following text I suggest working with a reputable performance parts house or speed shop when purchasing your parts. Over the years David and Waylon Magouyrk have developed a relationship with the guys at Birmingham Piston Warehouse, part of the Internal Engine Parts Group, in Birmingham, Alabama. It's nice to trade with stores that have stools in front of the counter. It means they don't mind you getting comfortable for a session of question and answer. It also means that the employees look you in the eye when they talk to you and they know that if they steer you wrong they'll get to look you in the eye again, too. This contact with the customer also gives them another advantage. They hear first-hand, from their customers, how different parts perform. Thus their opinion is based on something more than industry media. And this knowledge ranges over a wide array of products. You can leave with a standard kit assembled with reliable stock parts or you can leave with enough performance parts to burn your tires off in a matter of seconds, although it may require a second mortgage. Their contact information is in the back, so if you want to mix a little Southern hospitality with a great deal on parts, give them a call.

David and Waylon Magouyrk of Magouyrk Machining and Automotive. They were a huge help in putting together this book and this engine.

This is the parts counter at Birmingham Piston Warehouse. Finding a quality parts store with a knowledgeable staff is essential for your rebuild project.

Preface

Nobody popped out of the womb knowing how to build an engine. Well, maybe Smokey Yunick and Bobby Allison, but they're about it. The rest of us have to learn. In preparing a manual of this type, its creators are prudent to write to the least informed of the audience. In our case this is a person with no mechanical background who decides that they want to build an engine. I know a college psychology teacher who actually did this over a summer break. He looked like Mr. Magoo and had never turned a wrench in his life, but had always wondered about, as he put it, "the sequence of logical events taking place under the hood which allowed me to propel down the road." So one summer he bought a manual, took his car apart, and successfully put it back together. Thus, for the advanced mechanic, or even the accomplished shade-tree mechanic, some of the information and advice in this book may seem elementary. While it may be tiresome for the more experienced to wade through these bits, they are essential for the other side of the audience—the first-timer. In preparing this manual text I have tried to make it possible for someone who has never opened the hood to be able to successfully (and enjoyably) rebuild their small-block Mopar engine.

This book will guide you through a basic stock rebuild. Throughout the book I have scattered in a few performance options that can be accomplished fairly easily while doing a stock rebuild. Radically engineered performance engines are another matter entirely. If you are looking to build a 700-hp small-block, buy our book and read it for reference, but you will need additional help in achieving your goal. As well as telling you how to build your engine, I will also tell you why you are doing it and exactly what it accomplishes. Thus, when your build is complete, your knowledge of your engine's workings will extend past the nuts and bolts of the operation.

INTRODUCTION

What is a *Workbench* Book?

This is an S-A Design *Workbench* book. It doesn't present a hasty look at small-block Mopar engine building and modification, nor does it give vague advice or only cover the high points. Furthermore, this book doesn't require that you've had previous experience with engine building or a degree in engineering to use it. *This book is a complete reference that shows you **how to rebuild** a small-block Mopar; step-by-step, every step, with nothing left out!* Hundreds of photos guide you through the easy and "tricky" procedures, and photo captions explain exactly where to look for possible problems and how to fix them. This book shows you how to rebuild your engine and ensure that it's working perfectly.

However, this book is more than a "rebuild" manual.

The authors and the editors at S-A Design have packed this book with information about components and accessories, including a wide range of performance tips and modification procedures to improve power and economy—and we didn't stop there. We wanted you to get the same professional results on your first rebuild that the pros get after years of experience. So we've detailed the special components, tools, chemicals, and other accessories you'll need to get the job done right, *the first time*. You'll even find tips that will save you money without compromising "top-notch" results. To round things out, we've included a *Work-Along Sheet* to help you record vital statistics while you work on your engine.

This book isn't meant to replace other books on your bookshelf. (In fact, if you're looking for in-depth information on performance modifications or racing tips, refer to any one of several best-selling S-A Design books, including *Engine Blueprinting, How to Build Big-Inch Mopar Small Blocks, High-Performance New Hemi Builders Guide,* and *How to Install and Use Nitrous Oxide.* (Look inside the front and back covers for ordering information.) The book you're holding is meant to detail, like never before, the "workbench" procedures required to rebuild and assemble your engine—using the same tried and true techniques used by hundreds of professional engine builders—and prepare the finished engine for optimum street or strip performance. If these are your goals, you've got the right book.

Why This Book is Different

While virtually every other performance book is a series of "typical-looking" chapters, this *Workbench* book is quite different. Why did we make it different? The answer is simple: We had to! This book not only helps you become familiar with small-block Mopar engines and the tools and materials you need to work on them, it also shows how to rebuild an engine in your own workshop, step-by-step. This means that it must look different from other books. It must have hundreds of

INTRODUCTION

photos (more than 600!) to guide you through the entire rebuilding process. This book also illustrates many of the performance components, accessories, and upgrades that have been developed for the small-block Mopar engine. This additional information is easy to find and clearly separated from the step-by-step sequences. Through the use of "*Workbench Tips*," icon-labeled photos, and extensive cross-references, this book presents both stock and performance information and keeps each separate and accessible.

Text and Photo Chapters

The text and photo sections are the familiar part of this book. They consist of columns of text combined with photos, drawings, and charts. These familiar-looking pages contain the basic information you'll need to obtain the proper tools and accessories to begin specific building procedures.

Conventional text and photos are the traditional and most familiar way to present information about these wide-ranging topics. However, the best way to show the detailed procedures involved in rebuilding an engine is to show how *with step-by-step photos*.

Step-by-Step Photos and Icons

Each of the step-by-step photo sections includes a sequence of numbered photos and captions that illustrate virtually every operation involved in rebuilding a typical small-block Mopar engine for general street or high-performance use.

As we mentioned, the goal of this book is more than just rebuilding a stock engine. The step-by-step chapters also include many additional photos that show how to install performance or heavy-duty components, how to modify stock components for special applications, or even call attention to assembly steps that are critical to proper operation or safety. To keep these photos separated from the main rebuild sequence, we have labeled them with unique "icons." These symbols represent an idea, and photos marked with icons contain important, specialized information. An icon-labeled step may apply to your engine, in which case you should include the step in your rebuild. On the other hand, it may illustrate a modification that doesn't apply to your specific application; in this case, just skip it and continue with the next photo in the sequence.

Here are some of the icons found in S-A Design *Workbench* books:

Torquing Fasteners—Illustrates a fastener that must be properly tightened with a torque wrench at this point in the rebuild. The torque specs are usually provided in the step.

Special Tool Used—Illustrates the use of a special tool that may be required or can make the job easier (caption with photo will explain further).

Precision Measurement—Illustrates a precision measurement or adjustment that is required at this point in the rebuild.

Important!—Photo indicates a step in the rebuild that is very important for the correct assembly or preparation of components.

Safety Step—Indicates a step in the rebuild that is essential for the safe operation of the engine or to guard the personal safety of the rebuilder.

Critical Inspection—Indicates that a component must be inspected to ensure proper operation of the engine.

Performance Step—Indicates a procedure that applies to only high-performance or racing engines, or details a modification that can improve performance.

Economy Step—Indicates an optional modification or procedure that may improve engine efficiency and fuel economy.

Master Mechanic Tip—Illustrates a step in the rebuild that non-professionals may not know. It may illustrate a shortcut, or a trick to improve reliability, prevent component damage, etc.

INTRODUCTION

Notation Required—Illustrates a point in the rebuild where the reader should write down a particular measurement, size, part number, etc. for later reference.

Save Money—Illustrates a method or alternate method of performing a rebuild step that will save money but still give acceptable results.

The step-by-step photo chapters may include optional steps labeled with icons. This book also includes other optional information that, although it may not be essential for building a specific engine, the reader may find useful. These optional information "packages" are called *Workbench Tips*, and they can be found throughout the book.

Workbench Tips

This book contains *Workbench Tips*. They're easy to spot; look for a box with the "*Workbench Tip*" label at the top containing a group of photos and some text. These tips cover subjects that are generally too short for the text-and-photo chapters but present more information than a single icon-labeled photo. The author and editors selected topics that they felt would be interesting and valuable. Many contain hints that a professional may have discovered after years of work. For example, there are *Workbench Tips* on how to restore damaged threads, how to properly torque fasteners, how to use precision tools, upgrading engine components, sources for unique or special parts, and much more.

The *Workbench Tips* are not presented in a specific order. You can read the *Workbench Tips* one at a time as you progress through the book, you can look up specific *Workbench Tips* at any time, or you can even skip everything else and just read the *Workbench Tips*. However you choose to use *Workbench Tip* information, we hope it will add to your understanding of the small-block Mopar and help you get the most power, economy, and reliability from your engine.

Where to Begin

How to Rebuild the Small-Block Mopar is organized in a sequence that, theoretically, allows you to start at the first chapter and read straight through to the end. When you're finished, you should have a top-quality rebuilt engine. However, one reader may want to focus on the final assembly information in Chapter 5, while another may want information about a performance accessory described in a *Workbench Tip*, and others may be interested in the advice on the tools required for rebuilding, found in Chapter 1. Because of these wide-ranging needs, here are some tips for using this book:

If you're starting from scratch to rebuild a street engine: Start with Chapter 1 and read the whole book, in order.

If you have some experience and would like to assemble an engine from miscellaneous components: Start with Chapter 4 and review important issues that you need to discuss with your machine shop, then continue through the remainder of the book.

For all readers: Review the tables of contents and study any unfamiliar information until it makes sense. Carefully review and study the entire

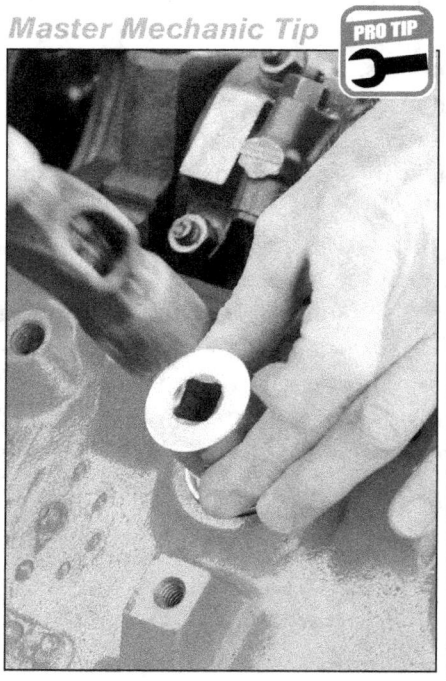

To drive the plugs you can use a special tool, but a large deep-well socket will do just as good a job. Drive the plug into the hole with steady blows.

This is an example of the hundreds of step-by-step photos in this book. The photos will guide you through easy and tricky procedures, while the captions explain exactly what to do, what not to do, and how to avoid problems.

rebuild sequence before you begin your project. The more you understand and practice these techniques, the more you'll benefit from—and enjoy—precision engine building.

Several other S-A Design books contain information that you may find very useful in your engine building project. Some of these books are pictured or mentioned here. If you would like a complete catalog of S-A Design publications, visit our website at www.cartechbooks.com, or call us toll-free at 800-551-4754.

CHAPTER 1

PREPARATIONS AND ENGINE REMOVAL

There are a number of television shows centered on automotive performance these days. From hot-rod building in California to truck performance here in the South, you can sit in your recliner and see a long-term project squashed into an hour or so. It's interesting that while you see great body work, custom upholstery jobs, and tons of aftermarket parts being bolted on, you seldom if ever see anyone building an engine. Inevitably when the chassis is ready and it's time for the next scene, our television comrades roll in a forklift with a big box, crack it open, and stand around "oohing" and "aahing" over a crate engine. Shame on them. There was a time when a true hot rodder knew the inside of his engine as well as the outside of his car. Perhaps it is because of a fear of the inside of an engine, or perhaps it is a need for instant gratification, that crate engines have become so prevalent. It is true that building an engine has many steps, each of which must be done correctly, but it is not beyond the average human being. A long time ago my dad, a mechanical engineer, told me a story about his first job just out of college (Auburn University [War Eagle!]) working at Marshall Space Flight Center. He was paired with an old-timer and sent to find a problem in an electrical junction box.

The engine's long run contained but one radical makeover. The Magnum series of small-block Dodge engines came on the scene in 1992 and 1993. The addition of multiple-point fuel injection and a roller lifter camshaft brought the 318 and 360 into the modern era (the roller cam did come first in 1987).

CHAPTER 1

When the old man opened the box and my dad saw the 50 million wires inside, he was exasperated and remarked, "How in the #*%$ do we check this thing out?" The old man turned and smiled and said, "One wire at a time boy, one wire at a time." That is the way to set your mind for your first rebuild—one wire at a time. Before you start it would be a good idea to read through the entire book so that you can get a feel for the project. But don't let it overwhelm you. You will learn a lot when you take your engine apart and things will begin to make more sense. Just remember, worry about the step that you are on and cross the rest of the bridges when you get there.

There are basically three types of rebuilds that you can do using this book. The first, which is the purpose of this book, is the basic stock rebuild. This is a complete rebuild restoring the engine to its original stock form (with the possible exception of over-sizing the cylinders) using stock components, some new, but others the engine's originals. If you just want your engine to be reliable and get you down the road this is the rebuild for you.

The second type of rebuild is what I will call refined stock. This rebuild is a semi-stock rebuild, adding non-radical performance improvements throughout the engine. Many of the performance improvements that I suggest will not dramatically change your engine on their own but will all add up to improve its efficiency. These are in the category of "as long as you are here." Some will cost a bit more so it is important to work up a pre-build budget before you start (remember, all those little things add up). The worksheet later in the chapter will help accomplish this task.

The third type of rebuild is the "my engine won't run and I need to make it go, doing the minimum amount of work over the shortest possible time and spending the least amount of money." I do not recommend this course of action but I have certainly been there myself and will do what I can to help out. A complete rebuild is best, but you gotta do what you gotta do.

The purpose of this first chapter is to get you to the point where your engine is on a stand ready to be disassembled. Before that can be done the infrastructure needed to complete the process must be present and ready to go. Tools and a workspace must be available, as well as a general plan of what the rebuild should accomplish. Lastly, this chapter will give a few hints and suggestions for getting your engine out of the vehicle and ready to go.

Step One: Before Reading On I Want You To Go Do Something

If you are committed to pulling your engine, we will go to step one before you read any further. Go out and purchase a can of penetrating oil. As is the case with most automotive chemicals, there are a number of choices out there. Over the years I have used purpose-brewed penetrating oil, as well as good old WD-40, and have had success with both. Once you have your penetrating oil in hand, pop the hood of your vehicle and spray every bolt and nut that you can see. If your engine is incredibly nasty you may need to brush some grit away before spraying. If any bolt heads or stud threads are caked with dirt or grime, clean them to the best of your ability. Nuts do not want to move down dirty threads. Pay special

As soon as you decide to pull the engine you might as well start coating the bolts with penetrating oil. There is more than one brand out there that specifically say "penetrating" on the label, but good old WD-40 will also do a good job. If you have the time, hit the bolts and nuts with a good spray every day for a week or so. It gives the oil time to penetrate and will make your teardown go much more smoothly. It's irksome to have a good rhythm going and have to stop for a frozen or broken bolt.

PREPARATIONS AND ENGINE REMOVAL

attention to any bolts that appear rusted or corroded, especially those used to secure the exhaust manifolds to the block and the collector pipes to the manifolds. Repeat the spraying process a couple of times a day. If you are fanatical about an unstained driveway you might want to put a piece of plastic or cardboard under the vehicle because you will get some dripping. If possible, begin this process a couple of days (or weeks) before you pull your engine as it gives the oil more time to penetrate and perform its duty. *Do not skip this step*, as penetrating oil will make your disassembly much easier.

Manuals and Information

Since Mopar put the LA and Magnum series engines in many cars and trucks over many years, it is not possible to give the details for engine accessories, plumbing, and wiring for each version. Thus buying a full vehicle manual on your particular make and model will be helpful. The three options suggested below will cover the removal and reinstallation of most parts of your vehicle from bumper to bumper. For general information at a low price I've been partial to Haynes manuals over the years but some prefer Chilton, which also publishes a full line of manuals. Most auto-parts stores will either have or be able to get you either of these. A wise purchase is a factory manual. These are usually year specific and will relate to one year's production run instead of covering multiple years like the Haynes and Chilton manuals. Your chances of finding a wiring diagram that matches the one in your vehicle are much better with the factory manual. They are more expensive than Haynes or Chilton manuals but are usually well worth the money. The other source of information is your local network of car

---

Differences Between Early LA and Later Magnum Engines

WORKBENCH TIP

While the basics are pretty much the same on all LA and Magnum small-block engines, there are some subtle—and important—differences. These differences are mentioned in the steps throughout the book, but this sidebar will give a quick view of the significant differences.

Blocks

If a replacement block is needed, make sure you get the correct block for your engine. Early LA blocks are not completely interchangeable with later LA blocks and Magnum blocks.
- LA blocks do not have the crank trigger mounting points on the back of the passenger side of the block.
- Dakota pickups have unique motor mounts.
- Early LA blocks (prior to 1987) will not interchange with 1987 to 1992 LA engines or Magnum blocks since they use flat-tappet lifters, not roller lifters like the later model blocks.

Cylinder Heads

LA cylinder heads have rocker arms that mount on a rocker shaft, while Magnum engines have rocker arms that are individually bolted on to the heads.

Magnum heads use 8-mm valve guides while LA heads use 3/8-inch valve guides.

Other

The roller lifter camshaft and throttle body fuel injection was introduced in 1987 on the LA.

Different roller camshafts and multiple-point fuel injection were introduced on the Magnum engines.

The LA 360 is an externally balanced engine, where some of the balancing is done by using a special damper and flywheel or torque converter that is out of balance by design. Don't mix and match these components on other engines since the engine balance takes these components into account.

The Magnum 5.9L engine is similar except that the imbalance of these components is less, and the counter balance on the back is on the flex plate instead of the torque converter.

HOW TO REBUILD THE SMALL-BLOCK MOPAR

CHAPTER 1

guys. Most communities have enough car enthusiasts to produce weekend cruises. Around my neck of the woods there are three or four gatherings within an hour's drive on every Saturday night during the spring, summer, and fall. They are usually at a large parking lot with the cars parked by type or manufacturer. Make your way to the Mopar guys and mill around meeting people. This can be a great source for used parts and machining connections, as well as endless pontification and suspect advice.

Workspace

"Billy's Home Garage" halfway between going up and coming down. Not everyone has a large, well-equipped shop, and over the years I have seen some incredibly nice hot rods that were put together in a one-bay garage much like this one.

You will need two workspaces to complete your project. The first one is where you park your vehicle so that you can remove, and later replace, your engine. It is imperative to get your vehicle on a flat, smooth piece of concrete to pull the engine. I've worked in hot apartment parking lots, cold gravel driveways, and weedy bug-infested side yards. When I was about 13, I watched my cousin pull a 426 Hemi from a Charger using a limb on a big oak tree in his front yard. I recommend none of the above but I know you'll do what you're going to do so I implore you—*be careful!* Engines and cars show no mercy when they fall on you. Jack stands cannot properly support a car on uneven surfaces, and if you hang an engine on something too weak it will come down in a hurry, and if you are under it, it will not care. So get your vehicle on a flat piece of smooth concrete where you can get the engine out safely.

The second workspace you will need is a place to disassemble and reassemble the engine. Really, you don't need all that much space but as always—more is better. One of the million stories I heard when doing NASCAR books was of Bobby Allison, back in the good old days, rebuilding

WORKBENCH TIP

A Little Bit of LA History

The 318, 340, and 360-ci engines were the backbone of the engine line coded "LA" by the factory. The first LA engine was a 273-ci unit introduced in 1964. The new LA engines would be the replacements for the A line of engines, which was produced from 1955 to 1966. The big improvements that the LA engines offered over the A engines was size and weight. The LA engine was substantially lighter, about 50 lbs, and thus the engine line was dubbed the LA, short for "light A." The engines were also smaller, as well, which meant that they could be offered in some of the small-body platforms offered by the Mopar trio. The LA engines used some internal components of the A engines but the heads and valvetrain were very different. The 1964 LA 273 V-8 had a cylinder bore of 3.63 inches and a stroke of 3.31 inches. The car had a 2-barrel carburetor, and produced about 180 gross hp. Within a couple of years the engine was putting out up to 275 hp when ordered with a performance option. The 273 stood alone in the LA lineup until 1967 when the 318 was introduced. The 318 had the same 3.31-inch stroke as the 273 but the bore was increased to 3.91 inches. The 340 followed the 318 into production the next year (1968). Like the 273 and 318, the 340 had a stroke of 3.31 in but the bore was again increased, this time to 4.04 in, to achieve the increase in displacement. Three years later, in 1971, the 360 was put into production. To get the 20 more cubic inches, the LA's stroke was increased for the first time. The 360's stroke was stretched to 3.58 inches and the bore was an even 4.00. The lifespan of the 273 and 340 was short. The 273 was discontinued in 1969 and the 340 in 1973, giving both engines a five-year production run. But the 318 and 360 became legendary. These two engines produced the vast majority of Mopar's V-8 HP for well over 30 years. The Magnum 5.2L (318) and 5.9L (360) were both used in the market until 2002 (a few 360s were installed in trucks in early 2003 in order to deplete the inventory).

PREPARATIONS AND ENGINE REMOVAL

an engine in his hotel room the night before a race. A well-organized single-bay garage will provide plenty of space for a rebuild as long as your vehicle is not in there with it.

During a rebuild it's nice to have space to spread things out. A thick piece of plywood on a couple of sawhorses it is the cheapest way to get some space, and it is easily stored when the project is finished and the garage again becomes a place to store a car.

A workbench or table will help when laying out and organizing parts. If you don't have one, an old door on a couple of sawhorses will suffice. It will be important to keep things off the ground and to try to avoid dirt contamination during the rebuild. If you are careful you can rebuild an engine making very little mess. Keep in mind that many heavy-duty cleaning products have very stout fumes that can travel impressive distances. If you bring an old dirty engine into the basement for cleaning, and that's where your air-conditioning return is located, you may fill your entire house with shop fumes.

Tools

If you already have a well-prepared shop, glance through the lists that follow and make sure that you either have or can borrow everything listed. If this is the first such project that you are attempting and have a meager tool collection, then read on.

Whether it's a rebuild manual or the assembly instructions for a bike that you are putting together for your kid on Christmas Eve, the beginning of all such works contains a list of things you will need. If you are a tool nut and can afford it, chase down that Mac or Snap-on truck and fill up your trunk with everything you may need and some things you don't. Mac and Snap-on make great tools. They seldom break and feel soooo good in your hand. But for the budget-restrained home builder there is a much more practical approach. It begins with a bit of philosophy. Never buy a tool until you need it. It may also make sense to rent some highly specialized, expensive tools. When you do need one, buy a good one and take care of it. I have owned a few high-end hand tools in my day and never had a complaint. But for the money, availability, and guarantee, it is hard to beat Craftsman. A good set of wrenches and sockets can be purchased at a very reasonable price and, if you watch the papers, are often put on sale. I have predominantly used Craftsman tools for years and have very seldom experienced failures. The couple of times I did have a problem were when sockets split when I was working on an extremely stubborn

Your rebuild will include many common tools. Some you will either have or can easily buy. Others will be well beyond your budget. Everything from a straight edge to a complete machine shop will be needed to properly whip an engine back into shape. It is important to weigh what a tool will cost against what it costs to have someone else do it. If this is likely to be your only engine rebuild you may want to sub out more operations. Don't forget to include the tools that you don't have in your budget.

HOW TO REBUILD THE SMALL-BLOCK MOPAR

bolt, and I could not really complain because considering what I was doing to it, if I was the socket I'd have broken, too. This brings up the other benefit of Craftsman tools. Sears stores are plentiful, and if a tool breaks a quick trip to the store will get you a free replacement on most hand tools. Of course, Snap-on and Mac guarantee their tools as well, but their truck is a lot harder to find on Saturday afternoon, while the Sears store doesn't move. There are many other brands sold at many other national retailers, and I am sure some are very good. Both of our national impersonal mega-hardware stores now have their own brands of hand tools, but with the longevity of my Craftsman tools I have had no need to try them out. Besides, it takes a half an hour for them to find someone who knows what a nail, is so I shudder to think how long it would take them to exchange a tool. Another rule of tools is that the more force used, and the more stress a tool will be put under, the higher the quality should be. If you don't believe me, wait until you have a cheap wrench break and you ram your knuckles full force into that sharp little bracket that is welded onto the frame. When it happens, the extra price for a reliable tool suddenly seems very reasonable. On the other hand, if you need a small pair of needle-nose pliers for nothing more than to retrieve a nut that fell in a hole, a cheap pair will do just fine.

Required Tools

Tools for the rebuild job can be broken down into two groups. The first group is tools that you have to buy. You cannot do the job without them and they will be handy to have around after the project is finished. The second group is tools that are required at specific times in the rebuild process and are often fairly expensive. If it is possible to borrow them you will be just fine. If you don't have a friend with a really well equipped shop, many auto parts stores have tool-loaning services. There are processes requiring special tools that you may elect to have your machine shop do. The cost of the operation on this engine may be much less than the cost of the tool. If you are starting from scratch your best move is to the Sears store. A fairly complete set of wrenches and sockets can be had for less than a couple of hundred bucks and will last a lifetime. A good set of combination wrenches has both open-ends and box-ends. When using sockets I greatly prefer the six-point to the 12-point. This designation is based on the number of sides and points where the socket fits to the nut or bolt. The six-point provides a much better seat against the bolt. Buy a set with 1/4-inch, 3/8-inch, and 1/2-inch drives. The 1/4-inch drives are good for light duty, the 3/8-inch for medium duty, and the 1/2-inch for heavy torque applications. One type of wrench that is not included in some sets is a line wrench. This is a boxed wrench with an opening in the end. It's used to loosen and tighten fittings that are usually brass or aluminum alloy and are susceptible to deformation, especially if open-end wrenches or pliers are used. Sears can also set you up with screwdrivers, pliers, and just about all of the other tools listed below.

Tools Required For Older Model Engines (Pre-Metric)

- Torque wrench
- 1/2-inch-drive ratchet
- Set of 1/2-inch-drive extensions
- Set of 1/2-inch-drive, six-point impact sockets

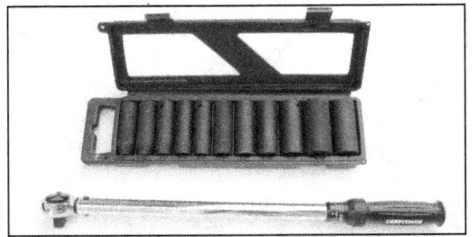

An accurate torque wrench will be a necessity. A set of 1/2-inch-drive impact sockets will make a good companion for your torque wrench and, if you opt for air tools, is also excellent for use with a 1/2-inch-drive impact wrench.

- 1/4-inch-drive ratchet
- Set of 1/4-inch-drive extensions
- 1/4-inch-drive swivel adapter
- Set of 1/4-inch-drive, six-point standard-well sockets, size 1/8 inh to 1/2 inch
- Set of 1/4-inch-drive, six-point deep-well sockets, size 1/8 inch to 1/2 inch
- 3/8-inch-drive ratchet
- Set of 3/8-inch-drive extensions
- 3/8-inch-drive swivel adapter

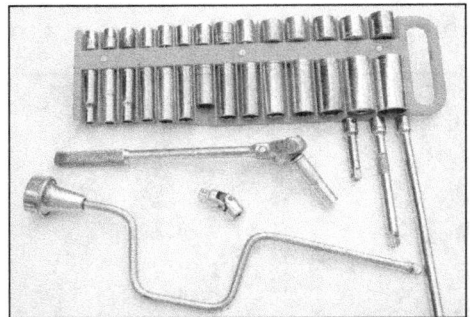

The trusty 3/8-inch socket will be your constant companion. A speed wrench will help with some jobs (especially if you are working without air tools), as will a ratchet with a tilting head. I've had this one (made by SKTools) for years and swear by it. A few extensions will be necessary, and a swivel joint will also come in handy. You might also consider investing in one of these magnetic trays to keep your sockets corralled.

PREPARATIONS AND ENGINE REMOVAL

- Set of 3/8-inch-drive, six-point standard-well sockets, size 3/8 inch to 1 inh
- Set of 3/8-inch-drive, six-point deep-well sockets, size 3/8 inch to 1 inch
- Set of quality flat-head screwdrivers
- Set of quality Phillips-head screwdrivers

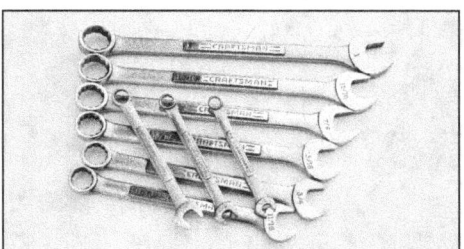

A set of combination wrenches (size 1/4 inch to 1-1/4 inch) is also a mainstay and will need to be purchased. If you are working on an older car, standard sizes will suffice, but if you are working on a later model it will be necessary to have both standard and metric. For some reason the geniuses in Detroit still cannot decide whether to go with standard or metric, so we have both on the same car.

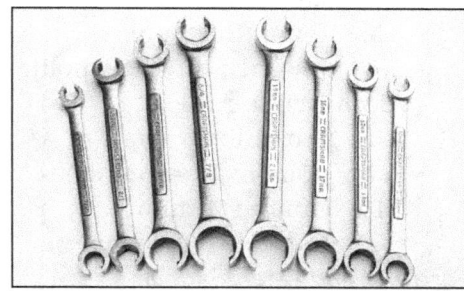

A smart purchase is a set of line wrenches (3/8 inch to 7/8 inch). They are so called because they are perfect for loosening fittings on fuel, transmission, and brake lines. They offer almost as much security as a box wrench (impossible to use on a line fitting) and much more than open-end or adjustable wrenches. One problem with a fitting and you will wish you had bought these.

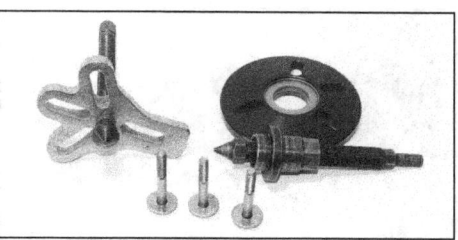

A puller will be needed for removing the harmonic balancer. The most common, and least expensive, type is on the left, while the type of puller on the right is a bit higher in price. It's worth it as this puller can also be used to press the balancer back on during reassembly.

Square-tip-drive tools will be necessary to remove threaded plugs in the block.

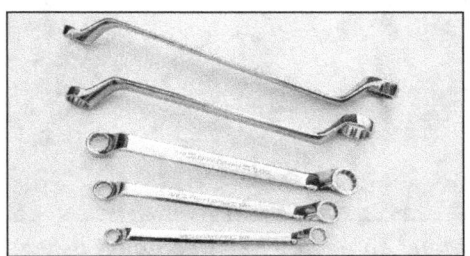

A set of these offset box wrenches is a nice addition. They are often able to reach bolt heads or nuts that are difficult to get a flat wrench on.

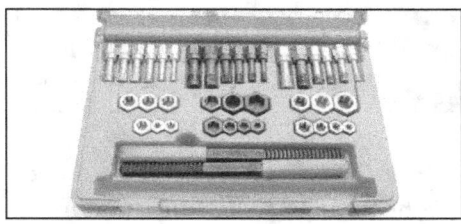

Craftsman makes these thread-chasing tools at a very reasonable price. It will be very handy to be able to clean up threads in the block and heads and on bolts and nuts themselves. Reassembling your engine will be much more pleasurable if everything threads together without a fuss.

I walked by these little ratcheting wrenches for years rolling my eyes. Then somebody gave me a set for Christmas and I find them in constant use. They are not made for heavy torquing (or un-torquing) but are a great time saver in long-thread situations.

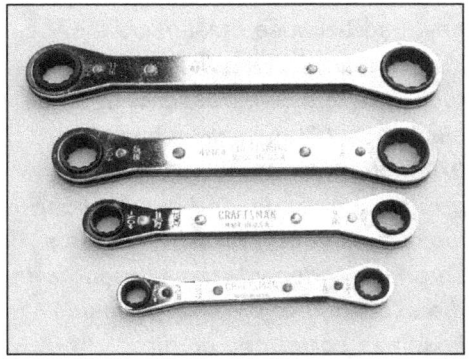

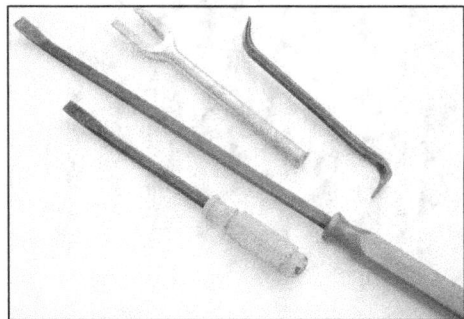

A couple of pry bars and one of those huge screwdrivers can come in mighty handy when manipulating the engine during removal and installation, as well as when setting belt tension on older models when installing accessories

---

HOW TO REBUILD THE SMALL-BLOCK MOPAR

CHAPTER 1

A variety of hammers will be useful during your rebuild. The small hammer is a $1.99 discount-bin special and is used for light tapping. The middle hammer has both a polyurethane and a rubber striking head. It's great for whacking on things that you do not want to mar or damage. The third hammer is helpful when you don't care so much about destruction and really want to smash something.

For Newer Model Engines (Post-Metric)

Everything listed above plus:
- Set of 3/8-inch-drive, six-point standard-well sockets, size 10 mm to 28 mm
- Set of 3/8-inch-drive, six-point deep-well sockets, size 10 mm to 28 mm
- Set of combination wrenches, size 6 mm to 24 mm

For 1992 and Later Magnum Multi-port Fuel-injected Engines

Everything listed above plus:

Important!

For 1992-and-later fuel-injected engines, a special tool will be needed to disconnect the high-pressure fuel line from the manifold that feeds the fuel to the injectors. Most parts stores will have these little plastic disconnect tools. This entire set, which handles line diameters from 1/4 to 3/4 inch, was only $12.00. Do not try to disconnect the fuel rail from the lines without one of these tools as you will likely damage the fitting and end up spending far more than the price of the special tool on replacement parts. You can disconnect the fuel runners and leave them attached when the engine comes out, so you may want to wait on this one until you decide your course.

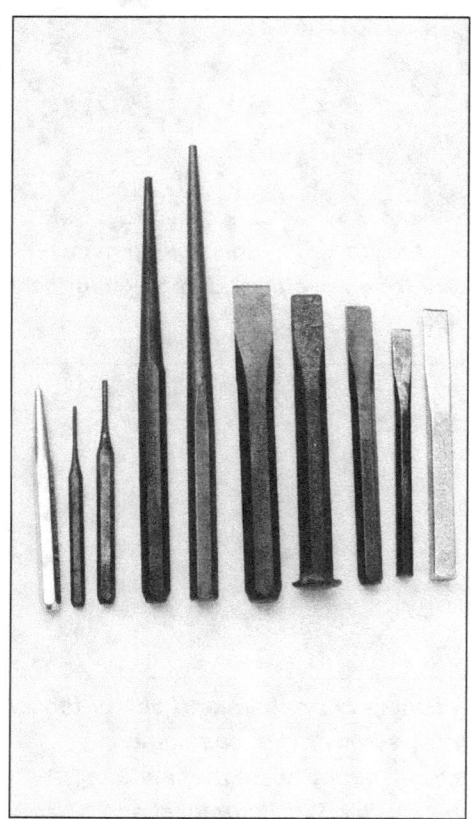

A set of chisels and drifts will be necessary during a couple of operations.

Many an engine has been built using only hand tools, but air tools are sure nice. For this project I bought a loss-leader item from one of those mega-home stores that are okay as long as you don't have to ask anyone anything because most likely they don't know what a bolt is. Anyway, they had this compressor with an air hose, 1/2-inch-drive impact, 3/8-inch-drive ratchet, air hammer, grinder, air nozzle, and a very cheap-looking paint gun for $300. It has a surprisingly decent warranty, and with the exception of the cheap leaking hose has performed admirably.

PREPARATIONS AND ENGINE REMOVAL

You will have to get under your car or truck during this project, so unless you have a lift, a jack and jack stands are a must. The jack that came in your car might be enough to change a tire, but I strongly suggest a small roll-around hydraulic jack. Regardless, jack stands are a must. Never get under a car that is not supported by a good set of properly placed jack stands.

To keep your floor clean and to properly contain waste fluids, a good drain pan will be needed. Any leakproof tub will suffice as a drain pan, but a unit like this one is very handy and quite inexpensive. This type of pan has a few distinct advantages. First, if you drop the drain plug it will not fall to the bottom of the pan. Second, when removing the pan from under the vehicle it is far less likely to slosh and spill. The side spout makes it easy to transfer the fluid into a container for proper disposal without making a mess.

While I've seen a few engines lifted with a come-along and a thick oak branch, the preferred method of lifting the engine will be with an engine hoist. A decent engine hoist will probably set you back a couple hundred bucks. Since they are relatively expensive and will only be needed when taking the engine in and out, the hoist is a great item to try to borrow or rent.

If you can borrow an engine stand, do so, but if not, bite the bullet and buy one. Many an engine has been built on the shop floor, but a stand will greatly eliminate the possibility of damaging the engine, getting dirt in the engine, and developing a sore back. A decent engine stand like this one can be picked up for around a hundred bucks, but, as this photo illustrates, it may be worth it to pay a bit more and get one with a catch tray.

Parts

If you're going to the effort to take it all apart, you might as well invest in some quality parts for when it all goes back together. At the least you will be buying timing gear, an oil pump, rings (and pistons if you oversize), main bearings, rod bearings, and gaskets. I went ahead and added fresh lifters and valves.

Regardless of the complexity of your rebuild, you will have to purchase some quantity of parts. For the basic, thorough engine rebuild, an engine kit is the way to go. Depending on your supplier, different kits may include different parts. The minimum purchase possible would be bearings, rings, and gaskets, re-using the rest of the engine's components. Other kits may include pistons, valves, an oil pump, valvesprings, a camshaft, and lifters. Make sure you know the exact contents of a kit before you purchase it. Kits are available from both local and national parts houses. Both sources can be adequate, but I suggest you consider the local shop where you can pull a stool up to the counter and have a talk. Other parts can be purchased piecemeal in the same manner.

This will inevitably lead to the price-vs.-quality question. Often at the parts store you will be given more than one price for the same part. The first may be a house brand with a 90-day warranty and the lowest price. The next may be a house brand with a lifetime warranty, and the third a premium brand (which probably has stickers on a bunch of race cars) with a lifetime warranty.

Some swear that the premium brand is the best. Others claim the parts are the same—it's the warranty and the premium brand's advertising budget that is the difference in cost. In this matter you will have to make up your own mind. I have used both low-priced house brands and high-priced premium brands from time to time and have truthfully had few problems with either.

My theory often revolves around how difficult the part is to replace later. In other words, I'm much more likely to buy a cheap alternator than cheap pistons. My recommendation on parts purchasing begins like my recommendation on tool purchasing—don't buy something until you need it. If you have an unknown problem, and begin tearing your engine apart and find that you have a cylinder-head problem, you may elect to leave the bottom end alone. If you find you have a bottom-end problem, you might want to leave the heads alone. If you are truly "building" the engine, then the engine kit is the best bet, but don't buy it until machining is complete. It is only then that you will truly know what you will need. If you buy a kit with .020 oversized pistons and the block ends up having to be bored to .030, then you have purchased the wrong stuff.

If you are going for what is basically a stock rebuild and are operating the engine under normal conditions, then the stock-grade parts you will get in the average engine kit will be just fine. High-dollar performance parts may be stronger (and will be more expensive), but if you are not operating your engine at high performance levels then you are gaining nothing. Just the same, if you are attempting to build a 318 that puts out as much HP as a 747, then you better buy the strongest parts you can find and have the checkbook to back it up. It is quite possible to rebuild two small-blocks and have $1,000 in one of them and $30,000 in the other. The final tally all depends on parts and machining choices. They will both be put together pretty much the same way. There are a few suppliers listed in the back that can both supply parts and service. Individual parts selections will be covered in more depth in Chapter 4.

Performance

After bringing up a $30,000 engine it's probably time to bring up the "P" word—Performance. Throughout the book there are some options that would fall under the category of performance improvements. Just remember that performance is relative. I'm at the stage of life where I'm getting old and worn out, so a performance engine for me has become one that gets excellent mileage, runs smoothly, and always cranks. When I was young and full of energy, performance meant HP output and nothing else. Mill off that choke, put a barely streetable cam in it, bolt on a set of straight pipes, and I was happy. Thus your performance engine may differ from your neighbor's. If you are building a 318 that will go in a truck used to pull a horse trailer, your definition of performance will be quite different from if you are building a 340 for a street rod for weekend cruises and amateur performance events. It just depends on what you need and what you want.

In truth, the concepts of engine engineering that will make an engine get better mileage and/or will make one more powerful are related. When dealing with a defined displacement, in our case 318, 340, or 360 ci, regular pump gas, and normal aspiration (no turbo or supercharger), the performance level for an engine will hinge mainly on the engine's compression, its ability to breathe, and the weight and amount of friction of the internal components. Thousands of man-hours and millions of dollars have been spent over the years figuring out how to massage these areas in order to make a small-block engine more powerful. And the search continues. The NASCAR guys run old-technology small-block engines that have been endlessly massaged. Although they run higher compression (12:1) than is practical on the street, they have a power output in the 800-hp range—all with a good old 4-barrel carburetor and solid lifters.

The weight of the engine components is pretty straightforward. You can do a curl with a 1-lb weight faster than you can do a curl with a 5-lb weight and use less energy doing it. Likewise, a lighter connecting rod or valve will move faster and will require less energy to make it do so. Friction includes how freely the connected parts turn where they are joined, as well as their aerodynamic and hydrodynamic attributes. Remember, the crankshaft is turning at tremendous speeds, so how it cuts through air and the oil in the bottom of the pan affects power. The other end of the equation, how well the engine breathes, refers to how much fuel and air you can get into the cylinder, how completely you can burn it, and how efficiently you can get exhaust out. There are a number of ways to do this. The intake runners of the intake manifold can be machined to perfectly match the ports in the cylinder heads. Likewise the exhaust manifolds, or headers' runners and the cylinder heads' exhaust ports, can be matched. Cylinder-head performance upgrades can include larger valves, special machining of the combustion chamber, and of course a cam that will open the valves farther and/or hold them open longer. Only after this has been done can a big old carburetor be mounted to dump more fuel into the engine.

Just remember that there are compromises to be made everywhere. Often the more HP an engine produces the less streetable it becomes. You may dream of an engine that turns 8,000 rpm, puts out 700 hp, and has a cam that thumps like a forge press while sitting at a red light. There's certainly nothing wrong with that, but if you have to drive the beast to work every day it may grow tiresome. If you are a relatively inexperienced builder and you are seriously considering major performance options, find a couple of good performance shops with the stools at the counter and have some good, long talks. Performance engines are balanced, not only weight-wise but engineering-wise as well. If you throw a huge carburetor on an otherwise stock engine you will be giving the engine more fuel than it can handle, which will actually hurt performance. Building a hot-rod small-block requires research and thought as well as money. This book is not a performance rebuild book, as that is a science of its own. However, I will offer some common performance suggestions that can be easily accomplished during a typical rebuild and will still allow a streetable engine.

If you are building (or rebuilding) your dream car, maybe you want to throw on a set of aluminum cylinder heads with big valves, a radical cam, and a high-rise intake. This brings me to the one irrefutable fundamental law of automotive performance. Speed costs—now how fast do you want to go? Leaving out the cost of tools, a 318 that's not too far gone can be built back to stock condition for about $1,000. This number includes a $400 budget for parts and a $600 budget for machining (you provide the assembly labor). The previously mentioned set of performance aluminum heads will most likely run you about $1,500. Things will add up quickly so do your addition before you order to make sure that your desires and wallet are matched.

Pulling the Engine

Depending on your engine's external condition, it may be a good idea to hit it with some degreaser and a hosepipe before beginning the extraction. A bit of cleaning will make the teardown a bit easier and will allow your wrenches to fit more securely on nuts and bolt heads. It's easy to get caught up in taking things apart. It can go quickly and you feel that you are getting a lot done. But there is a peril—putting everything back together. From the first time you pop the hood and begin the project it is prudent to proceed in an orderly fashion, to methodically tag everything that is taken off, and mark appropriate positions when necessary. Granted, your vehicle has only one radiator and it is pretty obvious where and how it goes back, but what about the radiator bolts? If you throw everything into one bucket how will you tell the radiator bolts from all of the other bolts you will be removing? Unless you have a remarkable memory, you will spend A LOT of extra time figuring out what goes where.

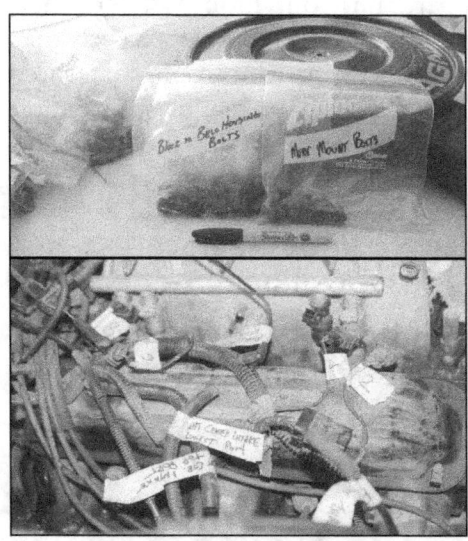

This $5 purchase will save more time and frustration than anything else. Unless you are intimately familiar with the model vehicle that you are working on, it is wise to get some bags, a roll of masking tape, and a Sharpie marker and mark and label all of the components that you remove during the project. Marking everything will slow down the disassembly process a bit, but will really speed up the reinstallation process and cut out lots of frustration as well.

Thus the first tools you will need are a roll of masking tape, a Sharpie marker, and a couple of boxes of Ziploc plastic bags. When something comes out of the car, bag it and tag it. It takes a bit longer but when you are installing your newly rebuilt engine you will make up the time tenfold by not having to figure out what goes where. Set the bagged parts and pieces aside for cleaning and inspection. Unless you are an experienced mechanic (and you probably wouldn't be buying this book if you were) it is a good idea to mark each side of electrical connections that must be taken apart. It all seems so logical when you pull it apart, but four months later when you are finishing the project that you told your wife would take three weeks, you will likely have forgotten most of what you thought you would be able to remember.

Hood Removal– Optional Step

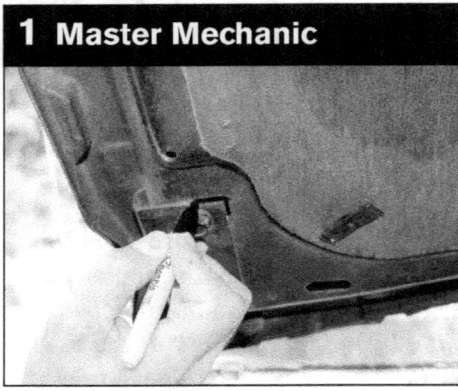

If you elect to remove your hood to pull the engine, you might want to mark the hood hinge positions before unbolting it. These marks will be very helpful in aligning the hood when it is reinstalled.

This step is not always necessary but for the effort involved can be worth the time. By removing the hood, the rear of the engine is more accessible and the likelihood of hitting your head is decreased significantly. Most hoods can be taken off by removing the bolts that attach the hood to the hood brackets. On later-model cars the hood-support device must also be removed.

There are a couple of tips that should be kept in mind when removing a hood. First off—mark the location where the hinge meets the hood. The connection points are slotted to allow the hood's fit to be adjusted. Taking a couple of minutes to mark the hood's location will save much time when the hood is put back on the vehicle. The other thing to keep in mind is that hood removal is a very difficult one-man job. In fact, without an overhead lift system it is close to impossible. The ideal number for hood removal is three—one to remove the bolts and two, one on each side, to hold the hood. This will be a step where talking a couple of friends or neighbors into helping will be of benefit. Once it's off, throw an old blanket over the hood to protect it and find a nice, safe place to lean it until the project is complete.

Draining Fluids

With the battery out and the airbags unarmed (if applicable) it's time to drain the oil and coolant from the engine. Drain the oil by removing the drain plug located on the bottom of the oil pan.

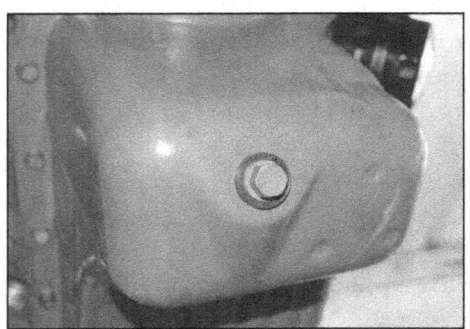

Before pulling the engine, drain the oil by removing the drain plug on the bottom of the oil pan.

The oil can be drained into a pan and then stored (I use old laundry detergent bottles) for recycling. Once the oil has drained, replace the drain plug. With the cooling system cold, opening the petcock valve located at the bottom of the radiator can drain much of the coolant. Over the years these have changed in design. The older ones are valved with a metal wing-nut-type actuator. Newer models may feature a plastic bolt that relies on an O-ring to form a seal. With the new type, unscrew it counterclockwise and pull. If you have one of the older types, twist the wing nut counterclockwise to open the valve. If one of these units has not been opened in years, it may be "frozen" to some degree. First, try to open the valve by hand. If the wing nut does not turn by hand a pair of pliers can be used to gain leverage—but *be careful*. When you try to open it, don't force it. Simply apply a small amount of even pressure. Petcocks are delicate bits of equipment and the worst thing that can happen at this point is that you deform the valve or rip the radiator where the valve is welded in. If the valve does function, the coolant will come out the center of the valve and if you are under the car and aren't ready for it you can get a face full, so safety glasses are prudent. With the drain open and a catch pan underneath, remove the radiator cap on the top of the radiator to relieve vacuum, allowing the coolant to exit more efficiently. When the draining ceases, hand tighten the wing nut on the petcock. *Never* attempt to remove the coolant when hot, warm, or anything but cold. Severe burning and blindness can result. If the valve will not open easily and you are fearful of disaster, it is time for Plan B.

PREPARATIONS AND ENGINE REMOVAL

This is an old-style radiator petcock. The wings of the opener are turned counterclockwise (lefty loosey) to open the valve. When the petcock valve is opened the coolant will flow through the center tube.

Later-model radiators will most likely have a plastic bolt like this one. This bolt can be taken completely out to drain the fluid. Be careful when replacing it in the radiator as the plastic threads are easy to damage if you cross-thread them.

Alternate Method

The coolant can be removed a couple of other ways, but they may not be quite as easy. The sticking petcock can be addressed later with the engine and radiator out. The petcock drains the coolant from the radiator at the bottom and the same can be accomplished by disconnecting the lower radiator hose. If the hose clamp is removed and the hose detached (or cut away) the coolant will drain. The problem is that it will come out in a gushing stream, both out of the radiator and out of the hose. It will be messy, and only the experienced will not be soaked with coolant. Another way is to cut or drill a small hole in the bottom of the lower radiator hose, which will be replaced anyway. This will allow for more controlled draining. If you do this, be sure to select a spot a couple of inches back from the hose clamp to clear the radiator's mounting tube for the hose.

Be responsible and collect your used fluids. Use some old jugs to store them until you can take them to a recycling center. Don't dump the waste fluids on the ground or into the sewer, as it plays havoc with water treatment, is bad for the environment, and gives the home mechanic a bad reputation.

Many auto-parts stores accept old oil and coolant, as do many recycling centers and municipal landfills. Do not pour the oil down the drain or onto the ground. You will probably be making multiple trips to the parts store before the project is completed so just take it along and dispose of it responsibly.

Unbolting the Bolt-ons

As this book deals with an engine that came in a very long list of vehicles, it is impossible to cover all of the individual differences in all models. As I mentioned before, a vehicle manual is a good idea. In place of specific instructions, the following section should help those who have not been through the engine-removal process. Before pulling the engine and beginning the rebuild, it will be necessary to remove all belts, hoses, wiring, and bolt-on components such as the alternator, power-steering pump, air-conditioning compressor, and distributor. This is a good time to make a small mark on the distributor relative to the block and/or manifold so that when you put it back in you'll be in the ballpark, timing-wise. Since the block's probably going to be cleaned, a pin-punch or chisel should be used, since hot-tanking will remove paint or Sharpie marks. I follow the onion process. I peel away from the outside in. As a general rule I proceed in the following order. This order may not be exactly applicable to your model, but it should be close.

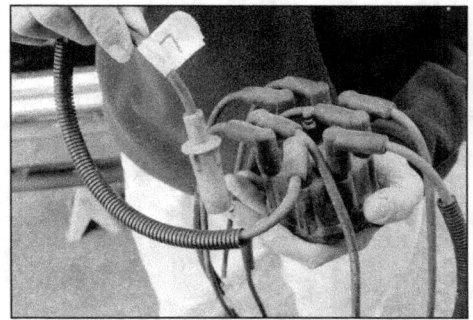

Disconnect the plug wires from the spark plugs and then remove the distributor cap with the wires still attached. I suggest a new distributor cap. The wires can be transferred one at a time from the old cap making it easy to figure out what length wire goes where.

I begin at the top of the engine, first removing the air-cleaner housing and any attached ducting, which is usually the first layer of the onion.

CHAPTER 1

The fuel-delivery system, whether a carburetor, throttle body, or fuel injection, can be removed at this point, but if at all possible I prefer to wait. Even though I will be building the engine I hate to drop anything into it, so I pull the intake off last. Next I move to the area in front of the engine, beginning with the fan shroud. This is followed by the removal of the belts and hoses. This can be followed by removing the alternator, power-steering pump, and air-conditioning compressor. Carefully disconnect any electrical connections along the way. (This is the last time I'll say this—be sure to tag, mark, identify, and store parts properly.) If your car is a later model it may be equipped with a single accessory drive belt. The method of belt removal should be located on a sticker on the fan shroud. It's a simple matter of releasing the pressure on the tensioning arm and slipping the belt off. Then the individual components are removed.

Unlike the other type of belt system, the single-belt setup's alternator, compressor, and power-steering pump are hard mounted and not adjustable. In older cars with multiple drive belts, the alternator, compressor, and pump will be mounted where they pivot and are locked in place on a bracket with an adjustable slide and a locking bolt in order to set the proper tension. Loosen the lock bolt and the pivot point will become obvious: the pivot bolt can then be removed. Watch what you're doing as this comes apart, because there could be shims or sleeves that must not be lost. Mark the wires and electrical plugs and where they enter the alternator before disconnecting. Then put the alternator and the appropriate bolts in a container for re-use. If the vehicle is so equipped, next the power-steering pump and air-conditioning compressor must be taken loose. While they are belt driven like the alternator, they are a bit different. Both are closed systems and contain hydraulic fluid in the power-steering system and refrigerant in the air-conditioning system.

You face a choice here. On many vehicles the pump and compressor can be taken loose and, although they are still attached to their respective hoses, can be pulled out of the way and secured to the frame or suspension with a stout piece of wire. This decision is partly based on the condition of the system and the budget of the project. If your vehicle has enough wear to warrant an engine rebuild, the chances are that it would not hurt to replace the power-steering hoses and the pump if necessary. Remember, there will never be a better time to do it. The decision on the compressor should be based on whether the system works. If it does, tie the compressor back with the hoses still attached. It should work just fine when you bolt it to your rebuilt engine. If the compressor is to come out, have an A/C shop evacuate the system before you take anything apart. When removing the A/C hoses always use a line wrench, and be careful, as the hoses can be delicate.

With the alternator, compressor, and pump removed, the fan and fan clutch can be removed. If your vehicle is a later model and has an electric fan, it's time for it to come out. The screw or nuts that hold either type in place should be easily identifiable. With the fan and fan clutch removed, the radiator can be taken out. On some models it may be possible to remove the engine with the radiator in the car, but I strongly suggest

The air blew cold in the project truck, so I saw no reason to open the system. The compressor was left connected and can be hooked back up when the engine goes in. This will also save the cost of evacuating and recharging the system. The same can usually be done with the power-steering system, although any vehicle in need of an engine rebuild probably could use new power-steering hoses as well.

PREPARATIONS AND ENGINE REMOVAL

removing the radiator for a couple of reasons. First off, radiators are fragile, and if things slam into it during the engine removal it will be bad. Second, on any vehicle that needs an engine overhaul the chances are the radiator could use a little attention, too. With the unit out it can be taken to a radiator specialist and cleaned or cored for a reasonable price. Your rebuilt engine will rely heavily on the radiator for cooling and there is no sense burdening it with a radiator that is not operating at peak efficiency.

Fuel System

Since the LA/Magnum engine family had such a long production run, your engine can have one of three basic fuel systems. Early 318s had carburetors, then throttle-body injection units, and finally a fuel-injection system. All three do the same thing; deliver fuel and air to the engine. All can be unbolted and removed from the engine after disconnecting any linkages, fuel lines, and electrical connections. If you don't understand where everything goes, you may want to take notes or a digital picture. Keep in mind that once the carburetor or intake manifold is off of the car it is possible to drop things into the engine. Even though it's the beginning of a rebuild, which is the best time to drop a nut into an intake port, there is never a good time to drop a nut into an intake port.

Warning—High-Pressure Fuel Lines

On a carbureted engine, a mechanical fuel pump delivers gas to the carburetor at about 4 to 7 psi. A late-model fuel-injected engine uses an electric pump that supplies fuel to a loop system that may run fuel pressure as high as 55 psi. This type of system draws gas into the fuel-injection system only as needed. The upshot of this is that when you disconnect the fuel line on a carbureted car a little fuel will dribble out. If a fuel line is disconnected on a high-pressure system, fuel will spray out with considerable force. As a result pressure must be bled from these systems before disassembly. Check your individual vehicle manual to see how this is done.

Exhaust Manifolds

Depending on the model of your vehicle, you may want to leave the exhaust manifolds on the engine until after it is pulled. If you do, the manifolds will have to be disconnected from the exhaust system. Instead of this you can unbolt the manifolds from the block and leave them attached to the exhaust pipes. This choice may be determined for you by the bolt's attitudes about coming loose. The bolts used to secure the exhaust system go through a significant heat cycle every time the engine is run. They are also pretty exposed to the elements. As a result they are prone to seizing and breaking. If at all possible I prefer to pull the engine with the manifolds attached. It's easier to get to the bolts and apply even pressure on the bolts with the engine on a stand. Hopefully you read the bit about penetrating oils and you have been using them, which will help a lot. With a six-point wrench or socket securely and squarely on the bolt head, try to remove it. A cheater bar can be used to gain a bit of leverage. When all of the bolts are removed the manifold is ready to come off. It may be necessary to give it a whack with a polyurethane hammer to get it to come loose.

Bell-Housing Bolts

The block will be attached to the bell housing with bolts around the perimeter of the front of the bell housing. On many engine pulls these will be some of the most difficult to

Once everything else has been loosened the intake can come off. Leave it on until the end to keep anything from getting into the engine.

HOW TO REBUILD THE SMALL-BLOCK MOPAR

get a wrench on. Once again, the advantage of multiple soakings with penetrating oil will be great. As these bolts are often difficult to get a wrench on, any help in getting them out will be most welcomed. With these bolts removed, the engine and transmission can be separated. Keep in mind there are steel pins that are in place between the block and bell housing. These will make it impossible for the block to twist in relation to the bell housing, so when the two are separated the block must come straight forward.

Engine Mounts

Engine-mount designs have varied over the years depending on the car or truck being produced. They all have one thing in common, though. They attach the left and right side of the block to the left and right frame or sub-frame. They are pretty straightforward, and it will be obvious how they unbolt. With everything disconnected and removed from the engine, and the bell housing and engine-mount bolts removed, the engine is ready to come out.

Position the vehicle in a convenient position to pull the engine. Keep in mind that when the engine comes out there will have to be adequate room to maneuver the engine hoist. The most common way to join

Use a length of strong chain to attach the engine to the hoist. The chain can be attached to the block or heads with bolts threaded through the chain. Make sure the bolts are threaded well into the engine before pulling commences.

Radiators and air-conditioner condensers are easily damaged. When you are pulling the engine free from the transmission it may take some prying and heavy pulling. If the engine comes free abruptly and swings forward it can quickly damage anything unfortunate enough to get in its way. A piece of 3/8-inch plywood held in place with a couple of C-clamps can help protect everything forward. This is especially helpful when pulling an engine alone.

PREPARATIONS AND ENGINE REMOVAL

Carefully guide the engine forward and upward slowly. As you begin the process keep an eye out for anything that might still be connected. When the engine clears the core support, pull it away from the vehicle. Never allow anyone to get under or too close to the engine. Go slowly and try not to let the engine start swinging.

With the engine out, lower it to the height of the engine stand and bolt it up. Make sure the engine is tightly attached to the stand brackets and that the bracket adjusters are tightly bolted to the backing plate. When rotating the engine on the stand, be very careful. Until the heads are off it will be top heavy, and once it starts rolling it will have a great deal of force.

and bell housings are reluctant to come apart so you may have to pry and wrestle with the thing for a while. As you bring the engine up and out, look all around it and make sure that all wires and hoses are indeed disconnected. Even the experienced can miss one little wire, and you don't want to yank it free without noticing. If you have to set the engine down after it is broken free but before you can pull it—if, for instance, you need to reposition the hook along the chain for better balance—you can slowly lower it back down onto the engine mounts. Before you do, make sure that you will not smash or pinch any wires, fuel lines, or brake lines.

Once the engine is high enough to clear the front of the engine well it can come forward. If your vehicle is still in a condition that allows it to

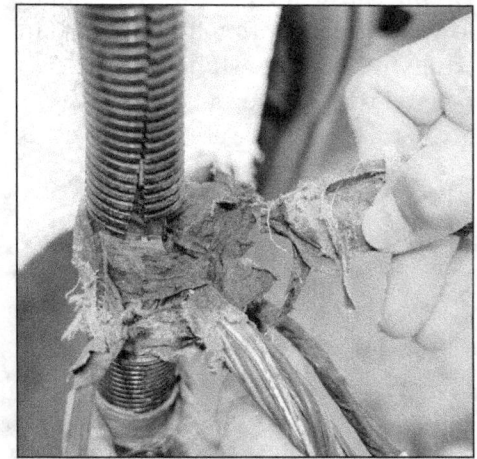

While this book deals with internal engine rebuilding, there are a few items that can be addressed while the engine is out of the vehicle. Inspect the wiring harness to make sure it is in good condition. The factory used wrap that tended to deteriorate over the years and lose much of its protective potential. Take a little time to pull it off and rewrap the wiring harness.

the engine and the hoist is with a piece of chain using bolts run through a chain link and into the cylinder head or block, at the front and rear of the engine. The chain should be run diagonally so that the engine won't roll when pulled free from the bell housing. Often, blocks

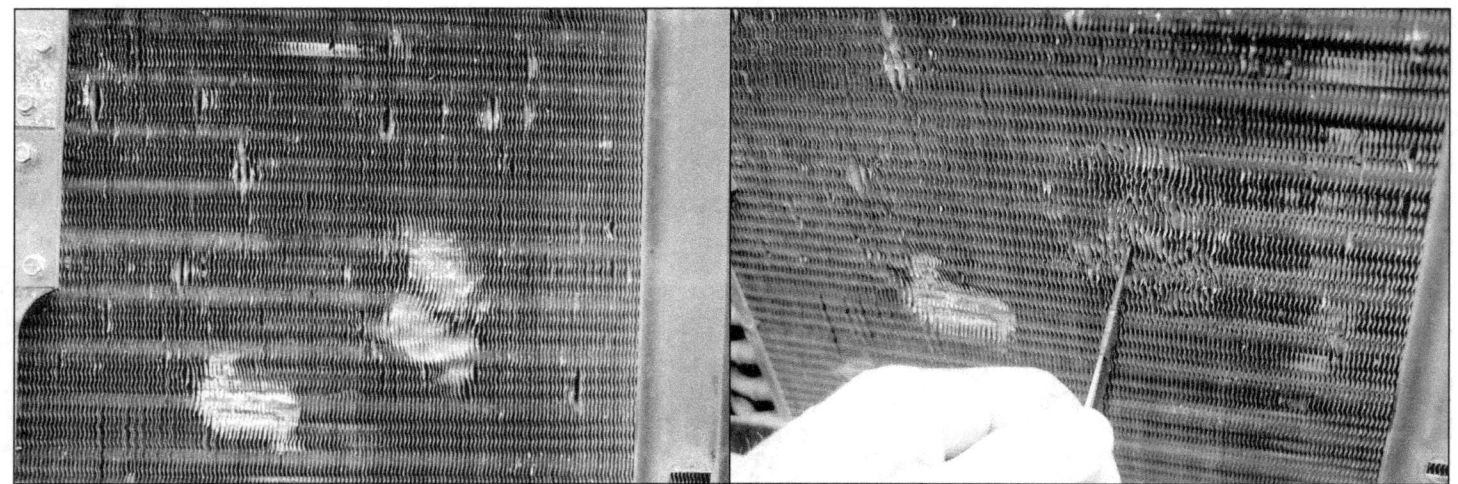

Radiators and air-conditioning condensers are often damaged over the years (usually by mechanics), and this vehicle is no exception. When the cooling fins are bent like those on the left they lose their efficiency. My weapon of choice to combat this is an old Rapala fillet knife. The thin blade is great for inserting between the fins and prying them back so they will allow air to pass through.

roll it may be better to push the vehicle away from the lift as opposed to pulling the lift away from the vehicle. When the lift is pulled the engine can swing around. This puts a lot of stress on the lift and it can bang into things. If the vehicle is pushed the engine can hang stationary. Either way, once the engine is clear of the engine well, lower it down to a level just above the ground for stability. At this point the engine can be cleaned up or, if it's not too dirty, bolted to the engine stand and rolled into the shop. If you are going to hose the engine down, either lower it to the ground or just over the ground. Try to refrain from hanging it high in the air on the hoist. The engine can now be rolled into the shop for disassembly. While the engine is out you may want to take the opportunity to address a few more items. Inspect the suspension, transmission, and wiring harness. There will never be a better time to address any problems.

If you have an automatic transmission, look for the dreaded front seal leak. I had enough of a problem that the tranny came out right after the engine.

If you have the time and inclination, there will never be a better time to check all of your steering and front suspension components and spruce up your engine well.

CHAPTER 2

DISASSEMBLY

Don't panic. To tell you the truth, the disassembly of our project engine was a dream. There was not a bolt, nut, or screw that caused the least bit of trouble. From the time we popped the hood from the time we put the disassembled engine in to soak, there was not a step that provoked the smallest desire to curse. May your luck run the same—but don't count on it. This was the only case of purely pleasurable disassembly that I have ever known. Chances are you'll encounter a bolt that breaks or a nut that someone used Vise-Grips on for years.

The first step in correcting any problem is to stop and think. Don't break a bolt, get pissed off, and make the situation worse. Everything can be fixed or replaced, so don't fret it. If you break a bolt off in the block, leave it if you can and worry about it later. If you get the nut that won't come off, you may have to go buy a small grinder and spend a half an hour grinding it away. If you run into a problem, stop and think (or go and get some advice) before you take rash action that may set you back in terms of time and money.

Chances are you won't have a NASCAR-sized garage for your project and will have to make do with anything from a basic two-car home garage to an apartment parking lot. Either way—stay organized. I cannot overstress the importance of keeping everything together and

At this point of the process the engine should be on an engine stand, ready to go. Use four quality bolts to attach the engine to the stand. The upper bolts here screwed into threads in the block while the lower bolts required backing nuts. Before you begin ripping the engine apart, give it a good visual inspection. Look for cracks, evidence of leaks, or anything else that seems to be out of the ordinary. If you find something, note it and pay close attention when tearing down that area of the engine.

organized. It will save time and money. If you don't, I guarantee you that it will take more time to find the right nuts and bolts than to mount a given component.

Lastly, it is important to keep your mind in the proper gear during disassembly. Proceed like you are an archeologist excavating fossil remains. That means go slowly, make sure that you do not damage anything, and closely inspect everything that you are working on. When in doubt, taking pictures can help you remember how things came apart later on.

1 Drain Fluids

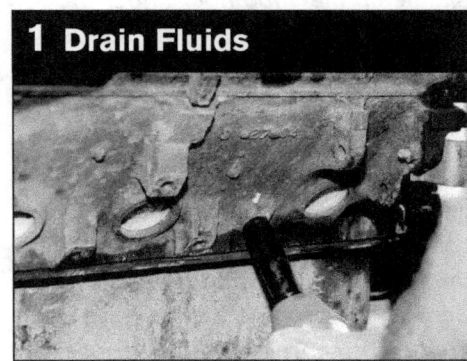

Remove the threaded plugs on each side of the block to drain the coolant that is still trapped in the engine's internal cooling passages.

HOW TO REBUILD THE SMALL-BLOCK MOPAR

CHAPTER 2

When you do, have a drain pan ready to catch the fluid. As mentioned before, transfer the used coolant to a closed container quickly, especially if you have pets. Many coolants actually have a sweet taste, and if your dog or cat drinks some it will kill them graveyard dead. Once the engine is on the stand and ready for disassembly, it is a good idea to have a piece of plastic on the shop floor under the engine stand if you (or your spouse) are one of those people who is serious about keeping the floor stain-free. While much of the engine's fluids were drained while the engine was in the vehicle, there will still be some residual oil and coolant inside that will escape during the teardown. Some newer engine stands have a built-in catch tray for fluids. Those of us stuck with an older model must rely on a discarded piece of cardboard or plastic (which is fine because my floor is already stained).

2 Remaining Bolt-On Parts Spark Triggers

If you followed my advice, the fuel system and intake were removed before the engine was pulled. Before tearing the internal components apart you must first unbolt any "bolt-on" components that remain on the engine. On later-model engines the spark trigger is bolted to the back of the block and reads the slots around the perimeter of the flexplate to initiate the ignition. Remove the two bolts that secure the trigger and store it in a safe place.

3 Mechanical Fuel Pump

Later model 318s equipped with fuel injection have an electric fuel pump mounted under the frame and will not be a factor. Earlier models of the 318, 340, and 360 have a mechanical fuel pump mounted on the right side of the front timing cover. The mechanical fuel pump has two bolts holding it in place.

4 Spark Plug Insulators

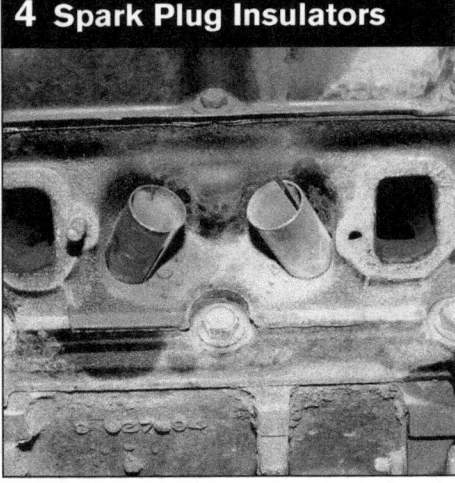

Your engine may have metal spark-plug insulators that are pressed into the cylinder head. Often these are ripped out and discarded during a rebuild, but this is a mistake. These sleeves insulate the plug boot and give extra security in keeping the plug wire firmly on the spark plug.

Grab the insulators with a pair of pliers and gently work them back and forth while pulling them up and out of the head. It may take a while, and you may distort the protector a bit, but they are malleable and can be straightened out once they are loose. Most are made of stainless steel, and a drill-powered wire brush will make them look new.

HOW TO REBUILD THE SMALL-BLOCK MOPAR

DISASSEMBLY

5 Distributor — Master Mechanic Tip / PRO TIP

Loosen and remove the bolt that secures the distributor clamp at the base of the distributor where it enters the block. With the bolt out, the clamp can be taken off and the distributor removed by pulling it upward. Store the distributor in a safe place to keep it from being damaged. This is a good time to make marks on the distributor and block so when you reinstall the distributor you're in the ballpark timing-wise.

Cylinder-Head Removal

6 Valvecovers

The first step in removing the cylinder head is to remove the valvecovers. These are secured with bolts and/or nuts on studs around the perimeter of the cover and may be accompanied with special spreader washers that more efficiently distribute the bolt's load and better secure the cover. If these are present, keep and re-use them.

There may also be wire clips located on the valvecover hardware. Locate and store all of these pieces, as they are small but important in keeping plug wires, electrical system wires, and vacuum hoses safely secured.

If it has been a while since the covers have been off, the gasket may stick to either the cover or the head. Don't worry about the gaskets' destruction, as it will be replaced. Any part of the gasket that is left stuck to the head or cover will be cleaned up later.

7 Cylinder Order — Notation Required

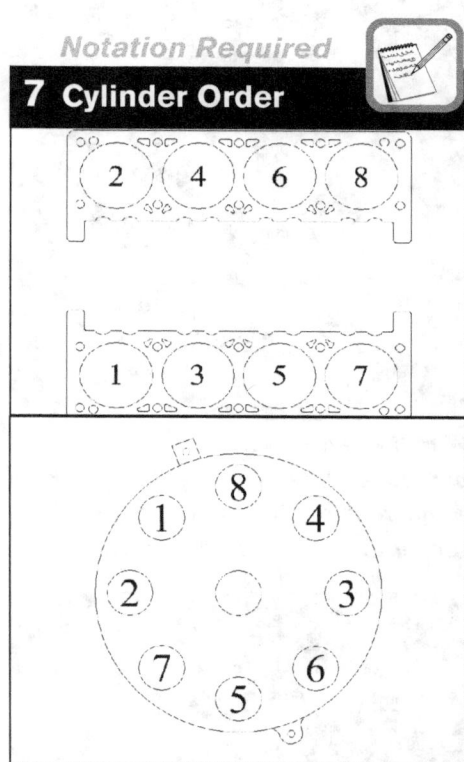

The first thing to do is to make sure that the cylinders are identified by their number prior to breakdown. For many parts it is imperative to keep the components for each cylinder with that cylinder. You should have your Ziploc plastic bags ready for the job so that when finished the number-1 intake components will be in one bag, the number-1 exhaust components in another, and so on. The reason for this is that until the engine is thoroughly inspected, it is not known what will have to be replaced. For instance, on a shoestring-budget rebuild, if the valve and valveguide wear is minimal, they can be re-used and should be replaced in the same position from which they were removed. If you don't want to use bags, special trays are available to store engine parts during a rebuild, but a creative mind and some old cardboard boxes and plastic bags work just as well and cost much less.

HOW TO REBUILD THE SMALL-BLOCK MOPAR

8 Rocker Arms

With the valvecovers removed you can begin the unbolting of the rocker arms. A single bolt on top of the rocker arm secures each rocker.

To save time you can run down the head loosening all of the bolts while you have your wrench out before removing any of the pieces.

After removing the nut the rocker can be lifted off of the post.

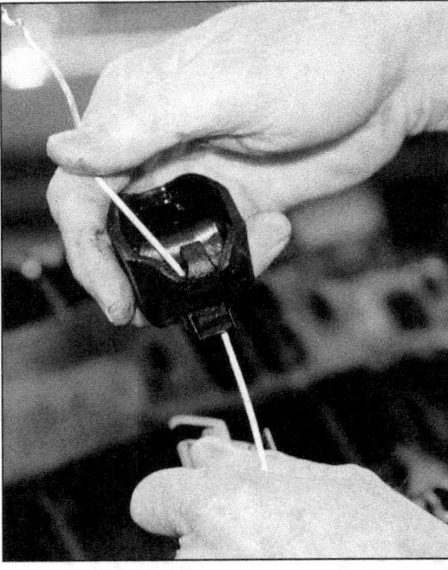

To help during the cleaning phase you can thread a piece of heavy wire (or coat hanger) through the center of the rocker. Make a note of the order in which they are strung on the wire so that they can be matched back to the proper cylinder after cleaning, if necessary.

9 Pushrods

With the rocker arms removed the pushrods are easily accessed.

Removal is a simple matter of lifting the pushrods out of the head. A cardboard box with 16 small holes punched in the top can be used to store the pushrods and to mark their location based on cylinder and valve.

Below the rocker arm is the guideplate, which is secured to the head with the rocker bolts. Once the rockers have been removed these plates will lift right out.

DISASSEMBLY

10 Head Bolts

The cylinder head is removed from the block by removing the 10 head bolts. Five of these bolts are inside the perimeter of the valvecover. When removing the bolts, begin the loosening by turning each bolt a quarter-turn at a time. Loosen the number-1 bolt a quarter turn, then number-2, then number-3, and so on. When all of the bolts have been relieved a quarter-turn, go back to number-1 and make another pass. Only when all of the bolts will turn by hand and the tension on the head is relieved should they be removed any faster.

The remaining five head bolts are outside the valvecover's perimeter. All of the bolts should be saved for cleaning and re-use.

Once the tension on the bolts has been relieved, they can be zipped out with an air wrench.

Leave the center outer bolt loose but threaded in a few turns so that when you pry the head off it will not fall on the floor or on your foot, or both.

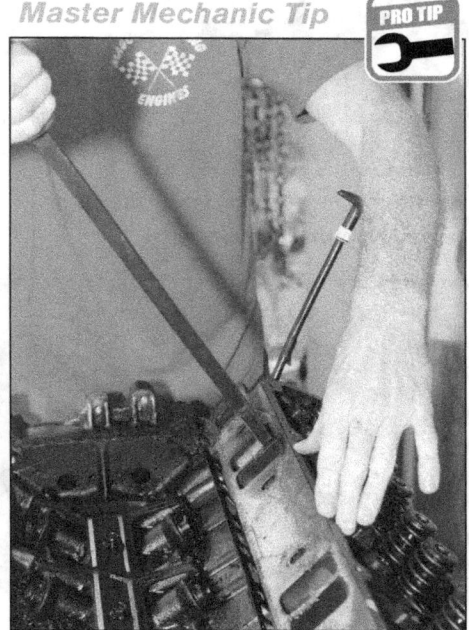

Master Mechanic Tip — PRO TIP

With all of the other bolts out, the head can be loosened from the block. If it is stuck (and it probably will be) place a piece of wood against the head and whack it with a hammer. Do this on each corner and try again to lift the head. If it is still stuck, a pry bar can be used, but don't get too crazy with it. First try the end of the bar inserted into an intake port to gain a bit of leverage.

If the head still won't come loose, you can pry it away from the block using the boss at the end of the head. If you use a bar in this manner apply steady pressure to insure you don't damage anything. *Do not* pry on or too close to the mating surfaces between the block and head. These are critical surfaces and must not be damaged.

When the head comes loose remove the center outer bolt and set the head aside for final cylinder-head disassembly.

Pry the head gasket up, pull it from the engine, and set it aside to be inspected.

HOW TO REBUILD THE SMALL-BLOCK MOPAR

11 Lifters

The type of lifter used will vary depending on your engine's age. Small-blocks from 1967 to 1987 will have flat-tappet lifters while those produced in 1988 or later will have roller lifters. The process for removing each is much the same.

Later-model engines will require you to first remove the hardware that retains the lifters. This spreader clamp is attached by three bolts and secures the retainers that keep the lifters in their bore.

With the bolts out the spreader clip can be removed.

With the spreader clip out, the lifter retainers can be removed.

It should be easy just to reach in and pull them out with your fingers.

Once all retaining hardware is off, the individual lifters can be removed from their bore. The lifters will be lifted straight up and out. Depending on the cam location some lifters will be easier to grab at the top than others.

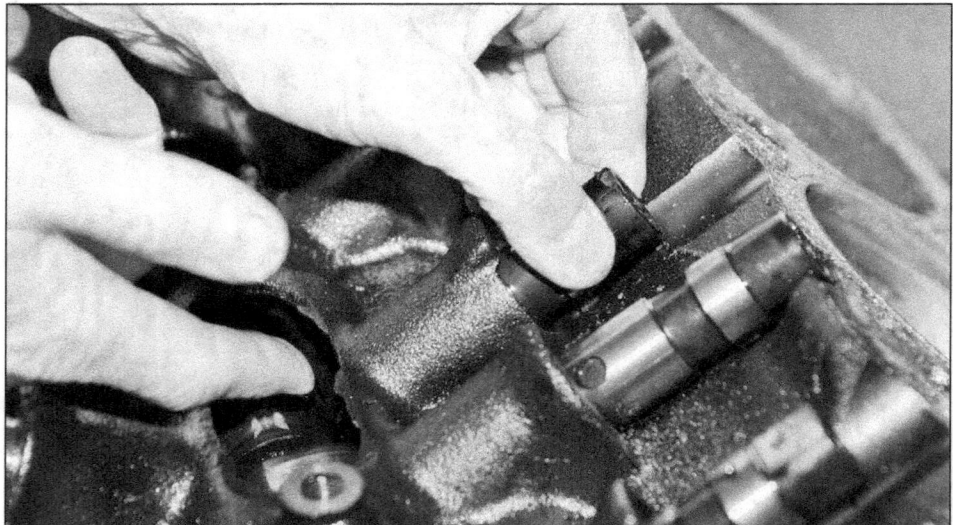

If a lifter is low in the bore you can stick a finger down by the camshaft to put some upward pressure on the bottom of the lifter. Reach into the engine with one hand and push the lifter upward until you can grasp it with the other. As you lift the lifters from the cam, take a peek at where the lifter meets the camshaft and note any unusual wear. If there has been a cam/lifter problem in the engine, the lifter may be damaged, or its shape distorted.

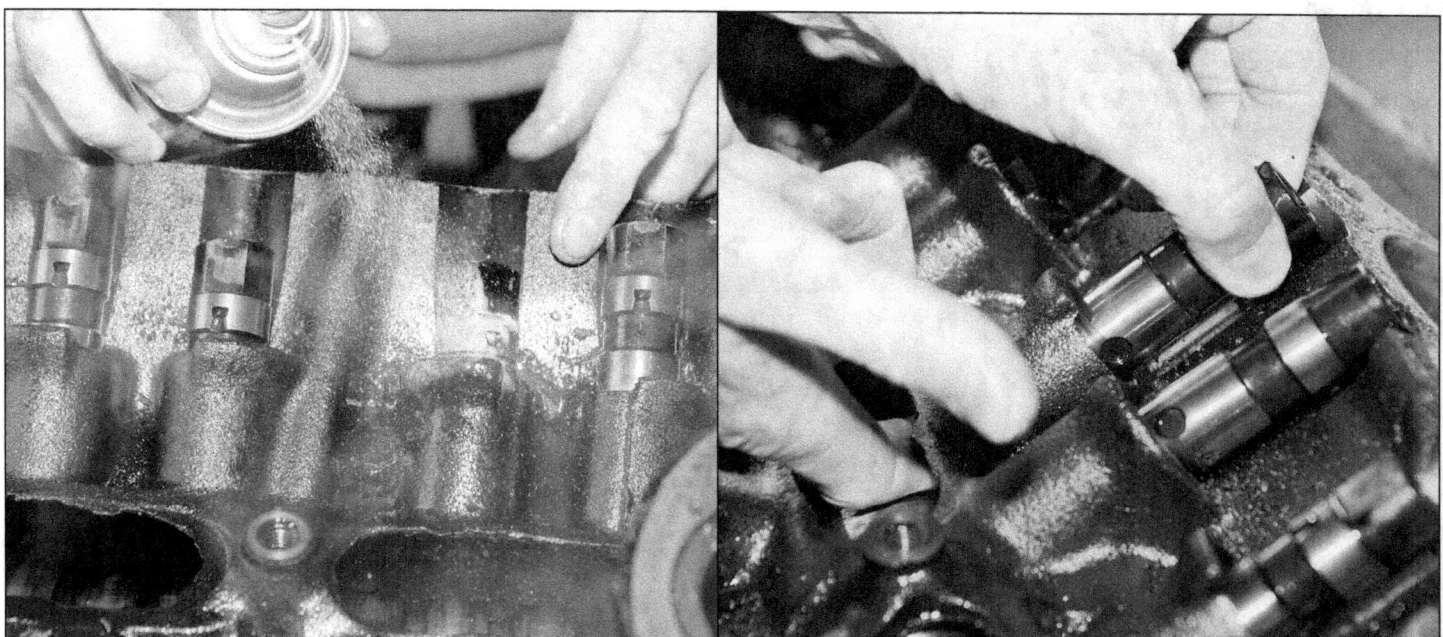

In a perfect world, all of the lifters would slide right out. However, they will often stick due to glazing, which often depends on the engine's history of oil maintenance. If a lifter has no apparent damage but sticks, spray a good aerosol lubricant into the bore at the top and bottom of the lifter and work it up and down. It may take a while to loosen it up, but often it will slide out. If it won't, or if the lifter has damage that will prevent it from sliding out of the top of the bore, it will have to come out the bottom after the cam is removed. When the lifters are removed they must also be stored with their location recorded.

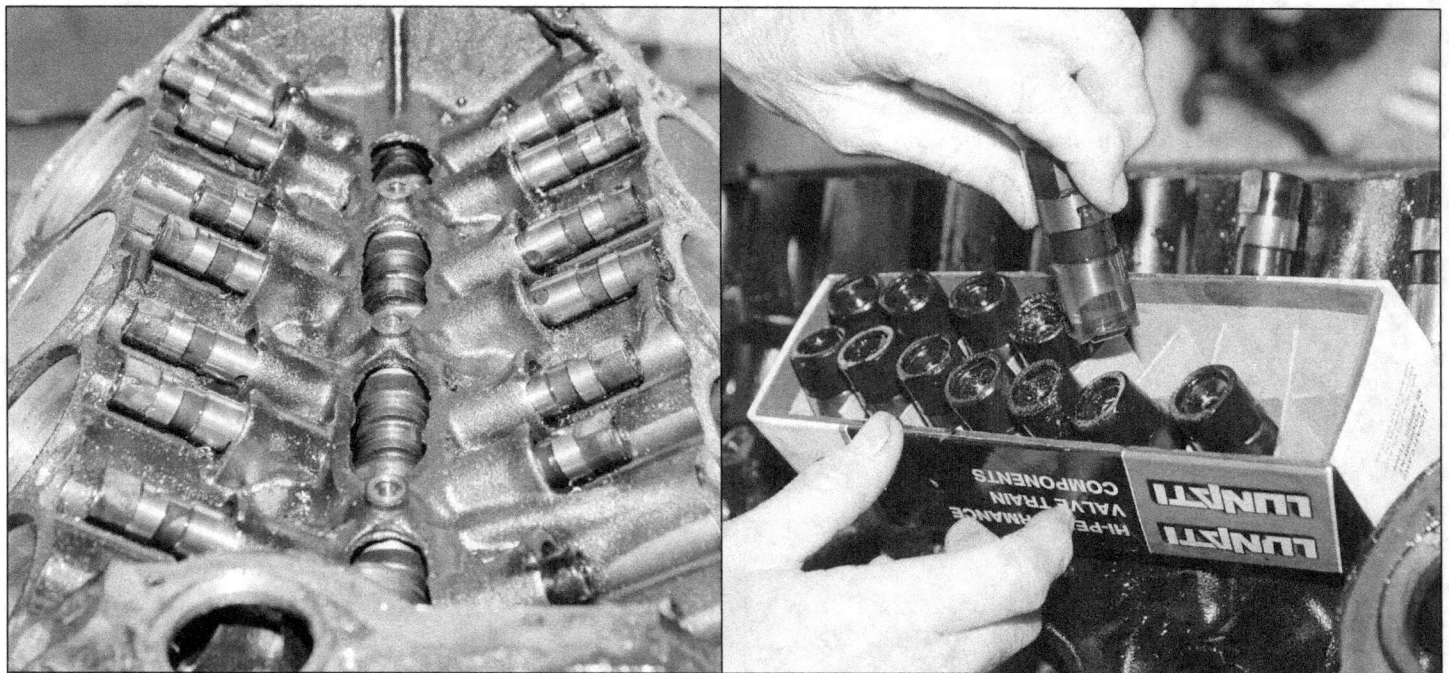

Once all of the lifters are loose they can be removed and stored. I used an old lifter box for storage, but any such device can be used to keep the lifters in the same order in which they were taken out of the engine. Even if you do not plan to re-use the lifters, it's a good idea to keep them indexed until the inspection phase is completed. A good detective never messes up his evidence.

CHAPTER 2

The Bottom End

12 Harmonic Balancer

With the top of the engine torn apart, it's time to start work on the front and bottom. The first piece to come off will be the harmonic balancer. Before the balancer can be pulled from the end of the crankshaft, the large bolt securing it must be removed.

With the bolt out the balancer is ready to have the puller attached.

Master Mechanic Tip *PRO TIP*

PRO TIP When the harmonic balancer comes off, pay special attention to the area on the balancer where the front engine seal mates. This area must be smooth and free of burrs to get a good seal where the crankshaft's end comes through the front engine cover.

13 Remove Oil Pan

Remove the bolts around the oil pan's perimeter.

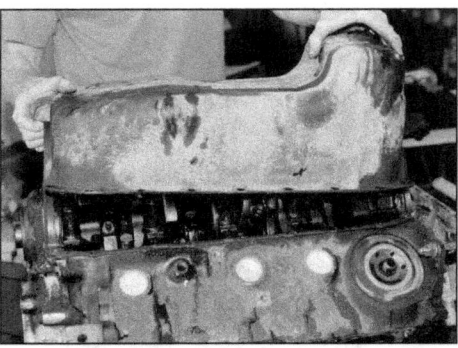

With the bolts removed the pan can be lifted free from the block. Set the pan aside to be cleaned.

There will be a gasket between the pan and the block that might be stuck to either or both. Like all gaskets, this one will be replaced, so peel off what you can and scrape the rest.

The puller will be attached to the balancer with three bolts. The threaded rod is then turned to pull the balancer from the crankshaft. Slowly turn the center bolt, increasing the pressure and pulling the balancer off of the end of the crank.

DISASSEMBLY

14 Oil Pump

After loosening the oil pan, the oil pump and pickup tube can be removed.

Critical Inspection

The screen at the pickup end of the tube may give some indication of the amount of junk that has been floating around in your engine. The above pickup screen looks pretty good for a four-wheel drive with 172,000 miles on it. If the screen is heavily blocked, the engine has certainly been operating with less than an optimal oil supply.

The oil tube is threaded into the oil pump, so it is a good idea to loosen it while the pump is still secured to the engine.

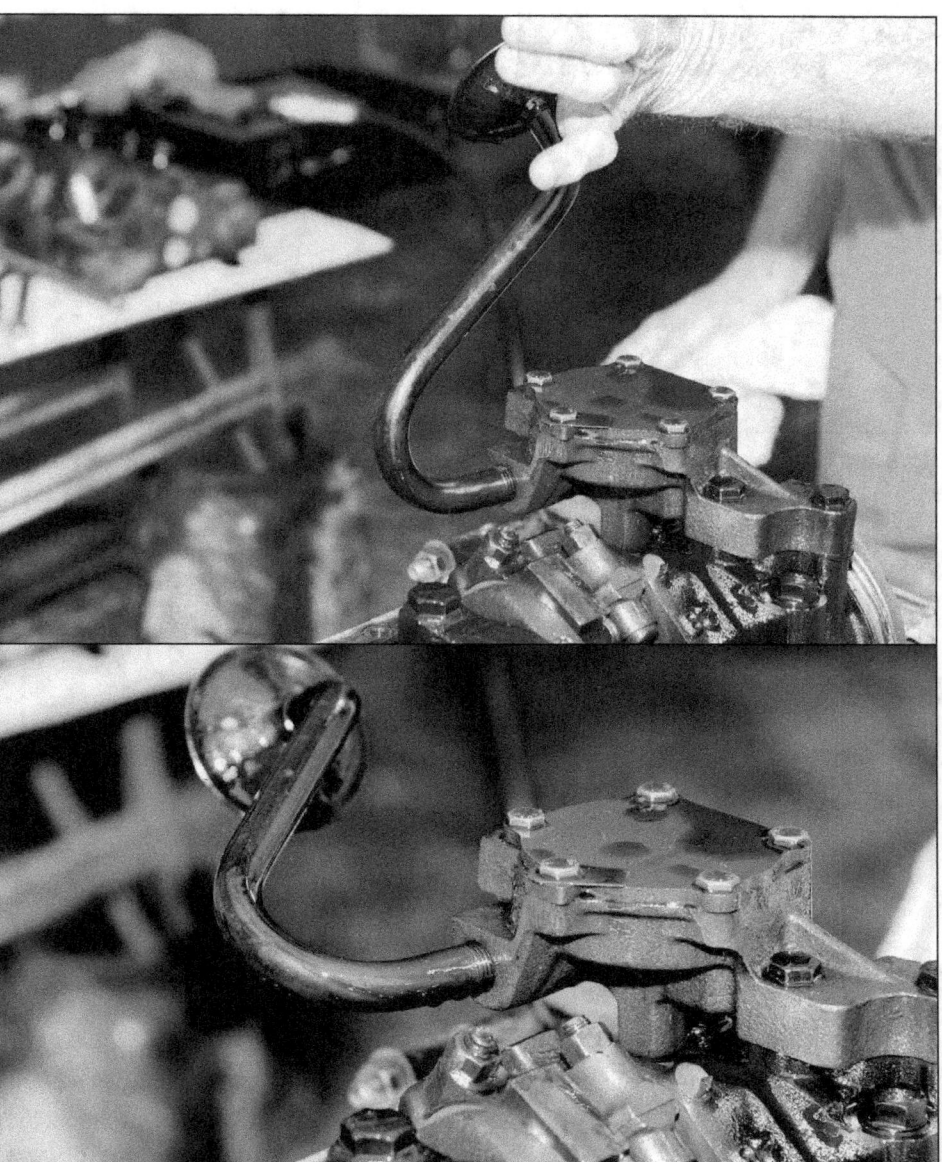

With the palm of your hand, push the tube to turn counterclockwise to break the threads loose. You will only be able to turn the tube about a quarter of a revolution, but the object here is just to break it loose. To fully unscrew the tube the oil pump must be removed.

To take the pump off, remove the two bolts securing it to the block. With the pump removed, unscrew the pickup tube the rest of the way and store it in a safe location. It will be cleaned and re-used on the new pump that you are going to buy.

HOW TO REBUILD THE SMALL-BLOCK MOPAR

CHAPTER 2

15 Oil-Filter Fitting

Rotate the block so that the oil-filter mounting point is accessible. The first step to its removal is to remove the double-threaded fitting that threads into the block and also has the threads to secure the oil filter.

With the double-threaded fitting removed, the backing plate can be removed, usually with little more than hand pressure.

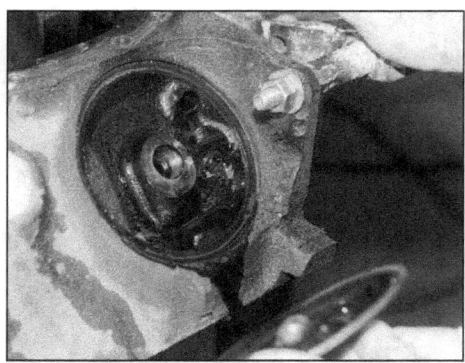

When the plate is lifted free be ready to catch the inevitable oil pocket still trapped under the plate. There should be a thin gasket under the plate that should be removed.

Use a deep-well socket to remove the oil-filter fitting. Slip the socket over the threads and secure it on the hex bolt. After breaking the threads loose the fitting should be easy to unscrew.

16 Front Engine Cover

With the balancer off, the front engine cover can be removed. The cover is mounted integrally with the oil pan, and while the job is usually possible with the oil pan on, it is much easier with it off. If the oil pan has been removed, the lower screws securing the bottom of the cover are already out. Proceed by removing the small bolts around the perimeter of the timing-chain cover.

Save Money $

$ With the bolts out, the cover is ready to be removed, but be careful. The cover may be stuck in place because of the gasket, and it is a relatively delicate piece. It is important not to mar or deform the surface where the cover mates to the gasket. Use a putty knife around the perimeter of the cover, gently breaking the tension between the gasket, cover, and block while pulling the cover forward.

DISASSEMBLY

17 Timing Chain and Sprockets

With the cover removed, the timing chain and gears can be inspected and removed. In an older engine it is likely that the chain has slack and is no longer within specifications, so plan on replacing the chain and gears.

To remove the timing chain, first remove the bolt located in the center of the camshaft gear. The cam gear is secured and located with a keyway.

With the bolt removed, slide the gears forward at roughly the same rate. The camshaft gear will come off of its shaft first, which will allow the chain to be lifted from the crankshaft gear.

The crankshaft gear can now be removed. Some gears can be pulled by hand and some cannot. If the gears are stuck, the best way to remove them is with a puller. Both two- and three-post designs can be used effectively. While a decent puller is not very expensive, it is often a free loan tool at some auto parts stores. If you do not have access to a puller you can use two strong screwdrivers or small pry bars to pull the sprockets, but I advise this to be a last choice. The puller is much more controlled, applies more even pressure, and is far less likely to mar the shaft.

18 Camshaft

The camshaft is locked in place with this plate located on the front of the block.

First remove the three bolts that secure the retainer plate and drip guide at the front of the block. Make sure to keep the drip guide that's secured by the plate's bottom bolt. This guide helps direct oil to the timing chain and is important for proper lubrication.

With the plate removed, the camshaft is ready to come out. The cam is secured with five bearings in a bore through the block; thus, the cam must come straight out the front of the block. As the cam is pulled out, the lobes will tend to hang up against the bearing bores. Hence, pulling it out can be like playing the game Operation.

HOW TO REBUILD THE SMALL-BLOCK MOPAR

As you pull the cam out you can reach into the block with one hand to help clear the lobes past the bearings. Try to take care not to bang the cam against the bearings.

When the camshaft is out, store it where it is safe and secure. If there were troublesome lifters that were still in the engine, lift them as far up the bore as possible as you slide the camshaft past them. An extra pair of hands may be useful here. Once the cam is out, the lifter can be pushed down to exit through the bottom of the bore and then lifted clear of the block. This will keep the damaged lifter from scarring the inside of the lifter bore in the block.

19 Pressed Plugs

Both the block and the cylinder heads in a Dodge small-block will have both pressed-in and screw-in plugs. The pressed-in plugs, often referred to as freeze plugs, are actually used to close holes necessary in the block-casting process. For the block to be properly cleaned, the plugs must be removed. Pressed-in plugs are actually simple to remove. With a chisel, tap one side of the plug, tilting it in the hole.

DISASSEMBLY

Then use a pair of pliers to remove the plug.

If you drop one into the block, don't panic, but do get it out if you drop it. A forgotten foreign object floating around in a block will inhibit proper coolant flow and most likely lead to trouble.

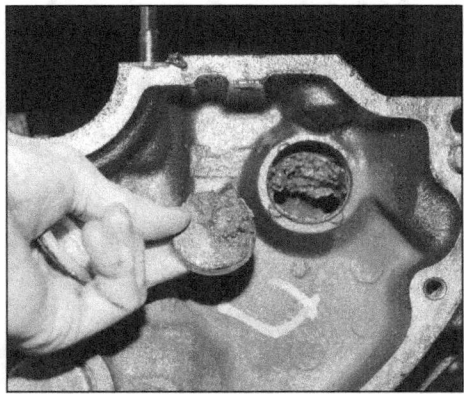

Don't forget to remove the plugs on the back of the block. These will have to wait until the block is taken off of the engine stand.

20 Pistons and Rods

This is another decision point for the home builder. If time's a-pressin' and the wife's a-fussin' you can take your engine in its current state (known as a short block, with the crankshaft rod and pistons still intact) and trade it in for another, remanufactured short block. It will certainly save you time, and could save you money, but if you elect this course of action you cannot say that you have "built" your engine. Buying a short block means you trade in what you have for a rebuilt block that includes the crank, rods, and pistons installed and ready to go. You skip the inspection, machining, and assembly, and bolt your heads to your new short block and go from there. There are probably good ones and bad ones out there, but if you stick with a reputable company you should be all right. Check out the recourse chapter in the back for a few ideas. If you are continuing to rebuild the engine, it's time to get to work on the underside.

Critical Inspection

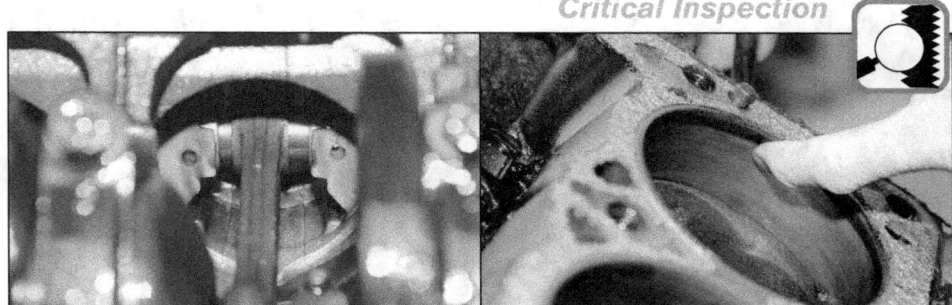

The rod and piston will remain connected while they are pulled from the top of the cylinder, so you will need to check the condition of the top of each cylinder. As an engine wears, the millions of times that the pistons go up and down take their toll. One wear characteristic is the development of a ridge of material at the top of the cylinder bore. Run your finger around the top of the cylinder to determine the presence of a ridge. If there is a ridge, it will have to be dealt with when removing the piston. There are two schools of thought here. The first method is to use a special ridge removal tool, which basically scrapes off the ridge. Some parts stores will loan you one, so check around before you buy one. The tool is run around the top of the cylinder, cutting away the ridge build-up. This will allow the piston to exit cleanly. The other school of thought is to ignore the ridge and pound the living snot out of the piston from the bottom side, busting it through the ridge. While this may sound archaic, there is a reason for it. When you (an inexperienced builder) take a tool to the cylinder you can likely do more harm than good. This is a critical surface and should only be modified with proper machining equipment. The good news is that the piston is aluminum and will give before the iron block when pounding it out. When pounding a piston out, put the end of a thick bar on the underside of the piston by the wrist pin.

CHAPTER 2

Notation Required

Before unbolting the rods, their position and pairing must be marked. With a hammer and a set of numeric punches, stamp a number on both the rod and rod cap to identify which cylinder it came from and which rod goes with which cap.

If you find your rods are already marked, check to make sure that they are marked correctly. If you can't buy or borrow numeric punches, you can use a sharp punch to put a single dot on the number 1 rod and cap with two dots on the number 2 and so on until you are putting eight dots on the number 8 cap and rod (which seems to take forever).

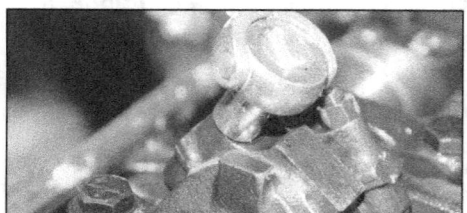

Once all of the rods and caps have been marked, they are ready to be unbolted. Using a socket, loosen the nuts that secure the rod cap on the threaded studs in the rod. Loosen the nuts evenly and stop when about halfway down the threads.

Once the nuts are halfway down the threads, whack the cap with a polyurethane hammer. This will loosen the bearing from the crankshaft and fully separate the cap and rod.

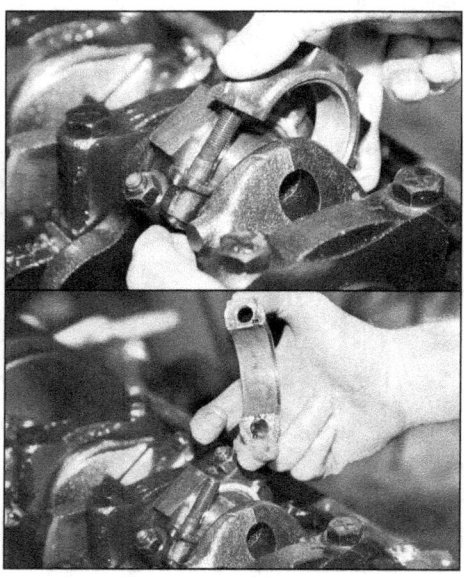

After removing the nuts from the studs, lift the cap from the rod. Make sure that the bearing does not drop out of the cap and into the engine.

With the rod cap off, the crankshaft journals are exposed. Be careful working around this surface, as it should not be scratched, dented, or marred in any way.

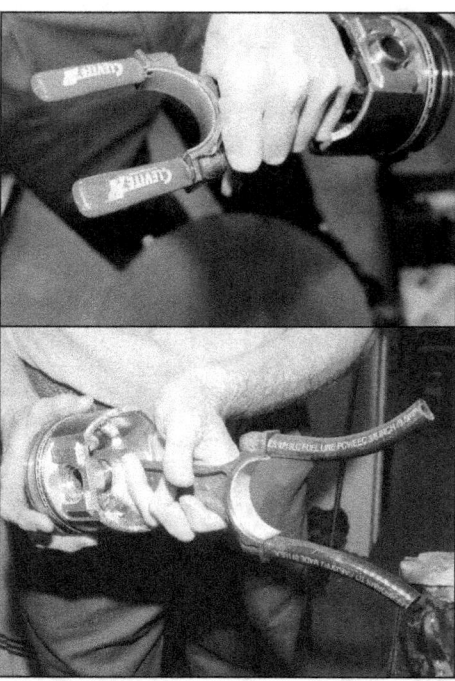

For the amateur builder it's not a bad idea to cover the rod bolts while they are pulled through the cylinder. Some purpose-made units can be bought, or you can slip a piece of 3/8-inch vacuum or fuel line over the stud before removing. Long pieces like this will center the rod in the cylinder and keep the threads from scratching the cylinder walls as the rod is moved through the cylinder.

While holding the rod in line with the piston, push the piston through the cylinder using a wooden hammer handle or a suitable replacement. Control the rod as much as possible during this step to keep it from damaging the cylinder wall.

DISASSEMBLY

As the piston clears the cylinder, be prepared to catch it. If there is any significant resistance, check the cylinder's top for a ridge. Repeat this process on all eight cylinders, carefully storing the pistons after they are out.

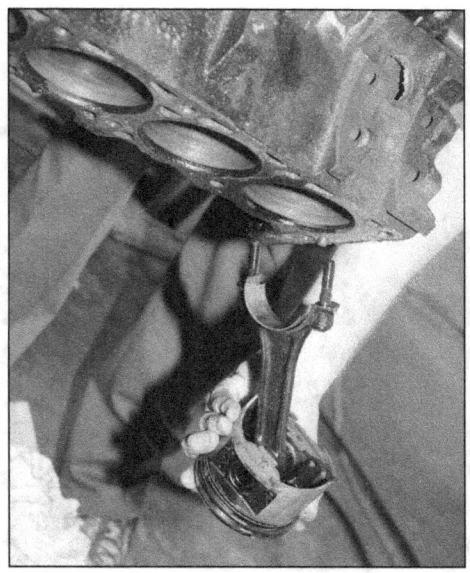

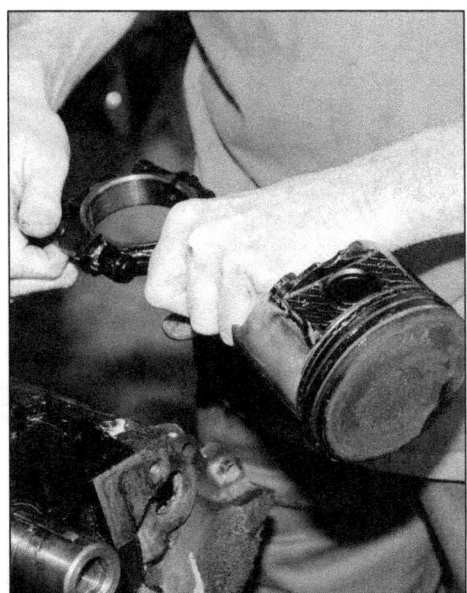

With the piston and rod assembly out of the engine, remove the bearings from the piston and rod cap, replace the rod cap onto the rod, and hand tighten the bolts. It is imperative that the same cap stay with the same rod throughout the rebuild.

A storage container made of two-liter drink bottles doubles well as a low-price piston tray.

Pistons and rods will need to be separated by your machine shop. The rod is heated and the wrist pin pressed in during assembly so a strong hydraulic press with special tooling is required for disassembly.

21 Crankshaft

With the pistons and rods out of the engine, the crankshaft can be removed. The crank is held in place with five main-bearing caps. Each cap is secured to the block with two bolts. Like the head bolts, the main cap bolts will be loosened a quarter-turn at a time until all can be turned with bare fingers.

Once loose, the bolts can be zipped apart with air tools.

When all of the bolts are off, the caps can be removed. This will likely require a few taps with a soft hammer to break the cap loose from the block.

HOW TO REBUILD THE SMALL-BLOCK MOPAR

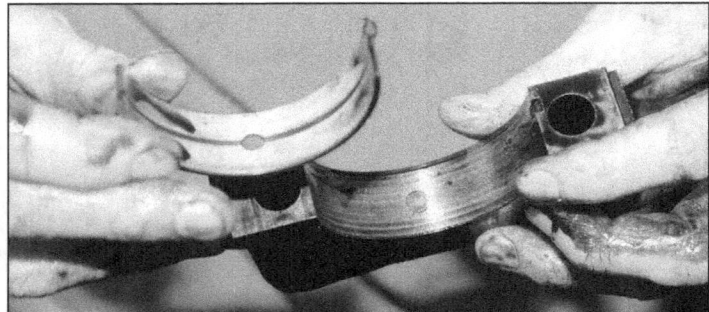

When the cap is lifted free, the bearing under the cap may be removed.

The rear seals should be removed from the cap and block. New seals will be installed during assembly.

When all of the caps are removed, the crank can be lifted out of the block. Cranks are heavy, so if you have a bad back it's a good time to have a healthy friend around. If not, use your engine lift to pull out the crankshaft. When in doubt use a lift, because under no circumstances do you want to drop the crank. Put the crank somewhere safe until you are ready to clean it. If transporting it, support it during transit so that it does not roll around.

22 Oil Pump/Distributor Driveshaft

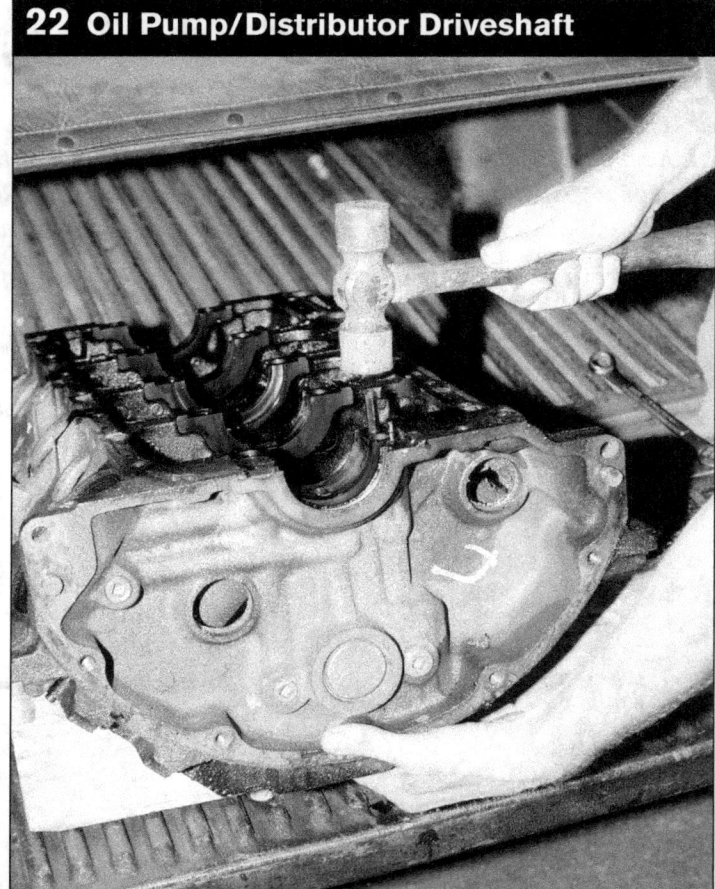

Once the crankshaft is out and safely secured, the block half of the bearings can be removed.

The gear and shaft that drive the oil pump and distributor shaft can now be removed. The base of the shaft extends out of the bottom of the block. With the block upside down, the shaft can be driven out. It will be removed through the bore where the distributor is located. First tap the bottom of the shaft with a polyurethane hammer. Do not abuse the shaft with the hammer. As you drive the shaft downward, be ready for it to drop out. If working alone, put something soft under the block to protect the shaft and gear in case it shoots out while you are tapping the shaft.

DISASSEMBLY

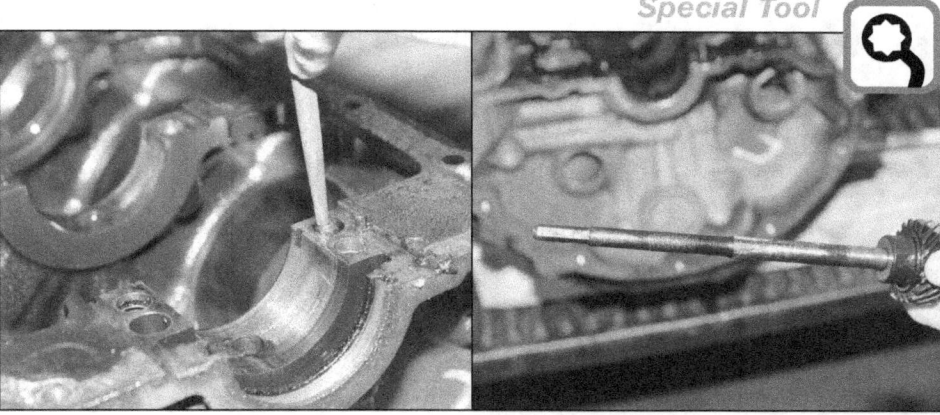

Special Tool

When the shaft becomes flush with the block, a long narrow drift can be used to continue driving the shaft downward.

With the shaft out, its brass bushing can be punched out.

23 Final Block Disassembly

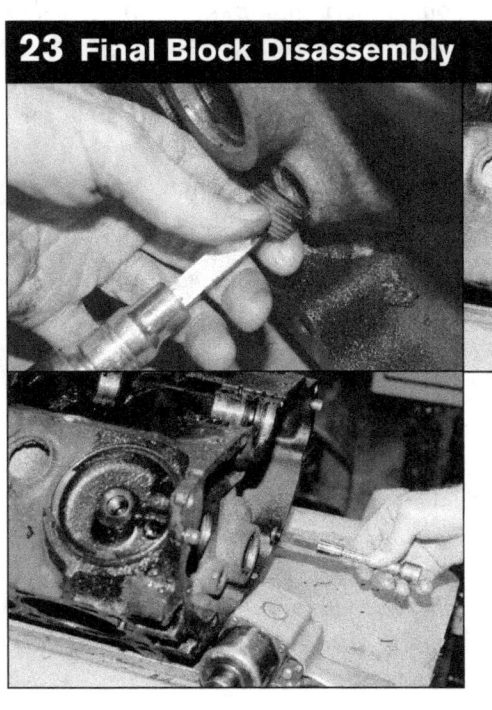

The various screw-in plugs around the block must be removed. With the block inverted, and looking from the rear, the plug to the right of the cam bore is removed. Once removed, look closely in the bore and you will see a second screw-in plug that must be addressed. Use a square drive and an extension to remove it.

With the rear plugs removed, the top, small pressed-in plugs at the front of the block can be removed. To do this you will need a long small-diameter punch that will extend all the way through the block. When the rod is inserted through the plug holes in the rear it will extend all the way through to the back of the plug. Then tap the rod with a hammer to punch out the plug.

24 Disassemble Cylinder Heads

With the cylinder head placed securely on a workbench, it's time to break it down to its base components. This will require a couple of special tools and a dedicated technique.

HOW TO REBUILD THE SMALL-BLOCK MOPAR

CHAPTER 2

The first special tool is a spring compressor. Buying a decent one will run you about $50, so unless you are going to build a lot of heads, it's a great thing to borrow or rent.

To begin the process, fit the spring compressor to the top of the valvespring against the retainer and the other side on the corresponding valve.

Activate the compressor to depress the valvespring. While the tool holds the spring in the depressed position, remove the two-piece spring keepers at the top of the valvestem. If they are stuck, use a pair of needle-nose pliers to extract them. *Be careful.* Valvesprings carry a good bit of pressure, especially when depressed, and once the keepers are out there is nothing holding the tension except the tool. If released the whole thing may go Wile E. Coyote on you and explode all over the room, and under the right conditions can certainly put an eye out. Once the keepers are out, slowly release the tool and remove the valve retainer and then the valvespring.

The valveseal should be removed with a pair of special pliers that are available at most parts stores. They can be removed with regular pliers in a pinch, but be careful not to damage any area of the head.

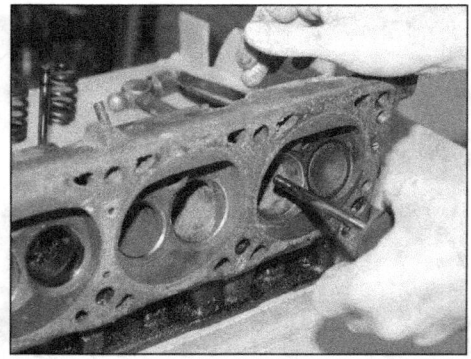

Once the valveseals are off, it's time to try to slide the valve through the head to remove it from the combustion-chamber side. If the valve sticks and will not slide through the guide *do not smash it with a hammer!* As an engine wears it is possible for the stem of the valve to develop a burr. Push the valve back into the head and visually inspect the valve's stem and rub your least calloused finger over it. If a burr is found, sand or file it off, removing no more material than necessary, and again try to slip the valve from the head. Remember, don't get impatient. An extra half hour on a single valve may save you a hundreds of dollars' worth of time, machining, and parts. When the first valve is out, repeat this process on the other 15 valves, making sure you keep everything organized.

DISASSEMBLY

When all of the valvetrain has been removed, the head is ready to be cleaned and then inspected. Set all of the parts aside while the bottom end of the engine is being disassembled.

25 Fuel Injection Intake Manifold

If you are building a 318 or 360 with fuel injection, you will have a few more steps than with a carbureted car.

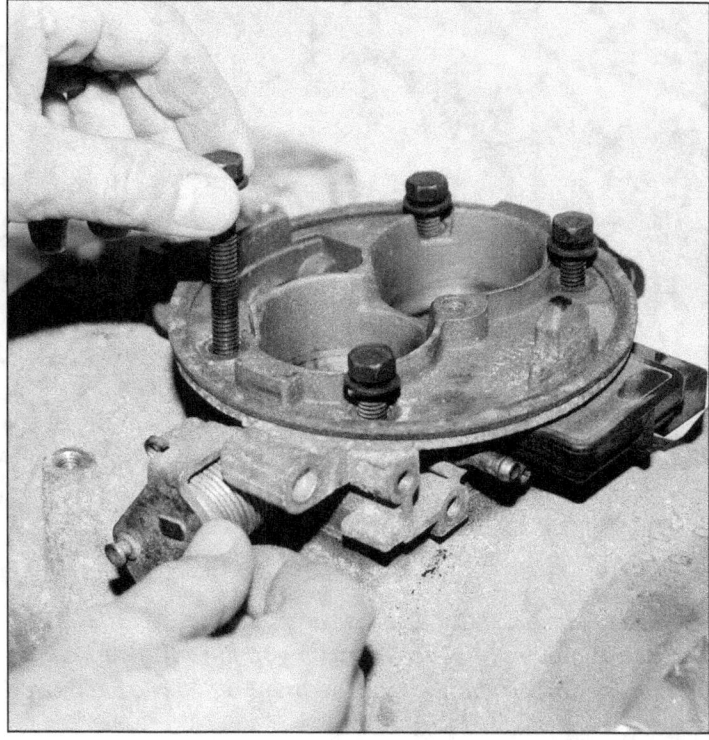

First remove the throttle body from the top of the manifold by removing the four bolts holding it in place.

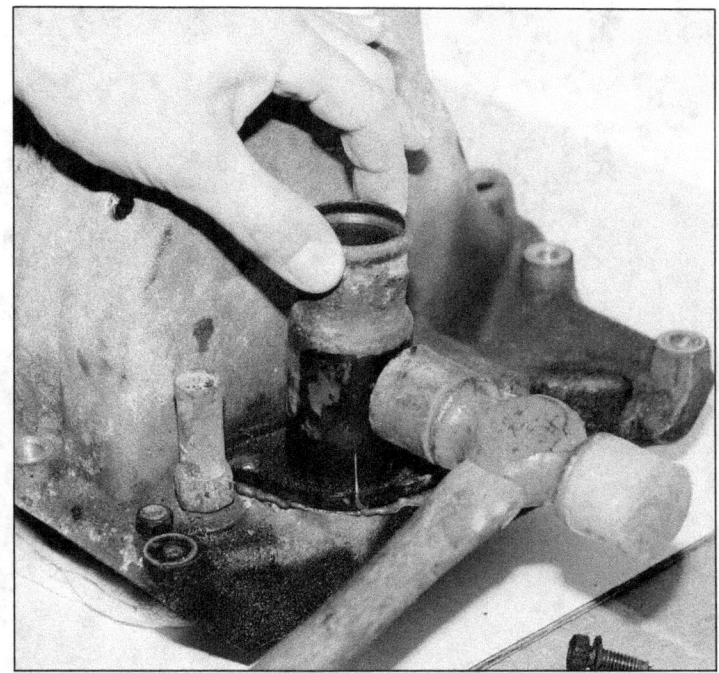

Remove the two bolts holding the thermostat housing to the manifold and lift it free. You may need the help of a rubber hammer if yours has been as thoroughly siliconed as this one. Discard the old thermostat and add this piece to your parts list.

HOW TO REBUILD THE SMALL-BLOCK MOPAR

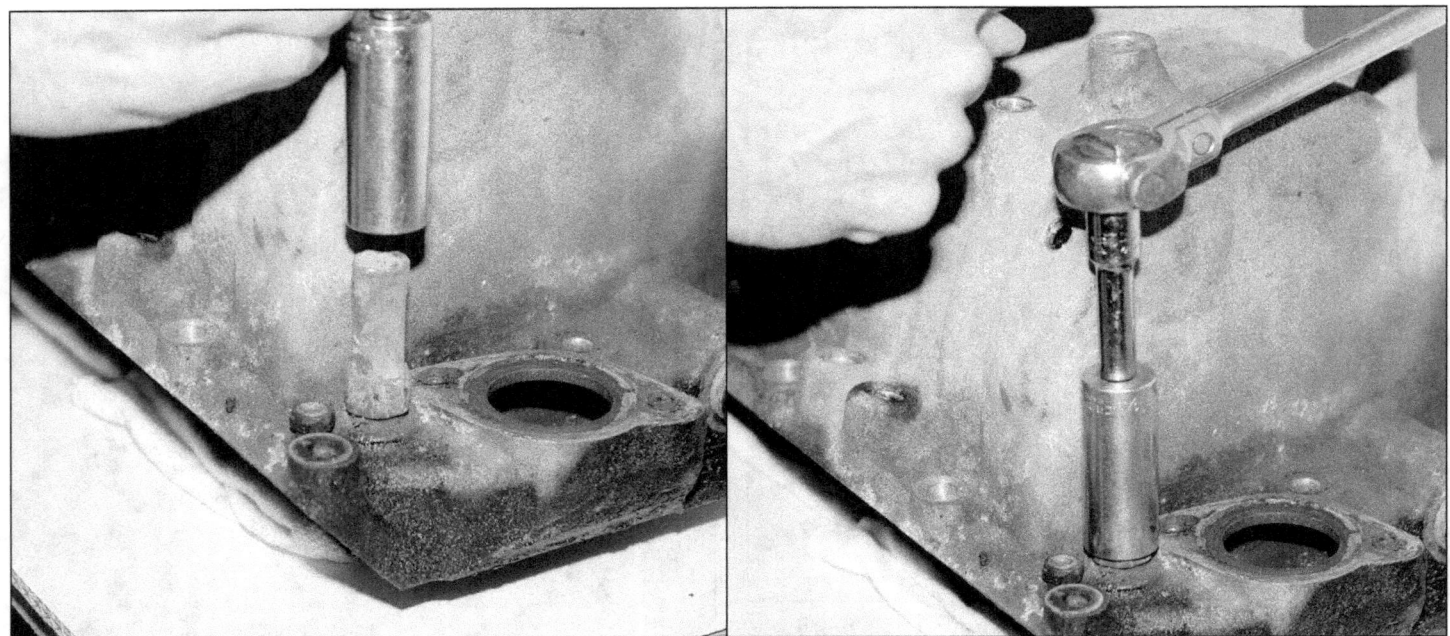

You can remove the hose fittings if you like. The vertical one can be removed with a deep-well socket while the horizontal one on the front of the manifold can be removed with a pipe wrench.

In order to manufacture the intricate shape, the bottom of the manifold is cast open and then closed with a plate. This plate is bolted to the manifold with a gasket in between. This seal is notorious for leaking, and it would be foolish to rebuild the engine and not address it, so remove the bolts and take the bottom cover off.

Scrape the gasket and put the plate away for cleaning.

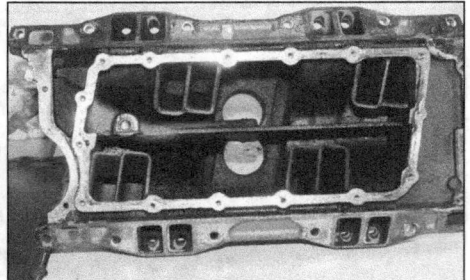

The manifold is now ready for cleaning. This one was not too bad in terms of oil leakage, but oil was beginning to seep into the intake. If this problem is not fixed, the oil blowing into the manifold will be burned and can be consumed rather quickly.

CHAPTER 3

CLEANING AND INSPECTION

At this point of the build you should have a block, two cylinder heads, and a bunch of dirty parts all marked and stored. Just how dirty they are, and your budget, can determine the cleaning method. There is more than one way to skin this cat, but some are better than others. Well, really one is better than all others. Proper cleaning is often the most undervalued and overlooked process in an engine rebuild. People are funny. They can be perfectly happy spending lots of money on things like spinning hubcaps and chrome alternator brackets, neither of which do anything for performance, but they'll balk at spending an extra hundred bucks to properly clean the block, cylinder heads, and other engine components. Do not make this mistake. All of the engine's individual components must be properly cleaned in order to perform a proper inspection. In addition, any contaminants that were in your used-up engine will go right into your rebuilt engine unless you get them out. In our opinion hot tanking is the optimal cleaning method. It requires a sub-contract operation and may cost a bit more than other methods, but it will do the best job, give the best chance of success, and clean your components without adding abrasive material to their internal passages.

Media Blasting

Media blasting refers to the use of steel shot, aluminum oxide, or glass bead to physically blast away anything adhering to the part. It is one of the most effective cleaning methods around, used at the factory to clean the sand cores from the blocks and cylinder heads after they are cast, and is a method that I do not promote using unless absolutely forced to. Some will disagree with this opinion and they may have their points.

My problem is that I do not want to introduce small steel shot or sand into the inside of my engine. Blocks and heads are relatively porous castings and it is about impossible to get out all of the blasting media. Thus any left inside is there to float around your engine until the end of time. It's like fingernails on the chalkboard. If you do elect to have engine components blasted with shot or sand, clean them extensively after you get them back. Blast them with water and then compressed air in every orifice and from every direction. When you think you have done a good job and can't possibly clean it anymore, do it six more times.

Hot Tank

How you clean your engine is your decision. You can get by with aerosol solvents and your garden hose—I can't stop you. But I strongly suggest you adhere to the following procedure. First off, home cleaning is a dirty business and will produce a toxic runoff that will either go into the ground or into the sewers. Second, home cleaning will not clean the engine components well. Metal parts are porous, and oil and grime gets into these openings and sticks. A cold hose in the backyard will not be able to rectify this. When the disassembly of the engine is complete, carry the block, cylinder heads, crankshaft, and rods to an automotive engine and machine shop and have them hot tanked. This process uses a heated caustic soda (sometime with agitation) to dissolve dirt and deposits on both the inside and outside of the engine. The heat and the caustic soda will allow the deposits locked into the pores of the metal to release. Some shops also use muriatic acid, another aggressive cleaner that is especially effective against rust. Once you establish where your components will be cleaned (it's best if it is the machine shop that you will be using), get a price in advance and make sure you mark everything you take to them both to keep everything straight and to make sure you get back the same pieces that you took in. You may elect to include items such as head bolts, valve hardware, valvecovers, the oil pan, and any other items that you want to get really clean. Small items can be put in a basket and then dipped in the tank.

Cleaning

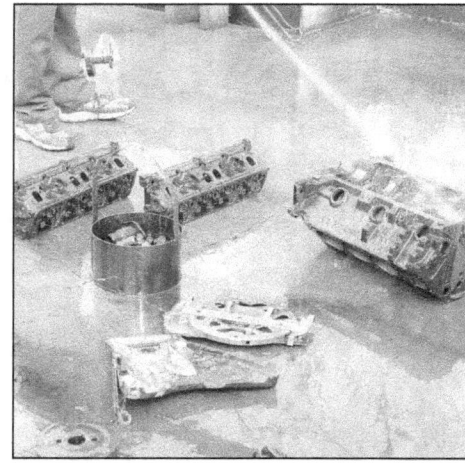

After the block, heads, and other parts come back from the shop, they should at a minimum be washed with a garden hose with a power nozzle attached. If possible hook your garden hose to your hot-water supply.

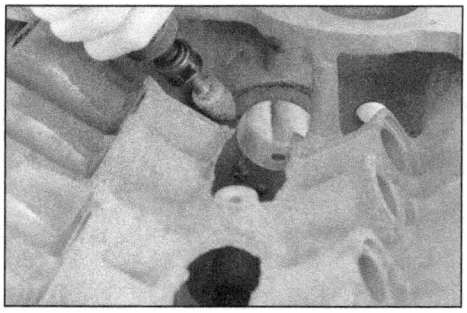

This is why my suggested method of hot tanking should be followed. The parts will come out extremely clean without the chance of blast media entering the block and heads. The oil and coolant passages will also be cleaned much better than with other methods. Your machine shop will also love you for bringing them parts this clean. Engine-machining centers use cooling fluids that should not be contaminated with used engine fluids.

Both inside and out, an engine will need a good cleaning before inspection can take place. Cleaning of the block and cylinder heads must include not only the exterior surfaces but also the internal (oil and coolant) passages. Over the life of the block, contaminants may build up in both systems, decreasing their efficiency and thus effectiveness. For proper cooling and lubrication these deposits must be removed.

CLEANING AND INSPECTION

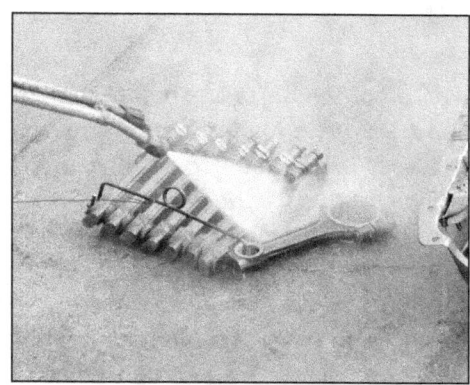

A better idea is to rent a hot-water/steam-pressure washer. Some machine shops offer pressure-washing services, and some probably do a good job. My advice is to get them to hot tank and rinse the parts, and steam them yourself. Hot-water pressure washers are not available at some rental places, but they are usually on hand at tractor and heavy-equipment rental stores. The last time I checked, the rate in my hometown was 60 bucks for a full-day rental. By renting the unit yourself you can accomplish a couple of things. The first is that you can spend a couple of hours cleaning your block and heads, which an automotive machine shop may not do. Plus, you can clean anything else around your house or shop. They are great for degreasing old engine compartments and the undersides of vehicles while they're in dry dock, as well as cleaning sidewalks or doing any other home chores.

When pressure washing the heads and block, stick the nozzle outlet in any port or cooling passage that is accessible. It will do wonders for cleaning internal passages.

Once the parts have been pressure washed, they should be set aside to dry. A haze of rust will appear very quickly, but don't be alarmed. It will not be a factor in the rebuild. As long as the engine will be machined in the near future you can leave it alone or, if the parts will sit in storage awhile before machining and inspection, they can be wiped down with a cloth dipped in clean engine oil.

A small brush can help clean bores and passages in the block and heads.

HOW TO REBUILD THE SMALL-BLOCK MOPAR

CHAPTER 3

Inspection

With all of the parts clean and on hand, it is time to start the inspection process. The final outcome of your engine rebuild will be very much dependent on a proper inspection of all of the individual pieces. Inspection methods for each individual component are in this chapter. It is here that you will measure and record critical dimensions on all of the working parts of the engine. This information will be used in the next

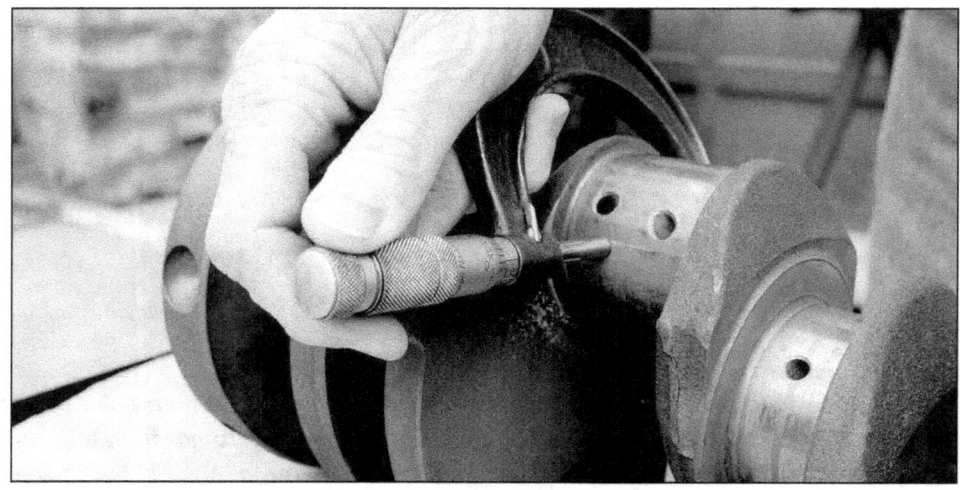

chapter to determine what will be re-used, what will be replaced, and what will be machined. Even pieces that you know you will replace should still be thoroughly inspected as they may indicate a problem. In the reference section of the book, there are a couple of checklists that you can use in place or use to make copies from. I suggest that you make a Xerox copy and put it on a clipboard. If you think this is a little nerdy, think again. Unless you are a seasoned engine builder they will make your task easier, and if you are a seasoned engine builder you probably don't need this book anyway. With some other book projects I had the opportunity to spend a good bit of time in many top-line NASCAR teams' shops, and when you walk through one of them you can't swing a dead cat without hitting a couple of checklists. Index your parts correctly and know the location of each it.

For the average rebuild, visual inspection will suffice on many parts, but there are some more advanced measurements that must be taken with some rather expensive tools. We'll start with the big pieces that may require machining, which will probably take longer than smaller items that can be purchased quickly. But first you'll need your inspection tools. The good news is that relatively few tools are actually necessary to properly inspect your engine components. The bad news is that a couple of the few that are needed are relatively expensive. If you think that this engine rebuild is a one-time deal, you might seriously consider allowing a machine shop to do your critical inspections, especially to the block.

There are two keys to proper inspection. The first is having accurate measuring devices. The second is using them in a proper manner. Engine inspection for a beginner and a professional engine builder are essentially the same process, but in practice will not resemble one another. The process that will be described in this book may take the better part of a day for a first-timer to complete, while an accomplished builder can accomplish the same in half an hour. This is due to the pro's familiarity with both the parts and the tools. If you decide to do the inspection yourself, do not be intimidated by this—just take your time. The goal is to get accurate measurements and not to impress.

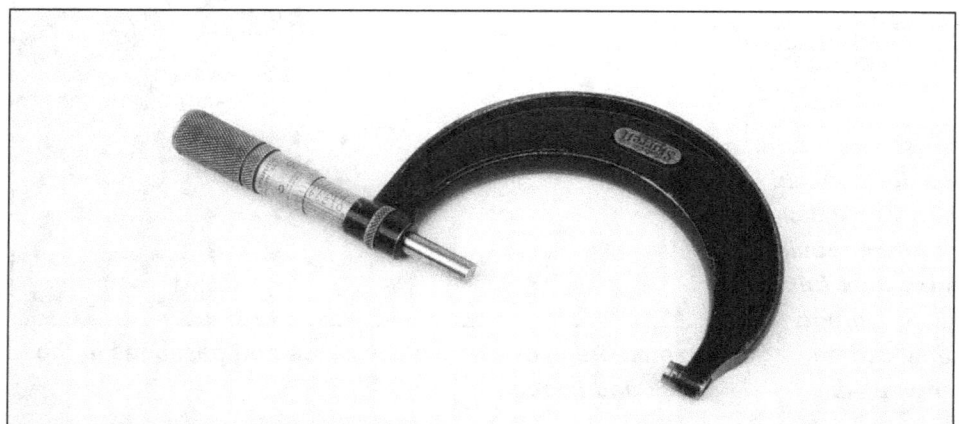

A micrometer is a measuring device that can measure both length and diameter. The C-shaped tool is straddled over the piece being measured and dialed in to get the exact measurement. Micrometers are reasonably affordable and are well within the budget of the average home mechanic.

CLEANING AND INSPECTION

A bore gauge is a tool used to measure the inside diameter of a bore. To properly inspect a block, a bore gauge must be used to measure all eight cylinders as well as the line bore. A good dial bore gauge and setting tool will set you back in the neighborhood of $2,000, which is why it may be wise to sub out this task to the machine shop.

Small dial indicators with a magnetic base can be picked up for a reasonable $50 or so.

Feeler gauges are an inexpensive way to accurately measure gaps. Feeler gauges come in sets and will have individual metal pieces that are produced to an exact thickness.

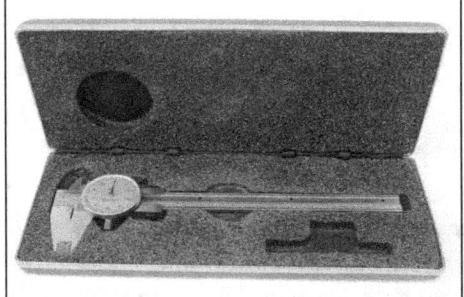

Like micrometers, dial calipers are used to measure lengths and diameters. Dial calipers come in the traditional style, both with a scale and needle, or can be purchased in the newer digital form. Dial calipers are good for quick measurements and are pretty accurate, but aren't as trusty as a good set of micrometers. A decent set of dial calipers can be had for about $30 and are a useful piece of a kit to have in the toolbox.

Block Inspection

With the block completely cleaned, inspection can begin. There will be more steps associated with block inspection than any other component. First, visually inspect every square inch of the block—inside and out. Look for cracks, chips, or any scoring in the cylinders. If you find a crack it may be repairable, but a replacement block may be necessary. A cracked block may not be the end of the world, but the repair will be beyond the capabilities of almost all home mechanics. Depending on the value of the vehicle in a classic-car sense, the location of the crack, and the overall condition of the block, you might want to strongly consider replacing the block. If you are dealing with a rare muscle car with the original engine I can understand the welding choice, but a sound, un-welded block is always preferred. Welding cast iron is difficult at best, and if the crack is in a hard-to-reach spot it may be hopeless. Either way, 318s and 360s had long production runs, and replacing a block is not too expensive. By the time you jack around toting your cracked block around and paying a good welder, the difference in cost may not be all that much. The 340 block had a much shorter production run and is, therefore, rarer. If you are intent on keeping the block, talk to as many people as you can to try to find a good welder. This guy will probably determine whether you ride or walk home after dropping a bundle on a rebuild.

If your block seems to be in pretty good shape, you will need to measure the cylinder bore and the line bore. The bore of each cylinder must be measured to determine wear and distortion. Chances are they will need to be machined to bring them back to cylindrical. The line bore must also be checked. Since this is the mounting bed of the crankshaft, it is essential that all of the mounting surfaces are smooth, the bore is round, and all are in a very straight line. A crankshaft's life is difficult. The math on the crankshaft on our project engine is impressive. The 15-year-old engine had 172,000 miles on it. Figuring an average of 30 mph at 3,000 rpm over its life, the crank has turned a total of 1,032,000,000 revolutions. In order to survive over a billion rotations, it must have a true axis on which to turn.

Measuring Cylinder Bore

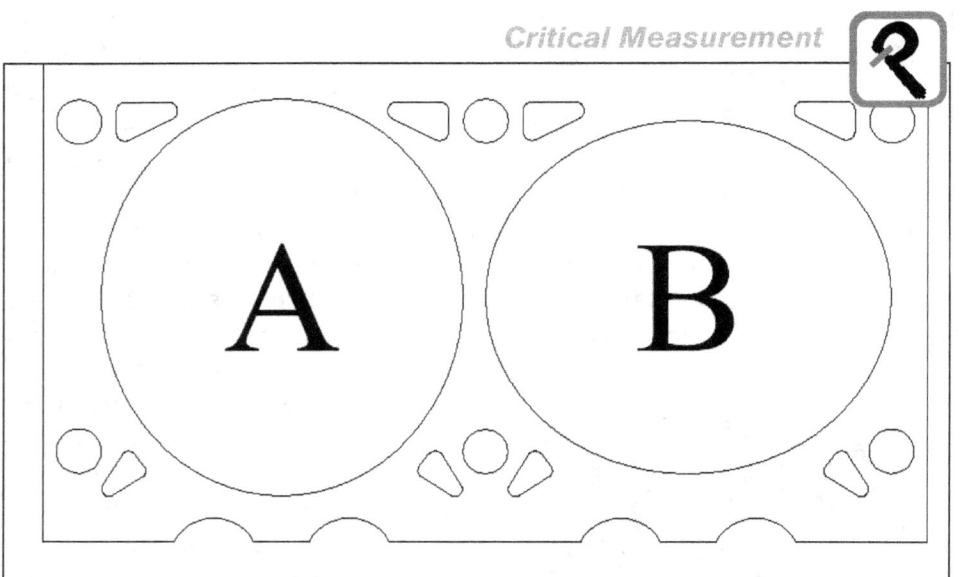

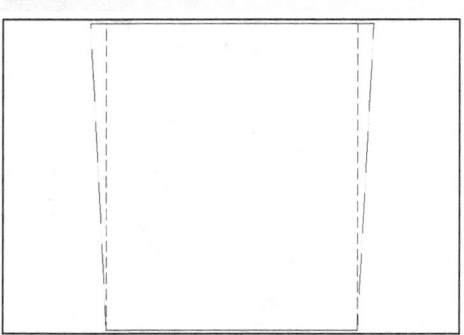

The other wear that must be checked is the bore's taper. Over the engine's life one or more cylinders may wear more on the top than on the bottom, or vice versa. Thus the taper is the relationship to the diameter of the bore vertically, or from top to bottom.

There are two main types of cylinder wear to be concerned with. The first is the concentricity of the bore. An engine starts its life with cylinder bores that are circular. As the engine wears the bore may become a bit egg-shaped. This may occur on one or more bores or on none at all. Thus the diameters of the bore are compared on a horizontal or side-to-side basis.

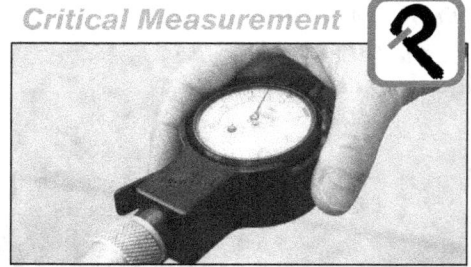

Each of the cylinder bores must be inspected, measured, and evaluated in the following manner. With a bore gauge, measure the diameter of the cylinder parallel to the crankshaft at the top (just below the top edge of the cylinder), the middle, and the bottom. Record the measurements.

Next measure the diameter of the cylinders at the same cylinder height locations perpendicular to the axis of the crankshaft, also recording the measurements.

These six measurements will be used to help calculate the condition of the cylinder. By comparing the measurements along the vertical lines (top to center and center to bottom) the taper of the cylinder can be calculated. By comparing the numbers on the horizontal axis, the roundness of the cylinder can be determined. A very slight amount of taper and out-of-round is allowed. Use the diagram and chart on the next page to guide your inspection and record your results. If there is a taper and/or an out-of-round problem, the cylinders must be bored.

CLEANING AND INSPECTION

Worksheet 1

Cylinder Bore Comparison Chart (1)

Cylinder 1
Top Parallel (A) _____	(C-A) _____	Top Perpendicular (D) _____	(F-D) _____
Mid Parallel (B) _____	(A-B) _____	Mid Perpendicular (E) _____	(D-E) _____
Bot Parallel (C) _____	(B-C) _____	Bot Perpendicular (F) _____	(E-F) _____

Cylinder 2
Top Parallel (A) _____	(C-A) _____	Top Perpendicular (D) _____	(F-D) _____
Mid Parallel (B) _____	(A-B) _____	Mid Perpendicular (E) _____	(D-E) _____
Bot Parallel (C) _____	(B-C) _____	Bot Perpendicular (F) _____	(E-F) _____

Cylinder 3
Top Parallel (A) _____	(C-A) _____	Top Perpendicular (D) _____	(F-D) _____
Mid Parallel (B) _____	(A-B) _____	Mid Perpendicular (E) _____	(D-E) _____
Bot Parallel (C) _____	(B-C) _____	Bot Perpendicular (F) _____	(E-F) _____

Cylinder 4
Top Parallel (A) _____	(C-A) _____	Top Perpendicular (D) _____	(F-D) _____
Mid Parallel (B) _____	(A-B) _____	Mid Perpendicular (E) _____	(D-E) _____
Bot Parallel (C) _____	(B-C) _____	Bot Perpendicular (F) _____	(E-F) _____

Cylinder 5
Top Parallel (A) _____	(C-A) _____	Top Perpendicular (D) _____	(F-D) _____
Mid Parallel (B) _____	(A-B) _____	Mid Perpendicular (E) _____	(D-E) _____
Bot Parallel (C) _____	(B-C) _____	Bot Perpendicular (F) _____	(E-F) _____

Cylinder 6
Top Parallel (A) _____	(C-A) _____	Top Perpendicular (D) _____	(F-D) _____
Mid Parallel (B) _____	(A-B) _____	Mid Perpendicular (E) _____	(D-E) _____
Bot Parallel (C) _____	(B-C) _____	Bot Perpendicular (F) _____	(E-F) _____

Cylinder 7
Top Parallel (A) _____	(C-A) _____	Top Perpendicular (D) _____	(F-D) _____
Mid Parallel (B) _____	(A-B) _____	Mid Perpendicular (E) _____	(D-E) _____
Bot Parallel (C) _____	(B-C) _____	Bot Perpendicular (F) _____	(E-F) _____

Cylinder 8
Top Parallel (A) _____	(C-A) _____	Top Perpendicular (D) _____	(F-D) _____
Mid Parallel (B) _____	(A-B) _____	Mid Perpendicular (E) _____	(D-E) _____
Bot Parallel (C) _____	(B-C) _____	Bot Perpendicular (F) _____	(E-F) _____

PARALLEL MEASUREMENT — A, B, C (SIDE VIEW, FRONT OF ENGINE)

PERPINDICULAR MEASUREMENT — D, E, F (SIDE VIEW, SIDE OF ENGINE)

Worksheet 1 Continued

Line Bore Comparison Chart

Bore/Cap 1

Front Parallel (A)_____ (C-A) _____	Front Perpendicular (D) _____	(F-D) _____
Mid Parallel (B)_____ (A-B) _____	Mid Perpendicular (E) _____	(D-E) _____
Rear Parallel (C)_____ (B-C) _____	Rear Perpendicular (F) _____	(E-F) _____

Cap 2

Front Parallel (A)_____ (C-A) _____	Front Perpendicular (D) _____	(F-D) _____
Mid Parallel (B)_____ (A-B) _____	Mid Perpendicular (E) _____	(D-E) _____
Rear Parallel (C)_____ (B-C) _____	Rear Perpendicular (F) _____	(E-F) _____

Cap 3

Front Parallel (A)_____ (C-A) _____	Front Perpendicular (D) _____	(F-D) _____
Mid Parallel (B)_____ (A-B) _____	Mid Perpendicular (E) _____	(D-E) _____
Rear Parallel (C)_____ (B-C) _____	Rear Perpendicular (F) _____	(E-F) _____

Cap 4

Front Parallel (A)_____ (C-A) _____	Front Perpendicular (D) _____	(F-D) _____
Mid Parallel (B)_____ (A-B) _____	Mid Perpendicular (E) _____	(D-E) _____
Rear Parallel (C)_____ (B-C) _____	Rear Perpendicular (F) _____	(E-F) _____

Cap 5

Front Parallel (A)_____ (C-A) _____	Front Perpendicular (D) _____	(F-D) _____
Mid Parallel (B)_____ (A-B) _____	Mid Perpendicular (E) _____	(D-E) _____
Rear Parallel (C)_____ (B-C) _____	Rear Perpendicular (F) _____	(E-F) _____

Measuring Main Bearing Bore

Critical Measurement

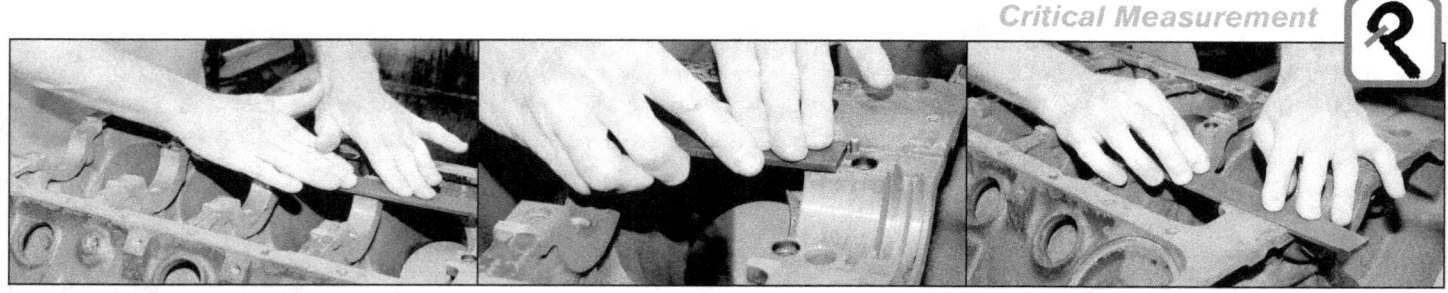

Fortunately the line bore of small-block engines tends to stay pretty true. To check the line bore, the main caps must be replaced on the engine and torqued down to the proper spec. Before replacing the caps, run a fine file over the mating surfaces of both the block's and caps' flat surfaces and edges to remove any burrs or obstructions. Use very light pressure with the file, as your goal is not to remove a lot of material but just to clean up the surface so that the block and caps mate well.

CLEANING AND INSPECTION

Clean the inside surface of the saddles and caps with acetone and a clean rag after filing.

Like the block, the caps should have their mating surface smoothed over with a fine file.

Make sure the caps are in the proper order and put them into place. It may be necessary to tap them with a soft hammer to get them to seat properly.

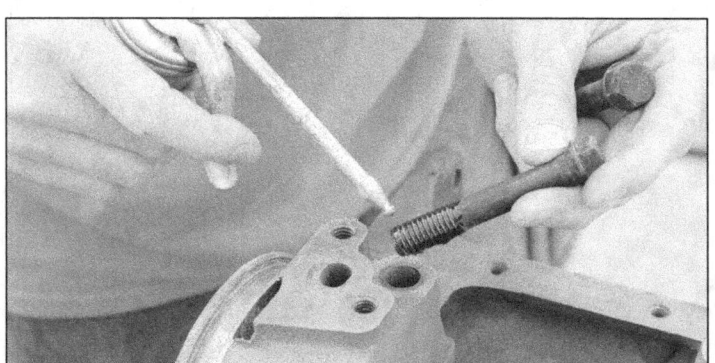
Before reinserting the main cap bolts, pre-lube both the bolts' threads and the threads in the block with engine oil.

Torque the bolts to the specifications listed in Apendix B.

HOW TO REBUILD THE SMALL-BLOCK MOPAR

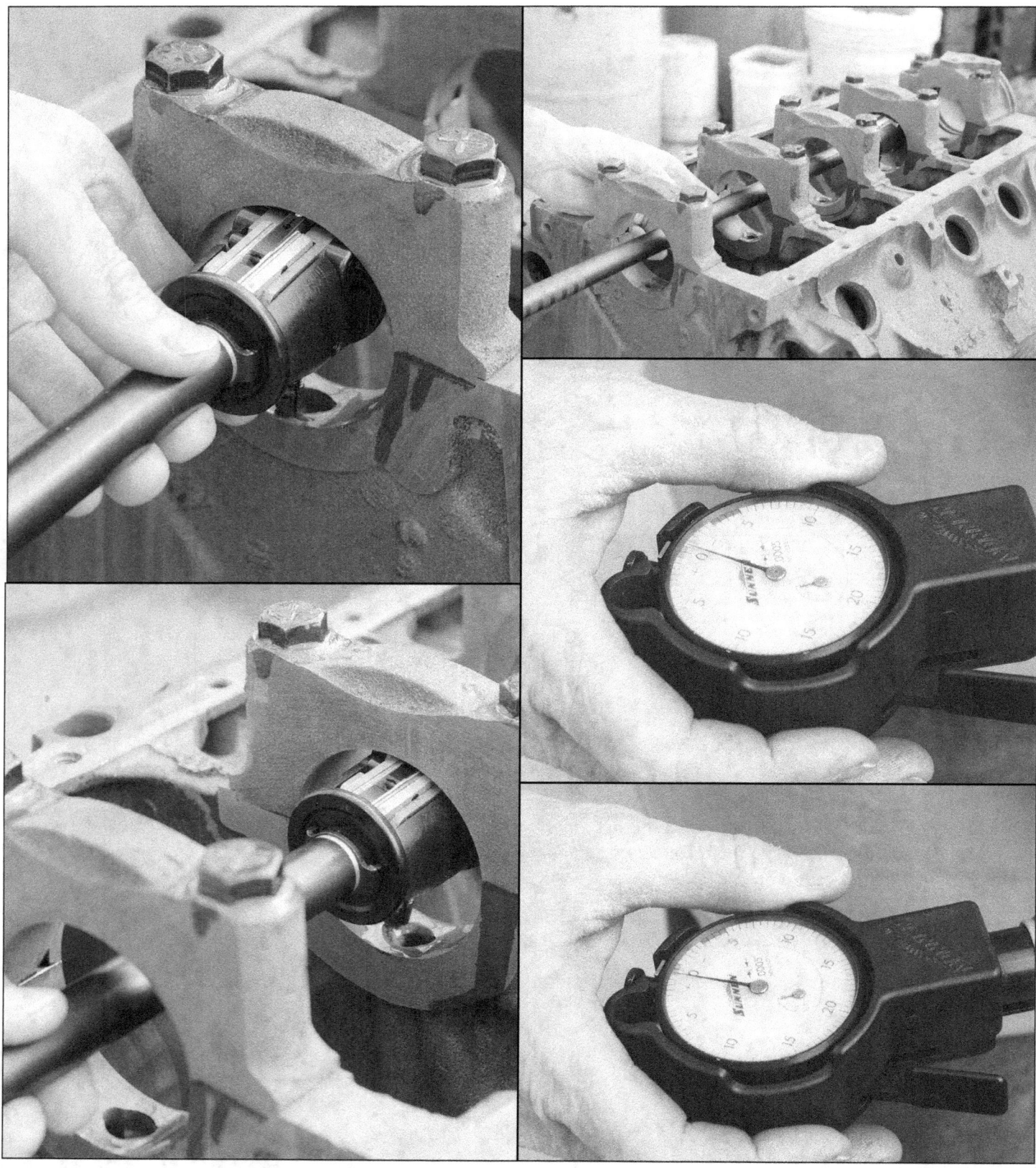

When all of the caps are torqued and in place, insert the gauge in each bore. You will measure in much the same way you measured the cylinder bore. Use the chart on the next page to record your inspection results.

CLEANING AND INSPECTION

Lifter Bores

Critical Measurement

Under normal wear conditions the lifter bores should not require radical machining for a typical rebuild. Unless you had a serious problem with a lifter, a good visual inspection supplemented with a finger rub should do the job. If the lifter bores are lightly scratched they can be smoothed over with a light honing.

Measuring the Decks

Critical Measurement

The block's decks are the surfaces that mate to the underside of the cylinder heads. Over a block's life this surface will not wear, but may distort and warp over time. When the engine is disassembled, stresses are relieved so the decks must be checked for flatness. Before the engine can be reassembled the surface must be checked to make sure it is flat. The best way to do this is to have a machine shop do it. This is accomplished with the block fixtured on a surfacing machine. If the block is properly set up, the cutting head will be a true 45 degrees from the centerline of the crankshaft.

Left: If a lifter bore has been damaged or is worn severely, it must be taken to a competent machine shop and sleeved. I could not find a sleeved Dodge around the shop, so this is a Chevrolet race block with sleeved lifters. The process of sleeving lifters for all blocks is pretty much the same.

A dial indicator is attached to the cutting head of the surfacing machine to take the measurements.

Worksheet 2

Main Bearing Bore

	High	Low	Variance
Bore No. 1			
Bore No. 2			
Bore No. 3			
Bore No. 4			
Bore No. 5			

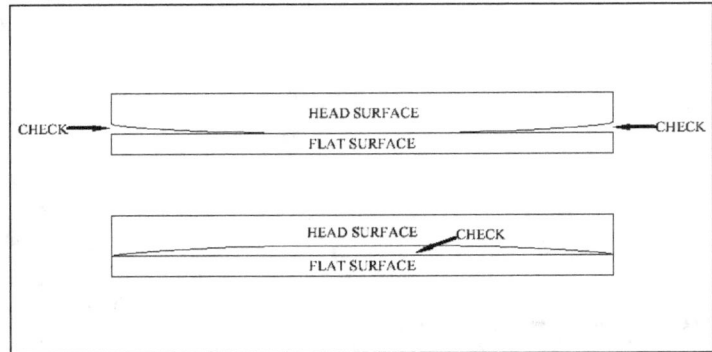

A common way to measure flatness is to lay a trusted straight edge across the deck in multiple directions and look for areas where the edge does not mate up to the deck. With the edge on the most secure point that can be found, and with your eye at the level of the deck, look to determine where the edge leaves the surface. Use a feeler gauge to measure the gap at its widest point. You will need to make multiple checks along both the length and the width of each of the block's decks.

Crankshaft

Critical Measurement

Before measuring the crankshaft, take a good look at the oil passages. Run a clean wire brush through all of the oil passages to make sure that they are clear and blow them out with compressed air. The oil passages should be cleaned as well as possible, as they are essential to keep the crankshaft and bearing surfaces cool and slick. If the main and/or the rod journals have excessive wear or damage, the crankshaft will have to go through a grinding operation. This means that the journals will be machined to a slightly smaller diameter. Check and record your measurements on the worksheet and store the crankshaft in a safe location. Just as the surfaces of the crankshaft saddles and caps must be the proper size and in alignment, so must the journal surfaces of the crankshaft.

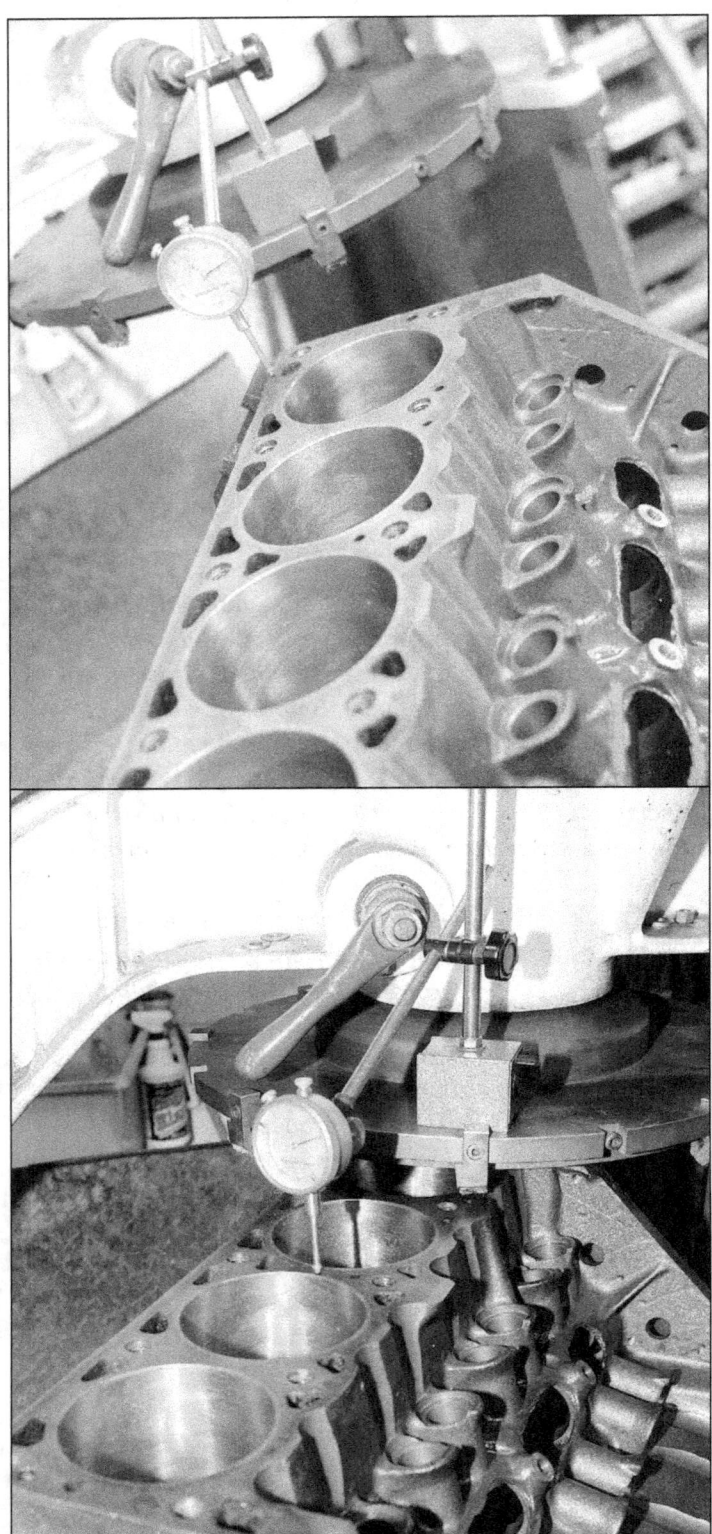

The measuring probe can be run across the head to take very accurate measurements and chart a true profile of the head. This may cost you a bit, but it's worth it to get an accurate assessment of your deck's flatness.

CLEANING AND INSPECTION

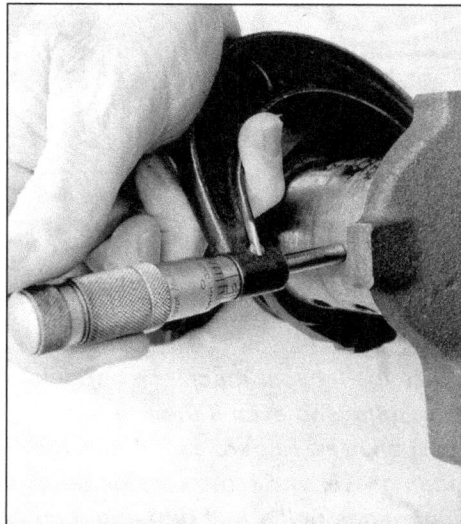

Use a micrometer to measure the journals of both the rod bearings' and main bearings' journals and record your results.

Feel around the rear of the crank where the rear seal meets the crankshaft. This dimension is not as critical as the main and rod journal sizes, but the surfaces must be clean and smooth for the seal to work properly.

Worksheet 3			
Crankshaft Journals			
	High	Low	Variance
Rod Journal No. 1	_____	_____	_____
Rod Journal No. 2	_____	_____	_____
Rod Journal No. 3	_____	_____	_____
Rod Journal No. 4	_____	_____	_____
Rod Journal No. 5	_____	_____	_____
Rod Journal No. 6	_____	_____	_____
Rod Journal No. 7	_____	_____	_____
Rod Journal No. 8	_____	_____	_____
Main Journal No. 1	_____	_____	_____
Main Journal No. 2	_____	_____	_____
Main Journal No. 3	_____	_____	_____
Main Journal No. 4	_____	_____	_____
Main Journal No. 5	_____	_____	_____

HOW TO REBUILD THE SMALL-BLOCK MOPAR

Connecting Rods

Critical Measurement

The rod's big-end bore can be checked by hand with a bore gauge, but I suggest you let your machine shop take care of it. Doing it by hand will take a good bit of time and gives questionable results, and even if the rod is still in tolerance there are a couple of things you will be having your machine shop do to it anyway. Regardless of how they are checked, the caps must be put back on the rods. Oil the threads, secure the rod in a vise, and torque the bolts to 45 ft-lbs. When torquing connecting-rod bolts, tighten them finger tight and then tighten one bolt a half turn and then move to the other and turn it a half turn. Then go back to the other bolt and repeat the process until the torque is at spec. The idea is to keep equal, or as equal as possible, pressure on the two bolts and thus the rod cap.

The quickest and most accurate method is a dedicated rod-bore measuring device like this Sunnen unit. Your machine shop can do them accurately and quickly, and it won't cost that much. If the rod is out of tolerance it can be replaced, or material can be machined from the inside of the rod and oversized bearings used.

Worksheet 4

Rod Big End

	High	Low	Variance
Rod No. 1			
Rod No. 2			
Rod No. 3			
Rod No. 4			
Rod No. 5			
Rod No. 6			
Rod No. 7			
Rod No. 8			

Pistons and Pins

Critical Inspection

Don't spend a lot of time on cleaning and inspecting pistons until the condition of the block is determined. If it is necessary to bore the block, new pistons must be purchased. If you are on a super-tight budget and the cylinder wear on the block is still in specification you can re-use the pistons as long as they are not damaged. I suggest you don't, as a set of stock pistons is not that expensive and will certainly mate better with a freshly bored or honed block. If you are going to re-use the pistons, visually inspect the surface of the piston inside and out, looking for visible wear patterns. Check every ring groove in the piston, making sure that they are clean and undamaged. If you are to re-use the pistons, and you marked everything as suggested in Chapter Two, then you will be able to reinstall the pistons correctly oriented in the cylinders they came out of.

CLEANING AND INSPECTION

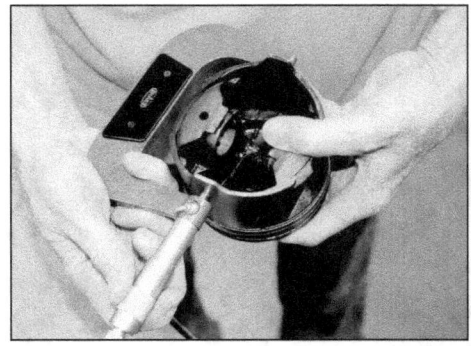

Measure the diameter of the piston, especially around the skirt at the bottom, and compare it with the specifications listed in the tolerance chart.

Cylinder Heads

Critical Inspection

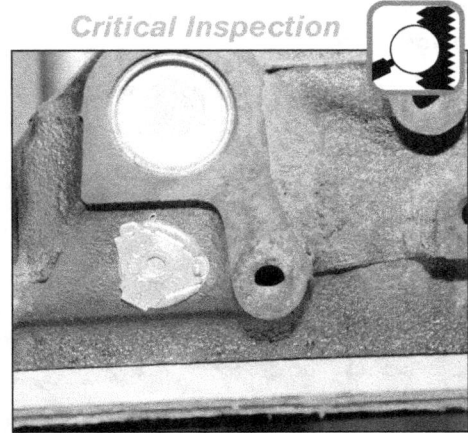

For cylinder heads to perform properly, each component must be within specification and the assembly properly performed. Over their running life, the cylinder heads will wear in a few critical places, and, like the block's decks, the heads may warp due to the tensions and heat cycles that they have been put through. With the heads disassembled per the instructions in Chapter 2 and cleaned per the instructions earlier in this chapter, the heads can be inspected. Start by giving the cylinder heads a good visual inspection on every surface for cracks or damage.

Like short blocks, heads can be purchased ready to bolt on with the machining done and the valves and springs installed. Purchasing remanufactured heads has advantages and disadvantages. The advantage is ease and speed. Throw your old head and your money on the counter and walk out with your heads. The disadvantage is that you don't know who built your head. This engine had one original head and one remanufactured head. The original head, which had many thousands more miles on it, had much, much better fit between the valves and the valveguides.

Valveseats

Critical Inspection

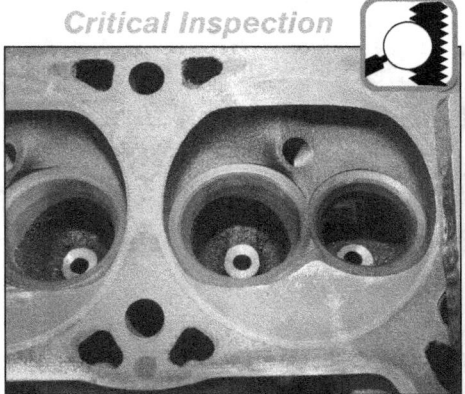

The valveseat is the area where the valve and head actually meet. For proper compression to be possible, the edge of the valve and the edge of the seat must be in good condition and properly machined. Check the seat for wear, cracks, or pitting. If the valveseats are worn the cylinder head will have to make a trip to the machine shop. I suggest you put this on your list of "must dos" anyway.

Valves

Critical Inspection

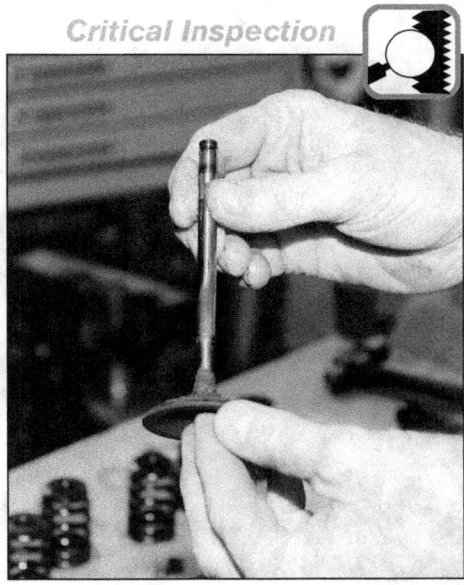

Clean the valves completely with solvent to remove any oil or dirt. Visually inspect the valve for any pitting, distortion, or unusual wear. Roll the stem of the valve on a flat surface to make sure that it is not bent.

Valveseals

Critical Inspection

Before the valveguides can be inspected, the valveseals must be removed. The condition of the valveguide can be determined with both a visual inspection and a mechanical check. A pair of special pliers like these should be used, but if used carefully a pair of regular pliers will suffice.

Valveguides

Critical Inspection

Partially insert a new valve in the guide and try to move it side to side. If you can feel play, the guide needs to be replaced. As the valves move up and down through the engine's life the wear usually occurs in the guide. The guide's function is twofold. With its close tolerance it keeps oil out of the combustion chamber, and it also locates the valve on the valveseat. The tolerance on the intake valve is a mere .001 to .003 inch total tolerance. This means it is .0005 to .0015 inch on each side of the valvestem. On the exhaust valve the tolerance is .002 to .004 inch, a bit looser—but not much.

Valvesprings

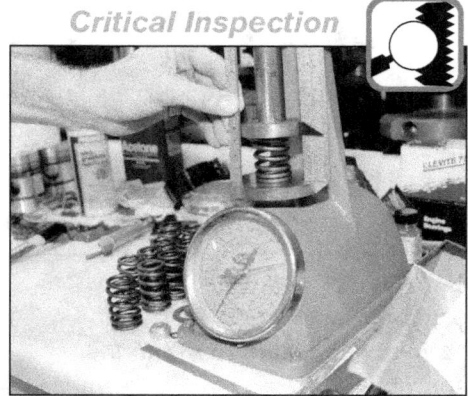

Critical Inspection

Valvesprings can be re-used if you elect, but they should be closely inspected. Their tension is checked with a special gauge that measures resistance at varying heights.

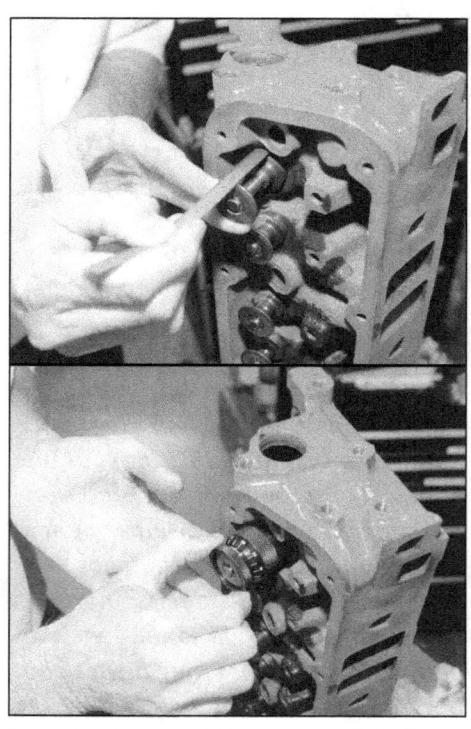

In order to match tension to height, the distance from where the valve sits in the head to the retainer at the top of the valve must be determined. This can be done with a 6-inch scale or, if you are a tool nut, with one of these special dial-type gauges.

CLEANING AND INSPECTION

Rocker Arms

Critical Inspection

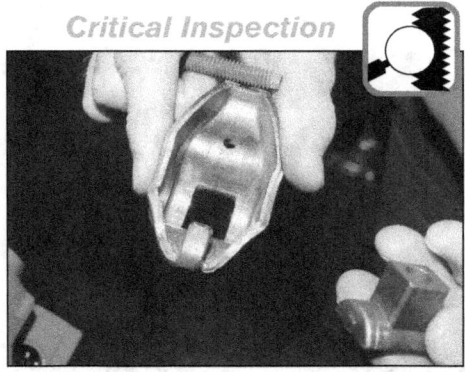

Closely inspect each rocker, paying special attention to where it meets the valve and the pushrod. Also check the pivot point where the rocker rides on the stud. If any of these areas shows excessive wear, cracks, or any other type of damage, they should be replaced.

Flat-Tappet Lifter

Critical Inspection

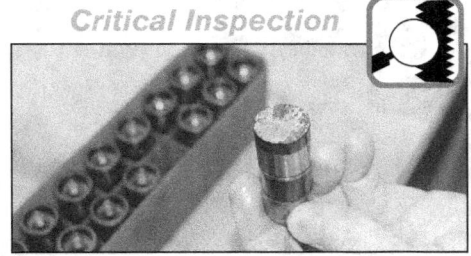

If you have an older-model engine you, will have flat-tappet hydraulic lifters. The hydraulic plunger in the lifter keeps the tension between the pushrod and rocker, eliminating the need for valve adjustments. If you are going through a rebuild on a flat-tappet engine, it is best to replace the cam and lifters. While they are heavily lubricated, it is still a metal-to-metal relationship that the camshaft and lifters share. If you do elect to re-use your lifters and cam make sure to mark the location of each lifter so that it can be reinstalled into the bore from which it was removed.

Roller Lifter

Critical Inspection

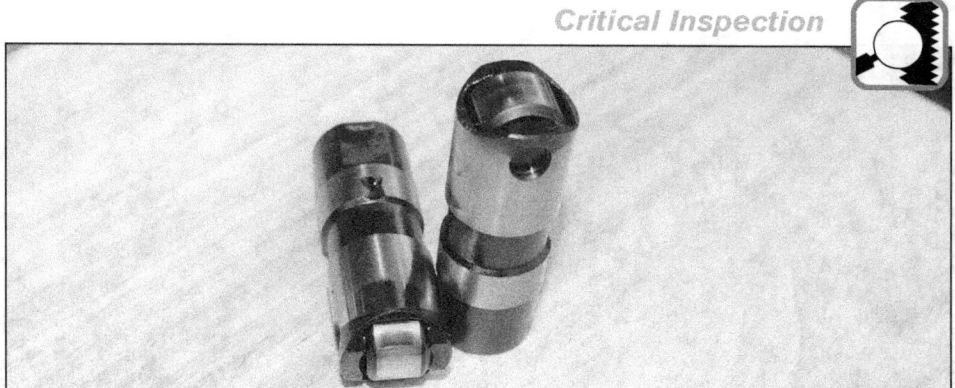

Later-model engines will have roller lifters like these. These began appearing on Mopar small-blocks in 1987 and continued when the Magnum versions of the 318 and 360 were introduced. The roller lifter is also a hydraulic lifter, but also has a small roller that rides on the camshaft in place of a conventional lifter's solid surface. This dramatically reduces the friction between the cam and lifter for better performance and longer life. Like flat-tappet lifters, roller lifters are best replaced, but there are a couple of companies (see Engine Resource Center section) out there that will refurbish them, which might save you a few bucks. Also, like flat-tappet lifters, if you re-use your roller lifters, return each one to its proper bore.

Pushrods

Critical Inspection

Pushrods can be re-used if they are in the proper condition. First, they must be straight. Lay each pushrod on a flat surface and roll it. If any amount of warpage can be found in any of the pushrods they all should be replaced. The pushrods are hollow, which allows oil to travel through them from the lifter to the top of the cylinder head in order to lubricate the valvetrain. These passages should be inspected and must be clear in order to properly lubricate the head. Pay special attention to the aperture that meets the lifter to make sure that its round shape has not been distorted. LA engines from 1967 to 1992 do not have the oil passages in the tappets, and oil is supplied to the head through passages in the block and heads instead of through the lifters.

Camshaft

Critical Inspection

Camshafts can be re-used under certain situations, but not in others. When dealing with a non-roller lifter, the wear between the lifter and cam can be significant. Check the camshaft for any wear on the lobes. If the cam shows any signs of wear it should be replaced.

Rod-Bearing-to-Rod-Journal Clearance

Critical Inspection

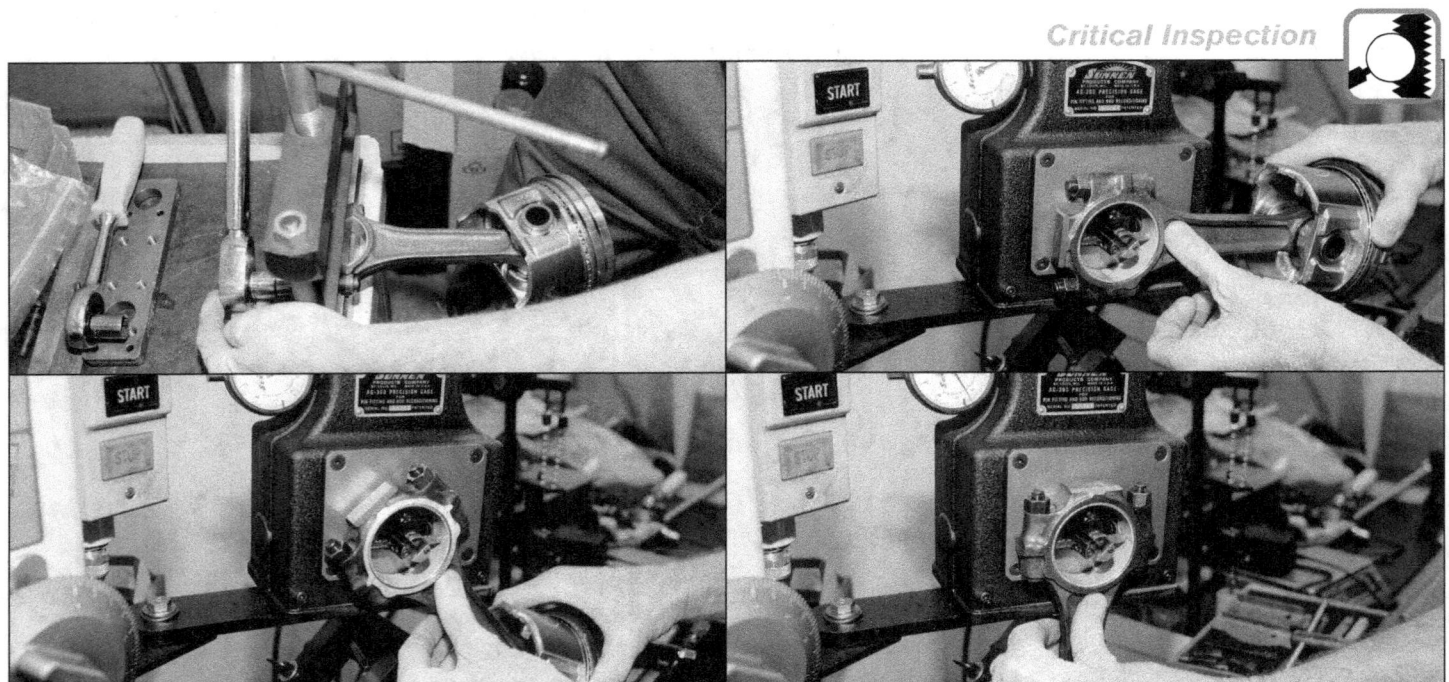

If you are doing no machining, or when the machining is complete, both the clearance between the rod bearings and the rod journals must be measured. First clean the inside of the rod bore and the bearings with acetone. Put them in place and bolt the caps on. Oil the threads of the rod bolts before assembling them. Torque the rods to 10 ft-lbs and increase the torque in 10-ft-lb increments, moving from side to side until they are at 45 ft-lbs. Then measure the inside diameter of the rod bearings. Record the numbers and subtract the rod journal size that you measured earlier from it. This will give you your rod-bearing-to-rod-journal clearance.

CLEANING AND INSPECTION

Main-Bearing-to-Main-Journal Clearance

Main-Journal Clearance

Critical Inspection

See caption on page 68

CHAPTER 3

Before placing the bearing halves into the block, do a final cleaning/wipe-down of both the bearing and its seat in the block. Acetone and a clean cloth (or quality paper towel) will suffice. Place the bottom of the bearing half into the journal of each main saddle. It should fit securely in the saddle with its edges flush and level. Once all of the bearing halves have been installed in the block, the other halves can be installed in the caps, and the caps can be bolted on. As with the block, clean the bearings and their mating surface on the caps. The bearing halves can then be put into position and the cap fitted to the block. The cap bolts can then be installed and finger tightened. Remember to put a few drops of oil or other favorite lubricant on the bolt's threads before installing it. Repeat this process until all of the bearings and caps are on the block. Once the bearings and caps are all in place they can be torqued and their diameters checked. The key to torquing the caps is to pull them to the block evenly. By evenly I mean side to side between the bolts. Do not torque one bolt to 85 ft-lbs and then the other. Torque the left bolt to 20 and then the right bolt to 20. Then take the left to 30 and then the right to 30. Use this method, increasing the torque by 10 ft-lbs per cycle, until the bolts are all torqued to 85 ft-lbs.

With all of the caps and bearings in place and torqued down, the inside diameter of the bearings can be checked. Using a dial bore indicator, rotate the tool around the inside of the bearing and record the size of the bore. Do this for each bearing. When all of the bore diameters have been recorded, measure the diameter of the mating journals of the crankshaft. Then subtract the size of each crank journal from the inside diameter size of the bearing and record the result. This is the crankshaft-bearing clearance. The tolerance of the crankshaft bearings to the crankshaft journal is listed in the tolerance chart.

Oil Pan

After the oil pan has been cleaned it should be inspected inside and out. Make sure that the surface that mated to the block is not distorted or marred, which might keep the block and pan from sealing and, thus, result in an oil leak. Oil pans on later-model engines are painted on both the outside and inside. This paint seems to hold up well under operation but can come loose during aggressive cleaning. If this happens, it is a good idea to get all of the paint from the inside to prevent any that has been weakened from coming loose and floating around the oil system. To fully clean the pan it may have to be chemically cleaned more than once.

Valvecovers

There should be no reason to change your valvecovers unless (a) you have modified the valvetrain, which may require taller covers, or (b) you really want to. If you put in beefy rocker arms and a high-lift cam it may be necessary to have more room under the cover. As far as dressing up an engine goes, you can go chrome or aluminum, smooth or ribbed. The choice is vast, but, with the exception of the aluminum covers being a bit lighter, there is no performance increase for the money. My advice is to repaint your stock covers and spend a hundred bucks somewhere else. If the covers have solidified oil residue or appear extremely dirty they should be hot tanked with the other engine components. If they are late-model parts they may be painted on the inside as well as the outside at the factory. If you hot tank them, make sure that all of the inside paint is removed.

CHAPTER 4

MACHINING AND CHOOSING PARTS

With all of the parts cleaned and inspected, it is decision time. The previous steps determined where your engine stands at this point. Now it is time for you to decide where you will take it. If you have nine kids and are doing a maintenance rebuild on your old rusty farm truck that you haul hay in, your goal will probably be getting by with the least extensive and thus least expensive rebuild possible. If you bought a bunch of Microsoft stock when it was offered and have no kids and an understanding wife, your engine may be open to many more options. Some choices will be made for you. If your block, is so worn that it must be bored then you have to buy pistons. If your camshaft has a lobe ground off then you will be buying a cam and lifters and replacing cam bearings. Some choices will be more subjective. These will be the things that you don't have to do but want to do. The process will begin with getting the block into shape. Follow through the next few pages, which will guide you through tolerance comparisons with corresponding machining operations, when they are necessary, what they accomplish, and what their process requires in other areas of the engine. Keep in mind that when a block is machined some of its critical dimensions will be forever changed. When the block is decked the surface of the head will move toward the crankshaft the distance of the amount of material that is removed from the block. If the cylinders are bored, oversized (larger diameter) pistons must be used. This is why it is critical not to buy parts until you know exactly where you stand concerning your block and cylinder heads. As you rebuild your engine you will face the same choice in every piece—re-use it, refresh it, or replace it.

Choosing a Machine Shop

If your engine requires substantial machining you can either shell out about $100,000 for the machines and tooling required to do the job right—or find a local automotive machine shop to do your work for you. Unless you live in a mechanical vacuum, start the process in the

Yellow Pages, supplemented by asking around. Most communities have weekend cruises somewhere close. Walk around and ask folks where a good machine shop is. Most car folks love to talk, so be prepared to get a 20-minute answer to a yes or no question. When you get some names of possible shops, go and pay them a visit. Most will give you an idea of what some standard operations will cost, but you must understand their reluctance to do so if they have not seen the block or heads. Some folks don't trust any shop that is crowded or messy. I would agree, except the best alignment shop and the best radiator shop I've dealt with are awful. You feel like you need a shower just driving by. Lastly, if you are a new builder going to the machine shop, don't pretend to be something that you are not. Most shops will gladly deal with a first-time builder but will probably be turned off by a pretend authority who has read five magazine articles and is trying to impress a guy who has machined and built a thousand engines. I've gotten a lot of mileage over the years with my stock phrase, "I'm an idiot but I've decided to *(fill in new venture here)*, can you give me some guidance?" Do not underestimate the value of having a good source for questions. If you find a good shop and they help you out beyond the call of duty, show up one day at lunch with a load of pizza and show your appreciation. The key is to build a relationship between you and your suppliers. Once a machine shop has been selected, establish what you will bring them and what you want done. This sounds ridiculous to mention but responsibility needs to be established. The machine shop knows that if the engine has a problem when completed that it will be your natural tendency to blame them for a machining problem instead of yourself for an assembly error.

Block Machining

With the measurement data collected during inspection, compare your block's critical measurements with the tolerances listed in the tolerance chart. If your block is still within specification as is, run the calculation again subtracting .0015 inch from your true measurements and make sure that it will still be within specification. This calculation is made because, regardless of what else you do to the block, it should be honed before reassembly. During a typical honing process about .001 to .0015 inch of material will be removed. Keep in mind that as the cylinder is increased in size, the gap in the rings will be wider. For every .001 inch the bore increases in diameter, the ring gap increases .003147 inch. If honing alone removes enough material to take the block out of tolerance it probably should be bored before honing. If the wear on the cylinders is enough to warrant a boring operation, the amount of material removed in the bore must be decided. If the measurements show that the block has been oversized before and cannot be bored any larger, the block will have to be replaced.

Cylinder Boring/Honing

In most situations a well-used engine will benefit from having the cylinders bored during a rebuild, even if it is barely in tolerance. All of the cylinders will wear a bit differently. A proper boring job will not only improve the individual cylinder shape, but will also improve their alignment relative to each other. If the block is to be bored it will require oversized pistons and rings to

The boring and honing machine will be used to clean up the engine's cylinders. The machine uses an articulated arm to move the tooling up and down in the cylinder. The tooling is flooded with coolant during machining to keep the block and tooling from building up heat. Different tooling can be used in the machine. The inserts in the above photo are the main cutting heads with two guide shoes and two diamond cutting inserts.

MACHINING AND CHOOSING PARTS

reassemble the engine. Since boring is a very common operation, oversized pistons and rings are plentiful. Common oversized pistons and rings come in .020 over, .030 over, and .060 over. As a rule it is a good idea to bore the cylinder as little as possible. An early 318/340/360 LA small block can be bored up to .060 over, though it's not a bad idea to have the block sonic checked for wall thickness. Chrysler and I don't recommend boring a 5.2L or 5.9L Magnum block by more than .030 inch. These blocks are made with a lightweight casting that doesn't have as much material in the bore wall as earlier LA blocks. As a result an engine can be bored more than once under most circumstances. This may especially be a concern on classic cars with the original engine that will gain in value. You don't want to max out the bore on the block unless you have to. Since the cylinders will have to have the same diameter, the most out-of-shape piston will determine the others' fate. After consulting your measurements taken during inspection, it is time to determine how much machining will be done to the cylinder bores.

The last operation is carried out with these special brush-type inserts. These leave the proper surface finish. When the block is bored and honed, the tooling leaves a pattern that is essential for the rings to properly seat. A boring machine moves the tooling up and down the cylinder, leaving a crosshatch pattern that intersects at roughly 45 degrees. This pattern is essential if the rings are going to properly seat when the engine is run.

The initial boring focuses on removing material. Honing follows it, which is a process more concerned with truing the dimensions and leaving the proper surface finish. This process begins with ceramic inserts on the machining head.

If you elect not to have the cylinders bored, a good machinist can do a decent honing job at home using a "berry" hone. These are available through most parts and engine shops. The brush can be attached to an air-powered drill or a regular electric drill.

When using the brush it is essential to keep everything well lubricated. Dip the brush in honing oil and insert it fully into the cylinder before turning the drill on. Once the brush is completely in the cylinder, start the drill and work the brush up and down. Your goal is to true up the cylinder and to leave the proper crosshatch pattern. If this is your first time, consult your chart and start on the cylinder with the least amount of wear. That way if it takes you a little while to catch on you won't be risking over-sizing a cylinder.

CHAPTER 4

The following chart shows the effect that cylinder boring will have on total engine displacement.

Bore Cylinder Engine				
Increase	Bore	Stroke	Volume	Displacement
LA 273 (1964-1969)				
Stock	3.630	3.310	34.256	274.048
0.020 Over	3.650	3.310	34.634	277.072
0.030 Over	3.660	3.310	34.824	278.592
0.060 Over	3.690	3.310	35.397	283.176
LA 318 (1967-1991)				
Stock	3.910	3.310	39.698	317.582
.0020 Over	3.930	3.310	40.105	320.842
.0030 Over	3.940	3.310	40.310	322.479
.0060 Over	3.970	3.310	40.927	327.413
LA 340 (1968-1973)				
Stock	4.04000	3.310	42.463	339.702
.0020 Over	4.06000	3.310	42.884	343.074
.0030 Over	4.07000	3.310	43.096	344.766
.0060 Over	4.10000	3.310	43.733	349.867
LA 360 (1971-1992)				
Stock	4.00000	3.58	44.988	359.901
.0020 Over	4.020	3.58	45.439	363.509
.0030 Over	4.030	3.58	45.665	365.320
.0060 Over	4.060	3.58	46.347	370.779
Magnum 5.2L (1992-2001)				
Stock	3.910	3.310	39.744	317.952
.0020 Over	3.930	3.310	40.105	320.842
.0030 Over	3.940	3.310	40.310	322.479
.0060 Over	3.970	3.310	40.927	327.413
Magnum 5.9L (1993-2003)				
Stock	4.00000	3.58	44.988	359.901
.0020 Over	4.020	3.58	45.439	363.509
.0030 Over	4.030	3.58	45.665	365.320
.0060 Over	4.060	3.58	46.347	370.779

When boring and honing is complete, a small chamfer is put around the top of the cylinder. This can be done with either a conical grinding head or a machine insert. The chamfer will ease piston installation and help ensure a good seat between the top of the block and the bottom of the head.

Decking the Block

The cylinder heads are torqued tightly to the block, and the two go through many, many heat cycles. When the heads are removed during disassembly, the tension is relieved and the surfaces can relax and move. If you are on a really tight budget and your block is slightly warped, you will most likely be fine putting the engine back together as is. If it is out of tolerance, or just a little out and you want to do a jam-up rebuild,

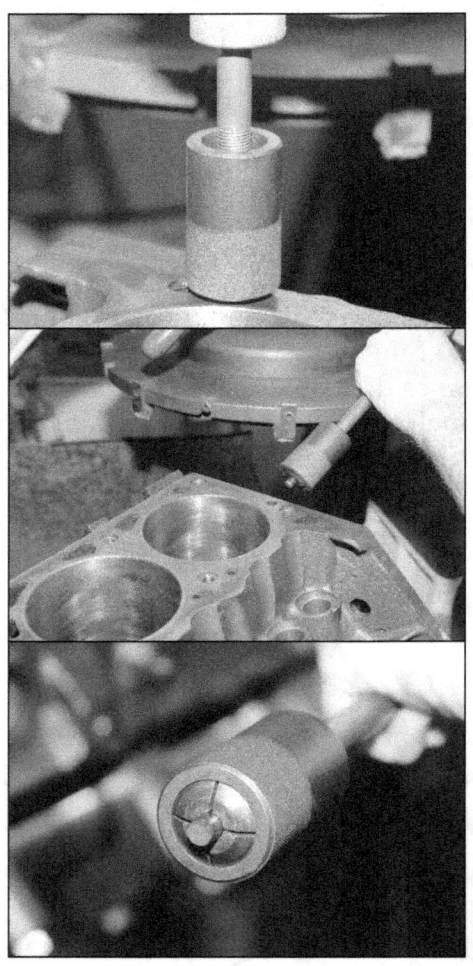

Before the block can be decked, the pins that locate the cylinder heads must be removed. To do the job right will require a special tool so you'd best let the machine shop do it. If you elect not to deck your block, the pins need not be removed during the rebuild.

MACHINING AND CHOOSING PARTS

have the block decked. Decking the block is a machining process whereby you remove material from the surface of the block that mates to the cylinder head. The flatter the surfaces of the deck and head, the better the head gaskets will seal. Just remember, every thousandth of an inch of material that you remove will move the cylinder head that far down toward the pistons. This changes the compression, the size of the combustion chamber, the distance from the lifter to the rocker arm, the distance from the valves to the pistons, and the mating surfaces of the intake manifold. Removing a few thousandths from the deck to flatten it out will not require any new parts. The minute changes in the aforementioned area will not be enough to worry about. But if you start taking off a lot of material in order to boost compression, be careful. New pushrods, and machining to the intake manifold, may be necessary.

The actual removal of the material is accomplished with a rotating head into which cutting tools are mounted. As the head rotates across the block's deck, it slowly cuts line after line of material. Only about .015 to .020 inch of material can be removed per pass. The project engine's decks were both warped a bit (about .012 side to side), so I ended up taking .015 off of each deck (you need to remove the same amount of material from each side).

Line-Boring/Honing

Line-boring refers to the machining of the block's main saddles and caps where the crankshaft rides. Using the measurements taken during inspection, consult the tolerance chart below to determine whether your engine needs line-boring or can just be line-honed. The crankshafts in small-blocks tend to stay pretty stable, so lining-bore a block isn't usually necessary. Compare the measurements taken during inspection with the work chart. If the block is still in tolerance, you can put the engine back together as is, but I would strongly suggest you line-hone the block. Like cylinder boring, line-boring requires a purpose-built machine. The caps are bolted back on the block and torqued to specification, and the tooling is inserted. Line-boring the block is much more involved. It's not just a matter of oversizing the bore like the cylinder. In order to properly line-bore, the bottom of the cap has some material machined off, the cap is replaced on the block, and then it is bored. Thus, when you line-bore the block, the crank moves slightly upward in the engine. How much it moves is dependent on how much material was machined off of the block.

If the block is set up properly during decking the new surface for the cylinder heads will be at a 45-degree angle to the camshaft and crankshaft bore, which are used to index the block on the machine. It is more common than not to find the decks of the block warped to some degree.

CHAPTER 4

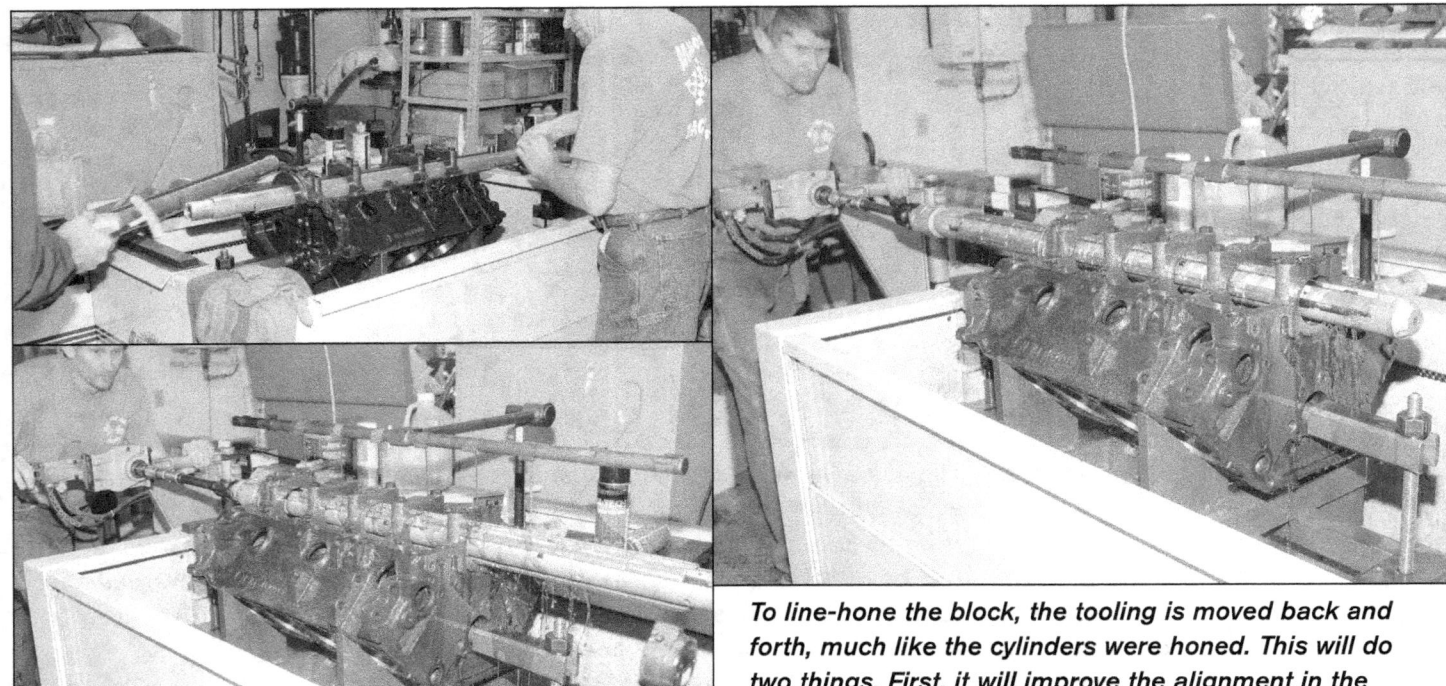

To line-hone the block, the tooling is moved back and forth, much like the cylinders were honed. This will do two things. First, it will improve the alignment in the crankshaft's support system.

Miscellaneous Grinding

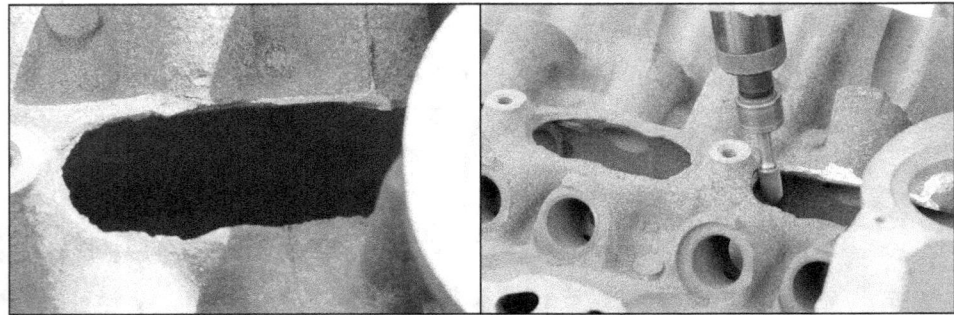

A couple of hours with a hand grinder can be an inexpensive way to improve your block. Here I found a decent-sized crack in the top of the block. Chances are it has been there since new and probably would remain in place, but I elected to remove it by grinding the area.

Second, line-honing will also leave a crosshatched surface in the block and cap, which is the optimal surface for the bearing to seat against when the engine is reassembled.

Master Mechanic Tip **PRO TIP**

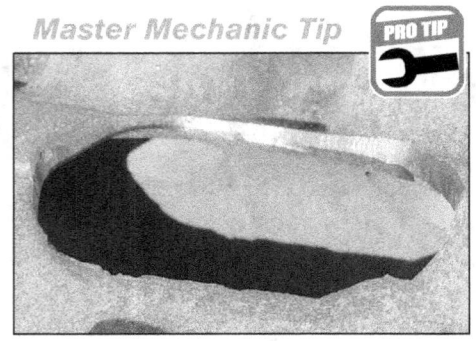

PRO TIP Run the grinder around the perimeter of all of the oil-return openings.

MACHINING AND CHOOSING PARTS

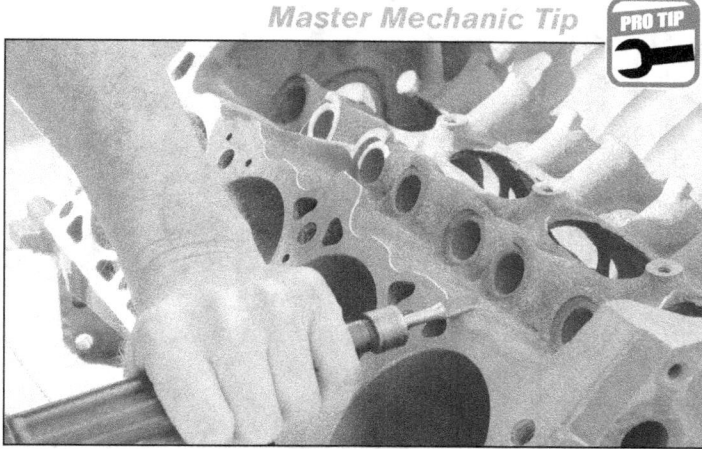

Master Mechanic Tip

Using the grinder to put a radius on the edge of the deck will help insure a proper mating to the cylinder head.

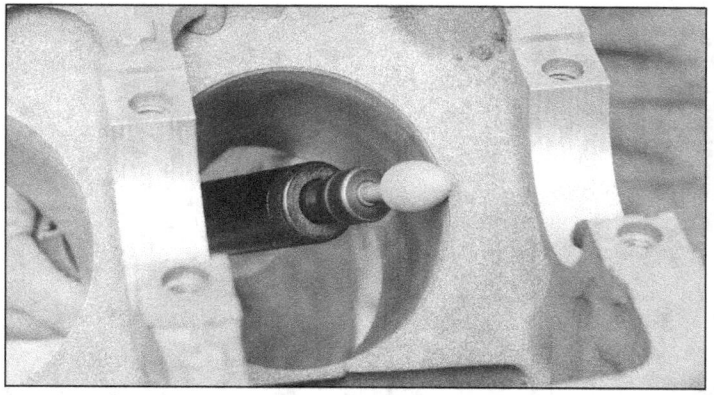

Use the grinder to radius the bottom of the cylinders to remove the sharp edges.

After the block has been machined it will again go through a thorough cleaning. Some of the small bits of metal that were machined off of the block will still reside within it. A good degreaser and steam cleaning is preferred. Your machine shop may take care of this step for you—if they do, make sure they do a good job.

Master Mechanic Tip

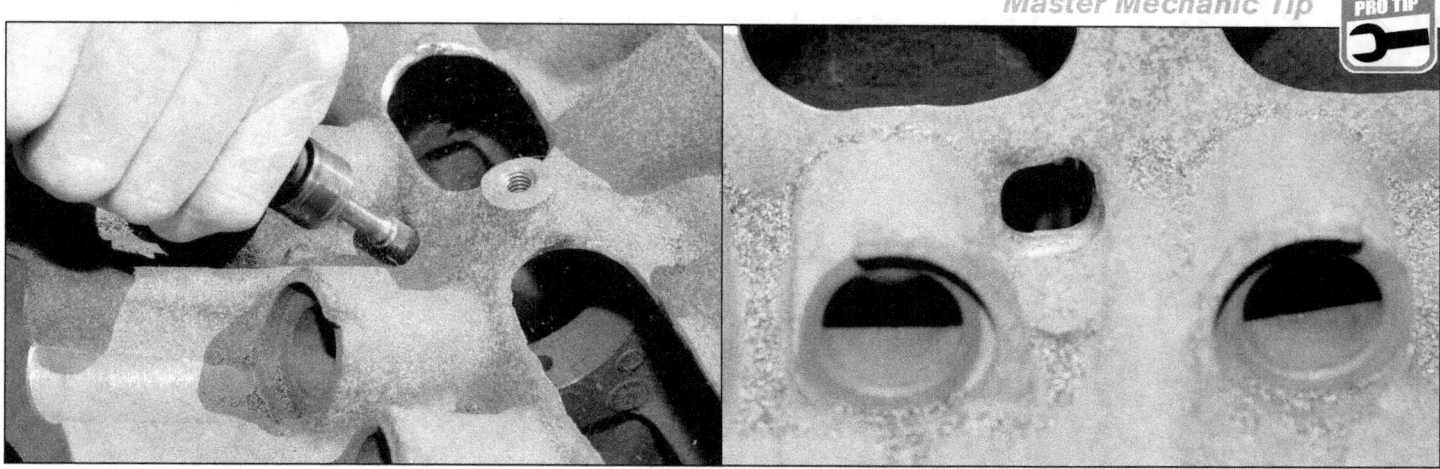

A smaller, more aggressive all-metal bit can be used to clean up the small oil-return openings.

Crankshaft

The crankshaft is one of those pieces that you hope you don't have to replace. If your crankshaft passed the inspection in the last chapter, there are a couple of little things that you might still want to do. If the crank is worn to the point that it is out of tolerance, then it must be ground or replaced.

To polish the crankshaft, it is mounted on a lathe and slowly turned. At the same time a belt sander is used on both the rod and main journals.

Master Mechanic Tip

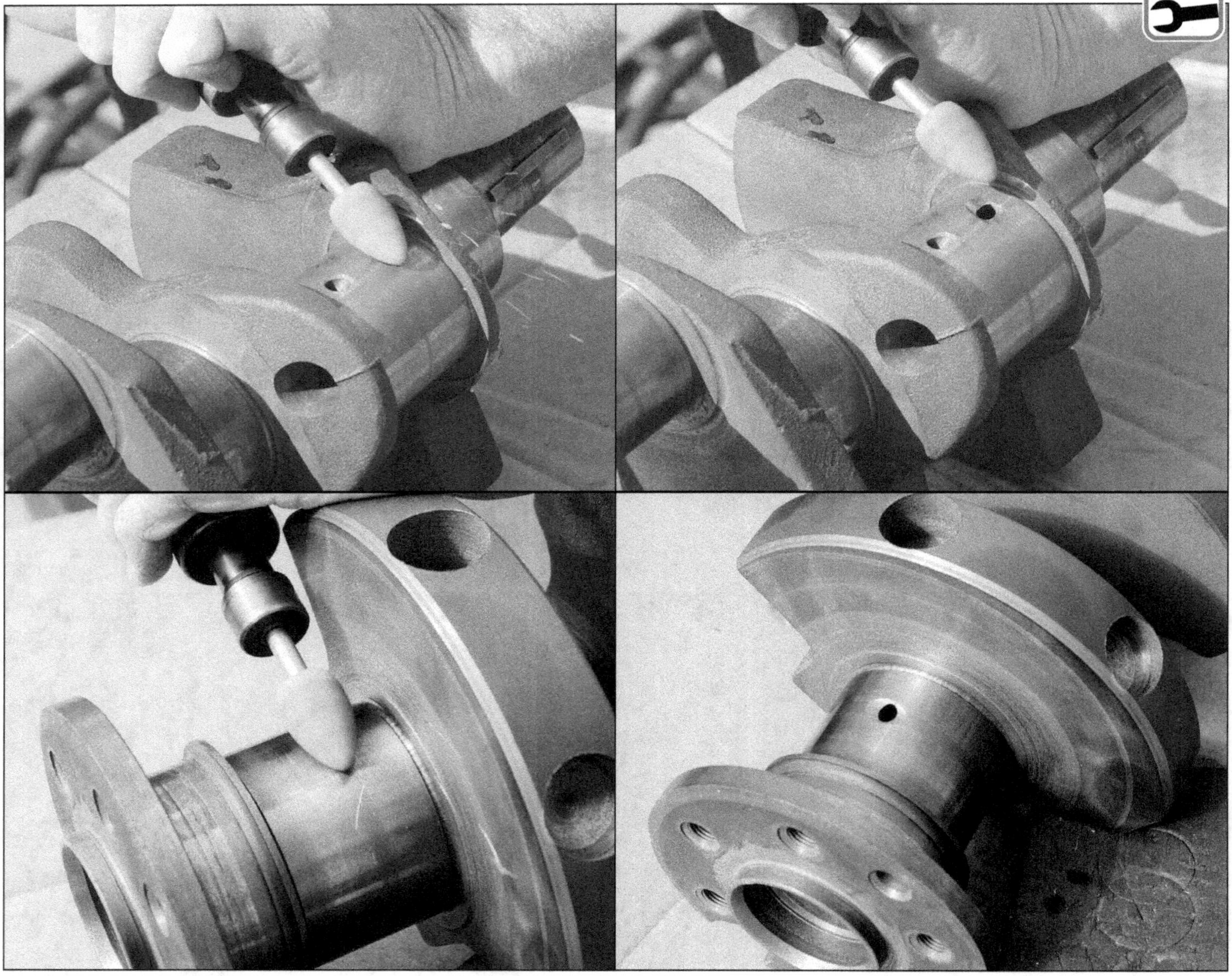

Use a conical grinder on the oil journals that lubricate the main and rod bearings. This will allow better oil flow to the bearing and better distribution around it. If you elect to do this, you will have to polish the crankshaft when finished.

MACHINING AND CHOOSING PARTS

The journals can be done by the old backyard method in a pinch. This consists of a cut sanding belt combined with a back and forth hand action. Use a 320-grit belt for the polishing operation.

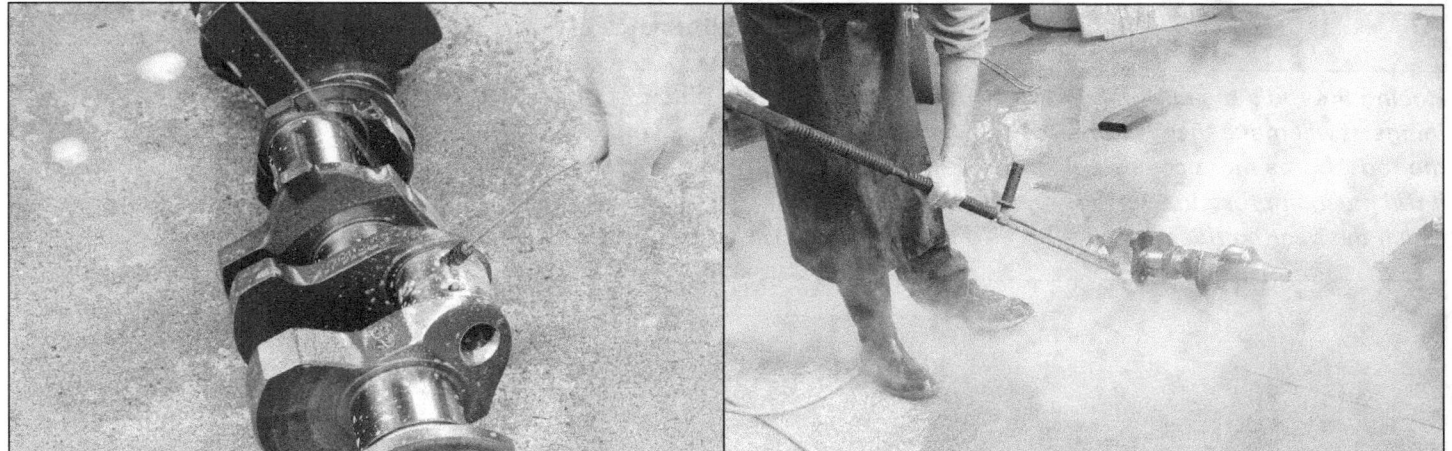

Like the block, the crankshaft must be thoroughly cleaned before being installed. Use a small brush with a degreasing agent in the oil passages. Then hit it with high-pressure water or steam if you have it. (Note: David is not a complete idiot, in case you noticed his one shoe/one boot setup. He lost his left leg a couple of years back in a motorcycle accident, so a wet left shoe is not an issue.)

Connecting Rods

Under most circumstances you should be able to re-use your connecting rods. You will have determined this with the measurements that you accumulated during inspection. If the rods are within spec it will be a good idea to hone them before reassembly. When the rod is honed, the bore of the big end is trued in diameter and concentricity, and a proper surface for bearing seating is left on the inside diameter of

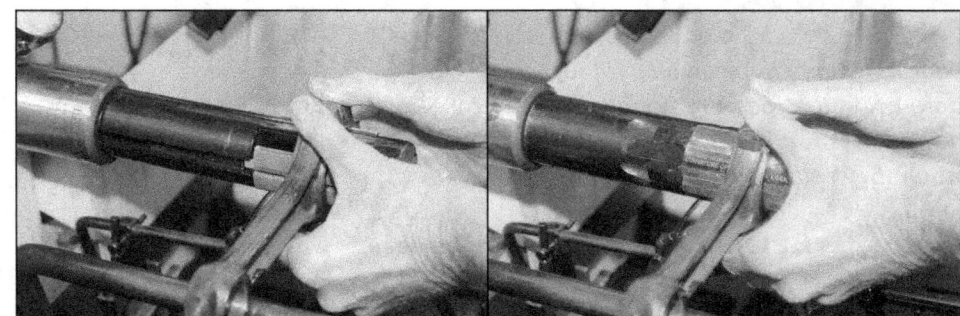

During the honing process, the rod and cap are bolted together and torqued to the proper tightness. The big end of the rod is run up and down a honing tool while being lubricated to prevent heat buildup. This is a Magnum rod that has a rectangular bump on the top of the rod. The LA rod is similar but is wider on the top, and does not have the bump on the top.

HOW TO REBUILD THE SMALL-BLOCK MOPAR

the big end. A thousandth or so will be taken off of the rod during honing, so make sure they will still be in spec. So much is riding on the rods and rod bearings that this is a step I would *not* skip.

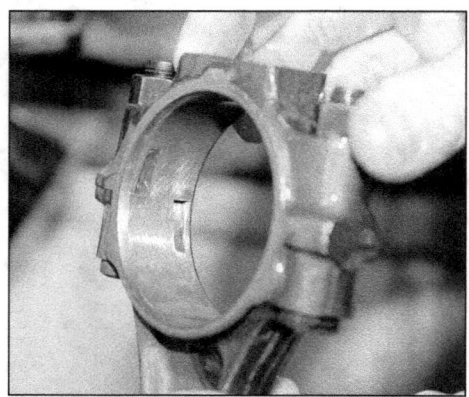
Honing the rod's big end will do two things. It will make the size of all of the rods' bores more consistent, and it will much improve the surface on which the bearing rides.

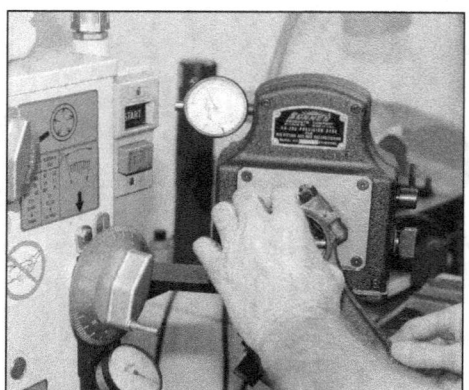
Your machine shop will check the bore when the rods are honed, but it never hurts to give them a once-over when they return from machining.

Balancing

As you begin your journey into the world of engines and performance, one of the first things you hear is the phrase "balanced and blueprinted." This is a broad term people use that is often a boast not understood. The phrase simply means special attention has been taken to ensure that all of the internal engine components have been matched both in terms of weight (balanced) and size (blueprinting). Balancing does a couple of things for an engine. It will remove vibration and will lower friction. If you elect to balance your engine, the chances are that a first-time amateur can exceed the factory in this area. When the average engine is built, it's brought into balance through the damper on the front of the engine, much like a tire is balanced with a counterweight. This eliminates some vibration, but the unbalanced components are still putting unequal forces on the internal components, especially the bearings. For everyday driving this is certainly adequate, and if you are on a tight time or cash budget you can skip it. The primary

The easiest way to check rod weight is with a purpose-built rig like the one pictured above. With a unit like this it is possible to weigh the rods three different ways. With the big end of the rod secured to the scale and the small end suspended, the big-end weight can be recorded.

components that should be balanced are the crankshaft, rods, rod bearings, pistons, pins, and rings. If you are good with tools (and have a scale, a grinder, and a drill press), you can do a pretty good job of balancing everything but the crankshaft at home. The crank you will have to sub out. A good digital gram scale that ranges from 1 gram to 1000 grams can be had for less than $100.

The rod's gross weight can be measured with the rod directly on the scale.

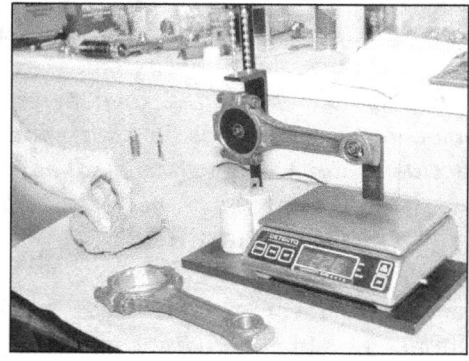
There are two ways to calculate the small-end weight. The big-end weight can be subtracted from the small-end weight, or the rod can be reversed in the jig and the small end weighed like the big end. Even if you can't afford a jig like this one, if you buy a scale, checking the rod balance at home can be accomplished fairly accurately by those who are ingenious.

You will also need a drill (preferably a drill press) and a bench grinder. Thus for about what you will pay someone to balance the pistons and rods, you can buy the tools (useful tools that you will use for other projects) that are required to do the job.

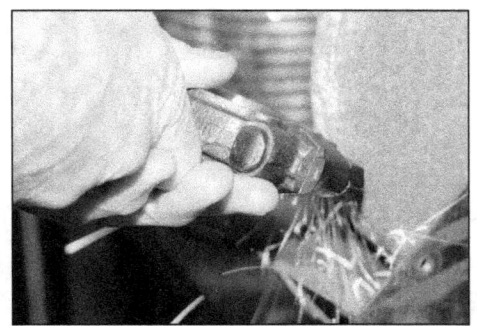

Record the rods' weights and sort them by heaviest to lightest.

Separate the rods based on their big-end weight. The lightest of these weights will be the goal weight. In this case the rods ranged in weight from a low of 516 grams to a high of 520 grams. All of the rods that are heavier than 516 grams, in our case five of them, will have to have material ground from the big end of the rod. The material should be ground from the boss on the bottom of the rod cap. Critical note: *Do not over-grind the rod. If your goal weight is 516 grams, and you have seven rods that are exactly 516 grams, but you over-grind the eighth until it weighs 515 grams, you now have to regrind the other seven.*

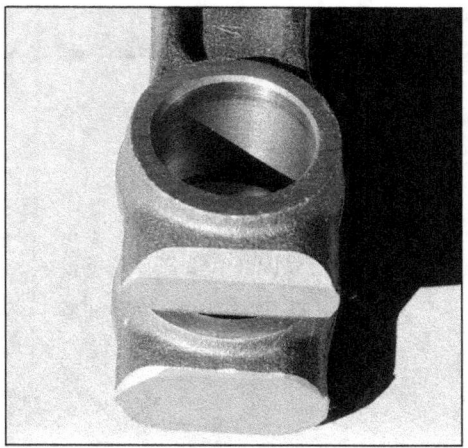

Once the big-end weights are all the same, weigh each rod conventionally, that is, just lay it on the scale. Record the weights and sort the rods by gross weight. Using the same process as with the big ends, sort the rods by weight, pinpoint the lowest weight, and prepare to grind the rest to match it. This time, however, the material will be ground from the small end.

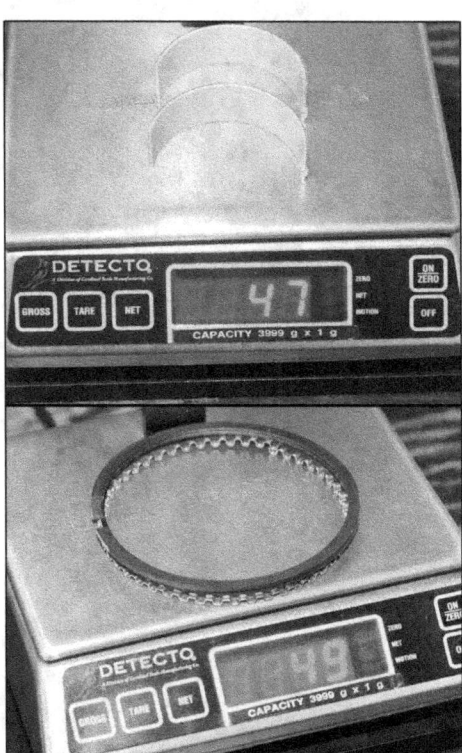

Once all of the rods are balanced, check the weight of the rod bearings and the rings.

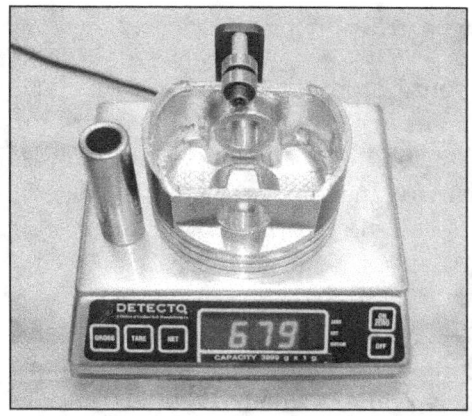

Weigh the pistons and pins together as a set and record your numbers. If there is a variance the pistons will have to all be taken to the weight of the lightest.

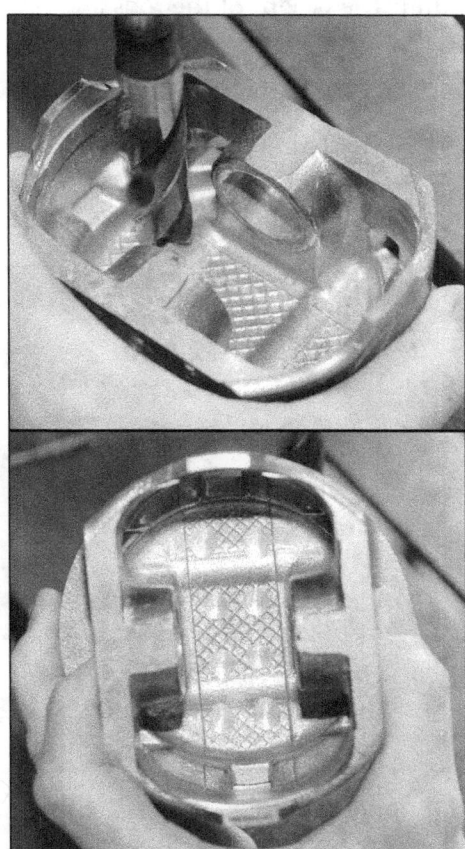

Use a drill press to make shallow dimples in the underside of the top of the piston. Many shallow holes are much better than a couple of deep ones. Space the dimples out as evenly as possible over the surface.

Balancing the Crankshaft

While you may be able to balance your pistons and rods, balancing your crankshaft will be beyond your home capabilities. Modern crankshaft-balancing machines are quite expensive. If you elect to have your crankshaft balanced, your machinist will need a number calculated during the balancing of the rods, pistons, bearings, and rings—the bob-weight. If you have any doubt about your balancing numbers, check them again. The bob-weight is the amount of weight that will be attached to each rod journal while the crank is turned on the balancing machine. These weights will mimic the weight of the rods and pistons as they rotate in the engine. The bob-weight is calculated as follows:

Big-end rod weight x 2
517 x 2 = 1034
Bearing weight x 2
47 x 2 = 94
Piston and pin weight x 1
768 = 768
Little-end rod weight x 1
225 = 225
Set rings weight x 1
49 = 49

Total bob-weight   2,170

Note: The LA 360 is an externally balanced engine where some of the balancing is done by using a special damper and flywheel or torque converter that is out of balance by design. Don't mix and match these components on one of these engines since the engine balance takes these components into account. The Magnum 5.9L engine is similar except that the imbalance of these components is different (less), and the imbalance on the back is on the flexplate instead of the torque converter.

Worksheet 5

Calculating Bob-weight

Big End Rod Weight	_____	x 2 =	_____
Bearing Weight	_____	x 2 =	_____
Piston and Pin Weight	_____	x 1 =	_____
Little End Rod Weight	_____	x 1 =	_____
Set Rings Weight	_____	x 1 =	_____
Total Bob-weight			_____

The crankshaft is first mounted on the balancing machine.

Then, if you balanced the rods and pistons, those numbers will be used to assemble the bob-weights.

Four bob-weights are assembled and bolted to the crankshaft on the rod journals.

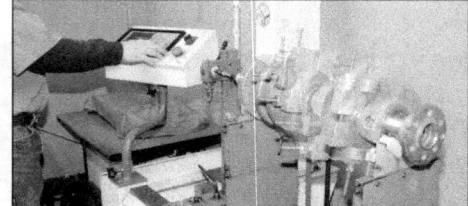

The crankshaft is spun and the machine's sensors calculate the degree of out-of-balance. It will give a printout of how much weight should be removed, and the location from which it should be taken off.

MACHINING AND CHOOSING PARTS

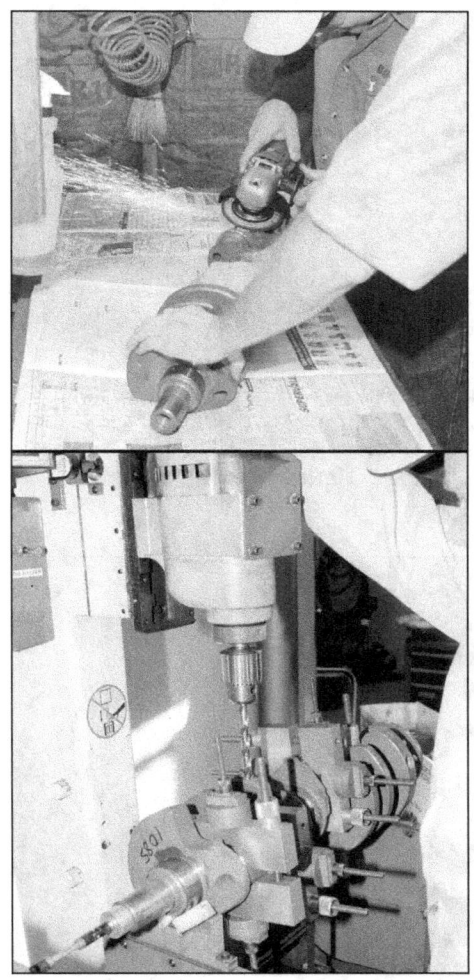

This crank had some flash in the area where weight needed to go, so I took it off first. The other weight removed was taken off with the drill press that is permanently mounted on the balancer.

Cylinder-Head Machining

When freshening up the cylinder heads, the work is primarily concerned with the workings of the valves. The first area of concern is the valveguides, which are the bores in which the valvestems reside. These position the valve in the cylinder head and are known as valveguides. The guides have to be strong enough not to wear but soft enough not to work as an abrasive against the valvestem. If the valveguides are out of tolerance, or anywhere close to out of tolerance, they should be bored and sleeved with replacement guides. Some people say you can just knock the old guides out and install new ones, but if you have a valvestem/guide alignment problem, this will not fix it, and your valves will not seal properly. A little extra expense here is worth every penny.

The second critical area of valve performance is the contact point between the edge of the valve around its diameter and the cylinder head. This area of the head is known as the valveseat. If the valve and the seat do not form a satisfactory bond, the cylinder will not hold proper compression. These two processes will require some special tooling, so unless you have a big budget and a lot of time it is best to let your machine shop handle this one.

Valveguides

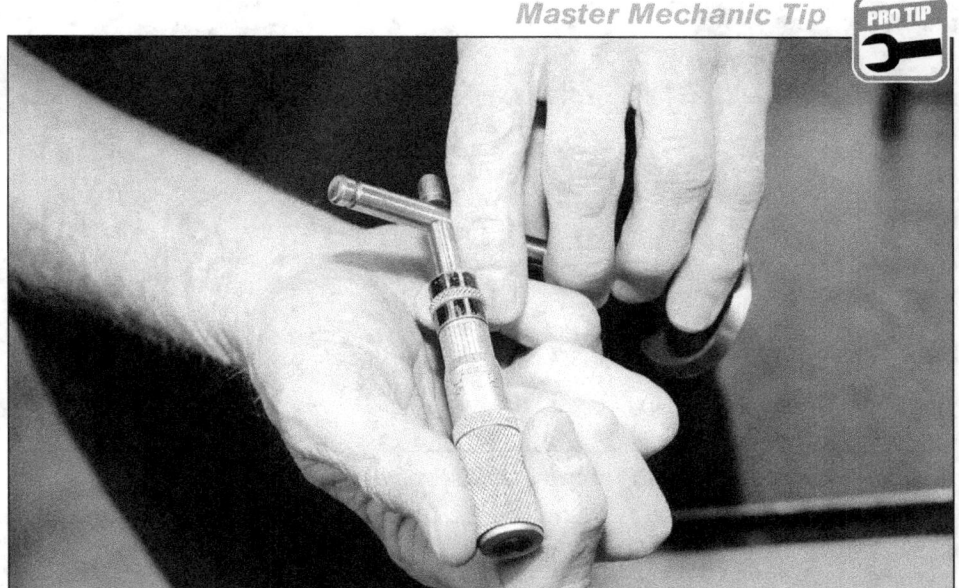

The guide's inside diameter is dependent on the diameter of the valvestem so it is the first item measured.

This burnishing tool is used to properly size the bore of the guide once it is in the bore.

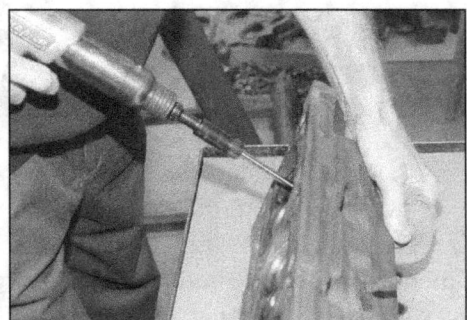

The burnishing tool is inserted in a hand-held air hammer and pounded down the length of the guide.

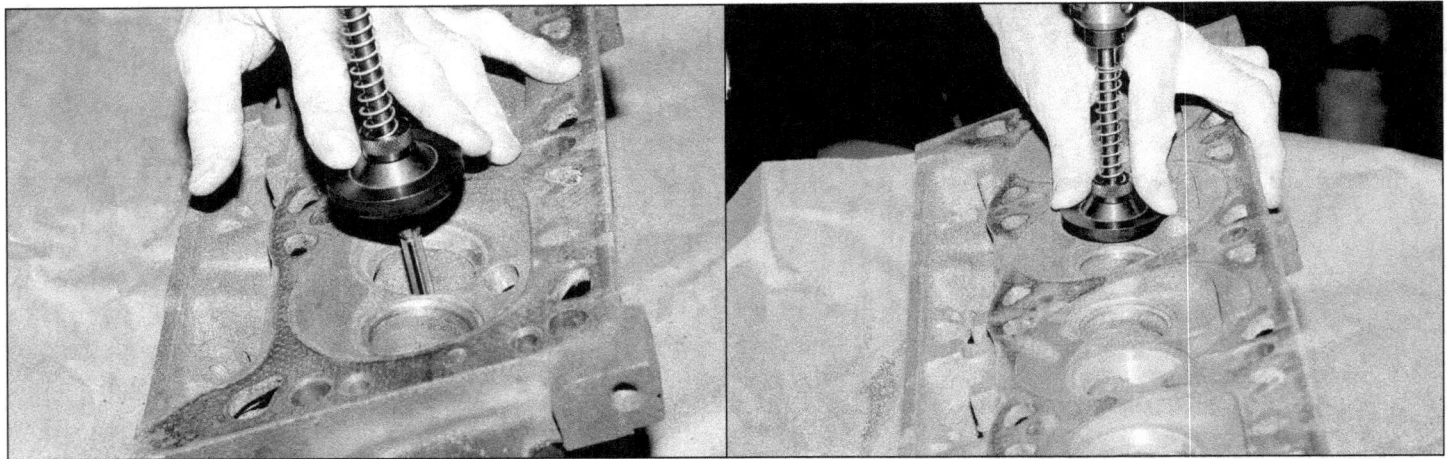

The old guide is reamed out with this tool. The black fitting fits accurately in the valveseat. Make sure that the fresh valveguide bore is aligned properly and thus that the valve will be aligned properly.

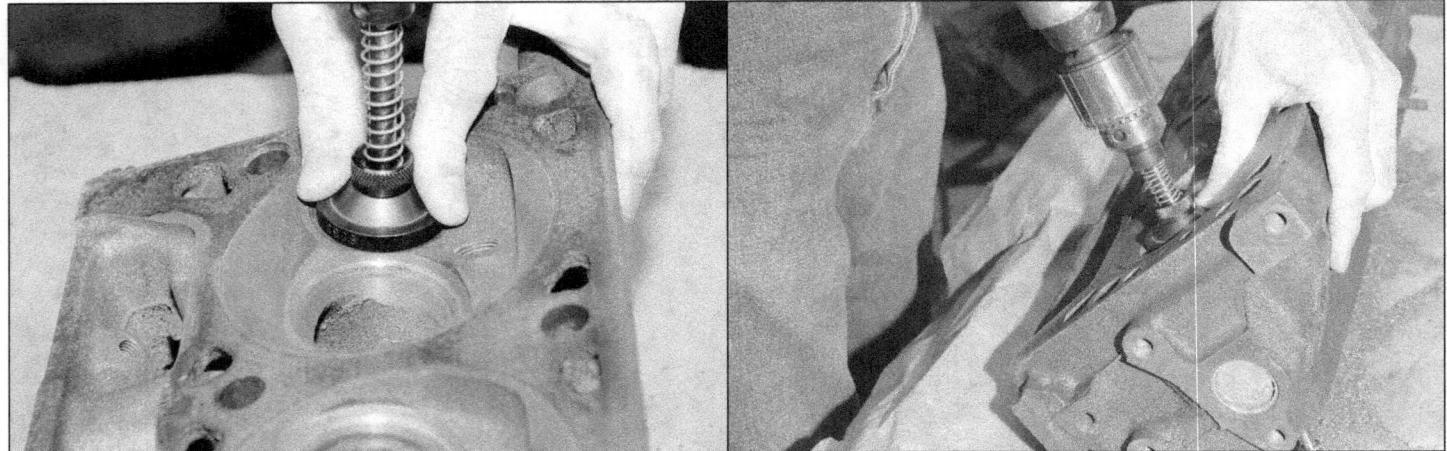

A smaller fitting is required for the exhaust valves.

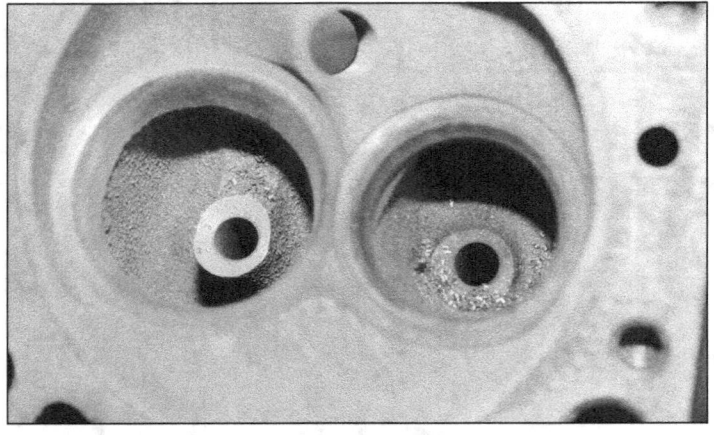

The new bore is now ready to have the guides pressed in. As with any operation using hand tools, the skill of the operator will determine the outcome. Valveguides can also be replaced using a head machine, and may well be if you sub it out. Either method can produce a satisfactory result.

When the old guides are bored out, a fair amount of material will be removed. The 8-mm bore on these heads was reamed out about .060 inch to accommodate the bronze guide inserts. Note that Magnum heads use 8-mm valveguides and LA heads use 3/8-inch valveguides.

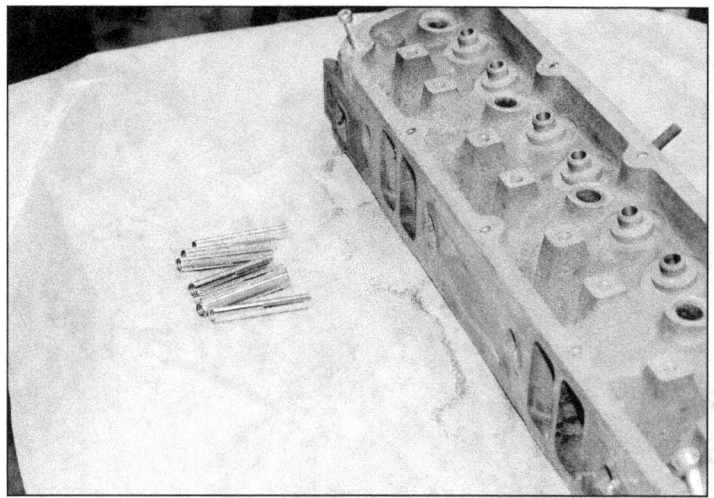

While there are different types of guides on the market, I used bronze guides. They offer both durability and good wear.

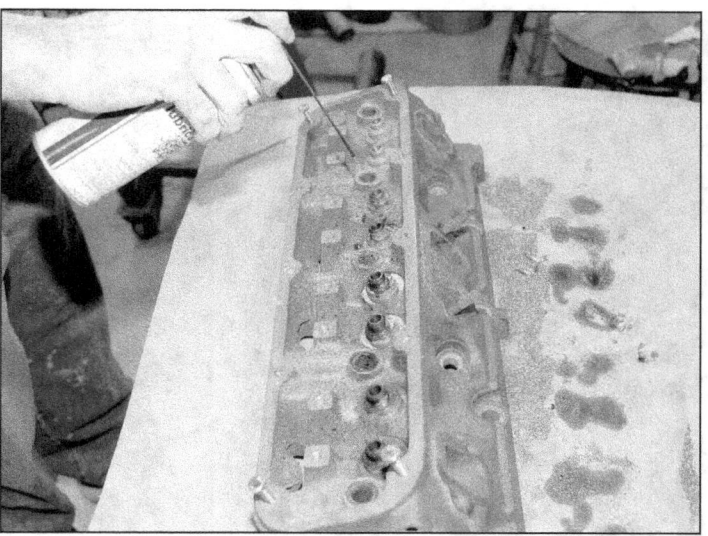

Once all of the bores are finished the new guides can be put in. First, spray graphite lubricant in each bore.

The new guides will be set into place with a hand-held pneumatic hammer and a special spring-loaded driving head. Each guide is hammered into the bore and into a very tight fit. The guide should be driven until the seat is flush with the top of the bore. The guides I used come with a chamfered top.

On the chamber side the guide will extend out of the bore and must be trimmed.

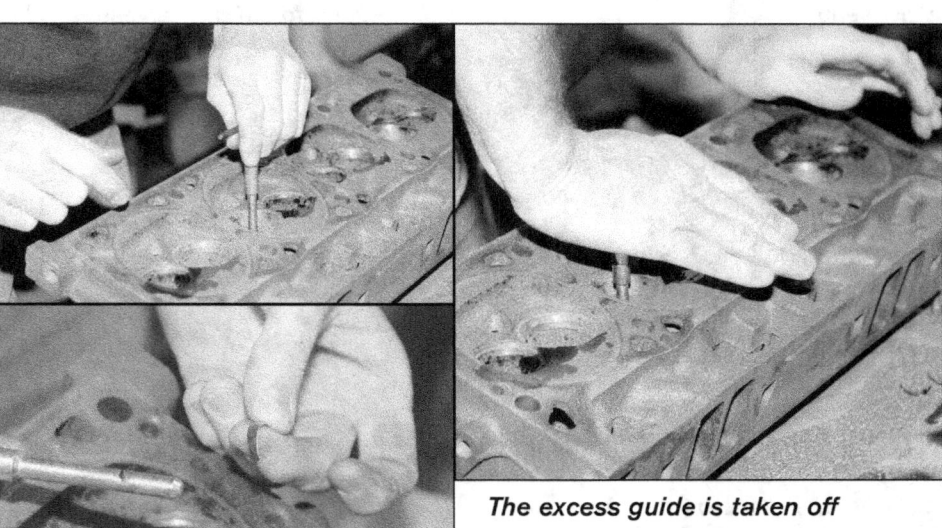

The excess guide is taken off by hand, using a trimming tool.

CHAPTER 4

A rotating cutting head is used to put a square machined surface at the top and bottom of the valveguide.

Installation and machining of the guides is now complete.

Valveseats

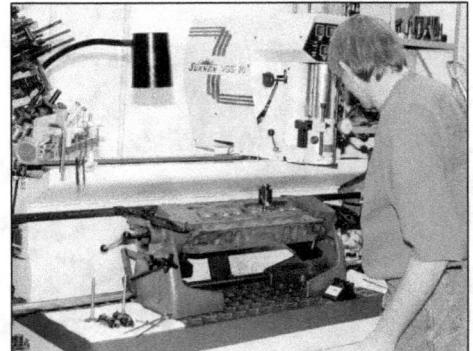

The next stage of cylinder-head machining will be on the valveseats and will take place on the head machine.

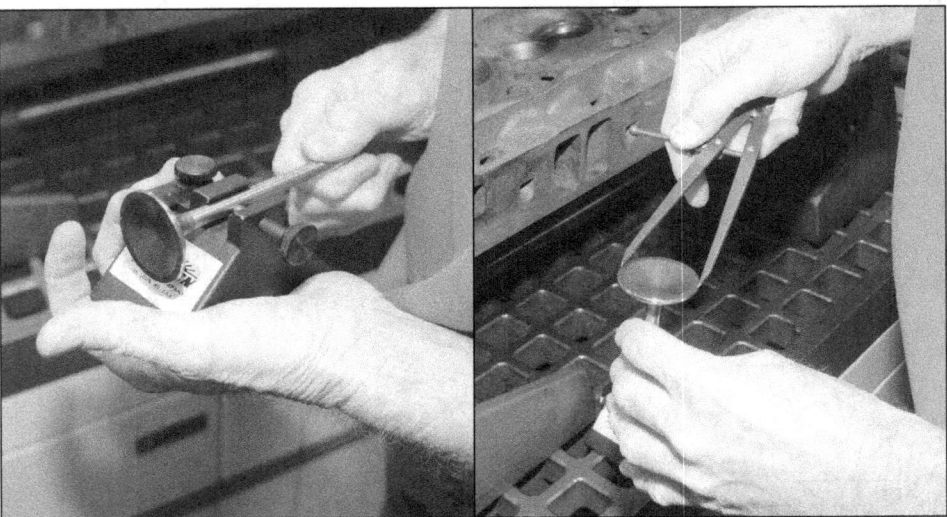

The cutting of the valveseats begins with a thorough measuring of the valve.

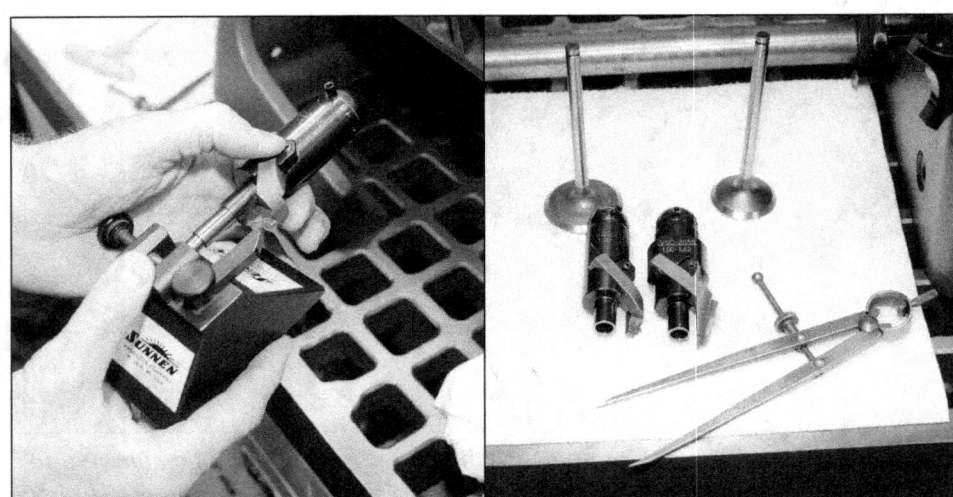

The measurements taken from the valve are then used to set the tooling that will be used to cut the valveseats. Because the intake and exhaust valveseats are different sizes, two pieces of tooling will be necessary.

The head is clamped firmly onto the head machine to eliminate movement.

An insert with a leveling gauge is inserted into the valveguide. This tool is used to make sure the head is level in the machine, and thus the boring will put the diameter of the valveseat perpendicular to the valveguide.

MACHINING AND CHOOSING PARTS

Machining begins with the smaller exhaust valveseat. The tooling turns and bores the proper three-angle profile in the head.

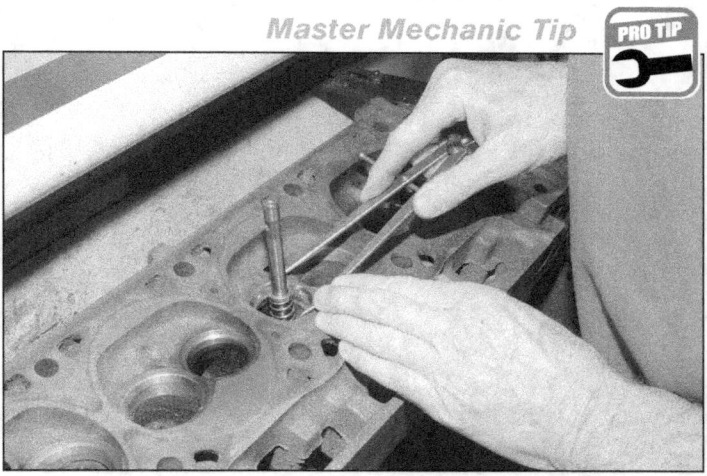

Master Mechanic Tip

After the first valveseat is machined a prudent machinist will check the diameter of the seat against that of the valve before proceeding.

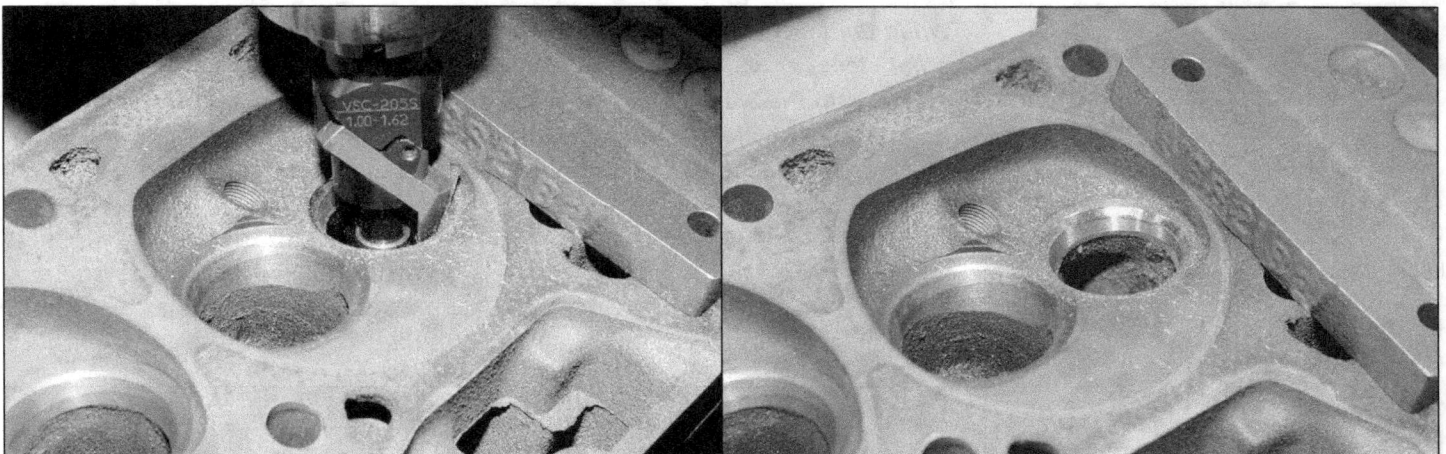

After the tooling is checked out, the rest of the exhaust valveseats can be machined.

When the exhaust valveseats are finished, the larger intake valveseats can be machined. The process will be the same as the exhaust seats, with the exception of the larger-diameter tooling.

The finished valveseats.

CHAPTER 4

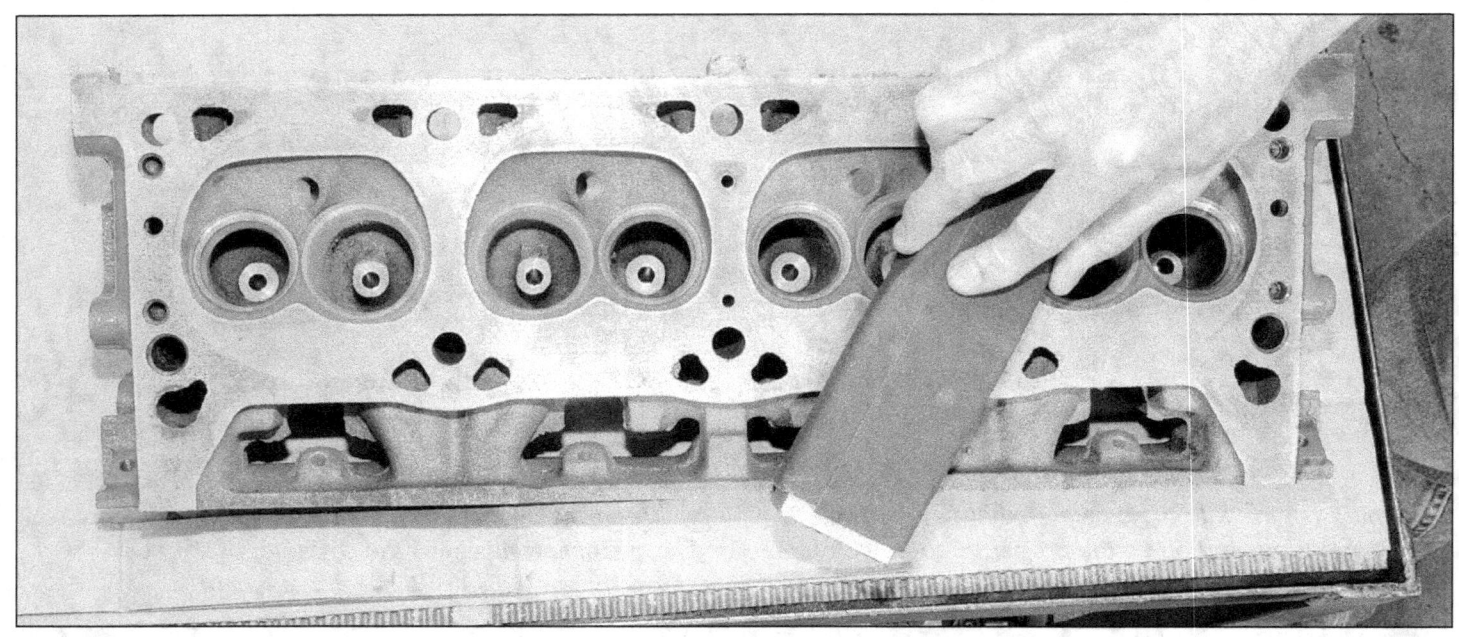

When the machining of the head is complete, a piece of sandpaper wrapped in a flat steel bar can be used to clean up the surface of the cylinder head that mated onto the block. When all of the machining is completed the cylinder head should be cleaned and pressure washed thoroughly to remove any chips that were produced during the machining process.

The Right Parts

Parts availability is greater now than at any point in history. Parts stores flourish. Aftermarket suppliers flourish. Added to this is the Internet, which has made purchasing from a myriad of suppliers easy—without

Your old valves can be freshened up and re-used in your engine if you like, but I prefer to use new valves if at all possible. If you have your machine shop grind your valves, they will grind a new three-angle surface on the valve's outer edge and will grind the top of the valve where it meets the rocker arm. This will probably be less expensive than new valves, but unless it is done with great care, the valves will not be as accurately ground as new valves, which are cut using CNC equipment.

With the proliferation of catalogs and Internet sites there are many choices when buying your parts. Maybe I'm still old-fashioned, but I would rather use a walk-in supplier where I can talk face to face with another human being.

MACHINING AND CHOOSING PARTS

even leaving the house. It has also revolutionized (and made so much easier), the task of finding used or vintage parts. Just go to a search engine and type in "318 valvecover" (then type in "Chrysler 318 valvecover" to get rid of the BMW stuff), and check out the results. There are parts out there from companies that have great reputations. Then there are mystery parts. To help you through this maze it is prudent to work with a parts store or a speed shop that offers personal service and advice. Local parts stores can be great but for an inexperienced builder the speed shop usually offers much better service. These people tend to know parts and engines. They have counters with stools. This indicates that they don't mind if you sit down and talk to them. Information adds value, and you might get a part slightly cheaper on the Internet but the face will not come with it. Call me old-fashioned, but I like to have a person who I can see if I have a question or problem. Keep in mind that if you buy off of the Internet and have a problem, at best you will only have the delay of shipping the wrong part back and waiting for the right one. It may cost you a week versus a 15-minute drive to the speed shop, so that 10 bucks that you saved wasn't really worth it.

Blocks

Your factory block is a cast-iron piece, and short of buying an aluminum block that is what's out there. If you find yourself having to replace a block you will have a few options open to you. A replacement block can be had at an auto-core shop or from an aftermarket manufacturer. There are a couple of source listings in the back of this book for national suppliers that will sell you a machined block with main caps. Another option is to go buy an engine from a junkyard or out of the local Buy/Sell section of the paper. Another method is to hit the local cruise-in on Saturday night, make your way to the Dodge mafia (they'll be camped out in a corner to themselves), and while complimenting their cars, mention that you are looking for a block. If you go the used-engine route remember that until you inspect it, you don't know if it is any better than what you already have in the shop. David Magouyrk has a saying, "If you buy an engine from a junkyard, you will have a junkyard engine."

If a replacement block is needed, make sure you get the correct block for your engine. LA blocks are not completely interchangeable with Magnum blocks, since they don't have the crank trigger mounting points (back of the block—passenger side), they don't have the special motor mounts used in Dakota pickups, and they won't work with the Magnum hydraulic roller tappets. Early LA blocks (prior to 1987) will not work in 1987 to 1992 LA engines since they are not set up to use the dog bones for the LA hydraulic roller tappets on those engines.

Short Blocks

Most auto suppliers, and a number of national order houses, sell what is called a "short block." When you buy a short block, you get a block with the machining done and the crankshaft, rods, and pistons installed and ready to go. Short blocks can be considered if you have to change your block. If you want to build your engine for the fun of it, don't buy a short block. But if time and money are factors, take a look at them. By the time you replace your block, clean, inspect, and machine it, buy parts, and assemble them, you may actually save money going with an assembled short block, but you will not be an engine builder.

Long Blocks

Buying a long block is essentially buying a completely rebuilt engine. Usually you will use parts such as the valvecovers, oil pan, and front engine cover from your original engine as well as the ignition and fuel system. A long block relieves you of any block, cylinder head, or assembly responsibilities. Both long- and short-block prices are contingent on turning over your engine as a core, so if you want to keep your stuff, the long or short block will cost more. As mentioned before, if you are working on a vintage car that will be shown and judged and you don't want to replace the engine, your decision may be forced. I would suggest that if it is a vintage car you will drive, put the original block into storage and build the car with a replacement.

Crankshafts

Crankshafts can be split into two main categories—cast cranks and forged cranks. Cast cranks are most often found in engines installed in everyday passenger cars. They are less expensive for the manufacturer to produce, are perfectly reliable for normal street use, and usually cost about half of what forged cranks cost. Forged cranks were installed in factory performance engines and have long been the favorite of hot rodders and racers alike. The forging process creates a better molecular structure within the crankshaft, making a forged crank a good bit stronger than a cast crank. Of course, the downside for the home builder is that they are more expensive. Other aftermarket crankshafts have been machined for better oiling. Another trick is to machine tapered edges on the crank's lobes. By improving the shape of the counterweights, it is possible to increase HP by decreasing resistance. If you are doing a stock rebuild, a cast crank is the way to go. If you plan to add significant power during your rebuild, break down and put in a forged crank.

Crankshaft Bearings

A high-quality set of bearings, like those produced by Clevite 77, is a must during a rebuild—end of story.

Connecting Rods

There are many types of connecting rods out there to choose from. For the most part, stock 318s came with forged steel rods. For stock-type applications and normal driving they are perfectly suitable. For more power-oriented options the choices are vast. Performance rods are machined from billet, or forged and then machined. There are I-beam rods and H-beam rods. There are also material choices, as they come in steel or some pretty tough aluminum alloys. The aluminum rods weigh less than their steel counterparts and will spin up faster using less power to move the rod and thus save more power to move the rear wheels. Of course, prices cover a wide range. Tell your parts supplier what you are after and see what he or she thinks.

Pistons

Piston manufacturers offer choices for just about everything that you can do for an engine. The stock piston is a flat-top aluminum model, and I suggest that is what you put back in. A discussion of all of the pistons out there would take up the rest of the book. Options include pistons made with the pin relocated to allow a longer rod to be used. Pistons are also made with valve reliefs cut in the top for high-performance applications. If you decide to use any of these, you are dramatically changing the geometry of your engine and are moving beyond the scope of this book. Most all are available in oversized models for rebuilds. The most common oversize pistons are .030 over and .060 over. As you plan your engine, make sure that the piston you choose is available in an appropriate oversize.

Rings

There are essentially two ways to go when choosing rings—moly or cast. To determine what was in your engine, remove a ring and twist it. If it breaks it's cast, but if you can bend it, it's a moly ring. Regardless of what was in your engine, you will have to decide what you will be putting back in. The advantage of moly rings is better performance in high-heat and high-stress conditions. Moly rings will also operate better in poor conditions such as hard-use four-wheel-drive vehicles that are more likely to get a little grit in the oil or to run hotter due to a radiator that is half covered with mud. Cast rings have been run in cars for years and for regular driving are perfectly acceptable. Cast rings are also a bit easier on the wallet. It will be your choice, but as long as you are there I'd put a set of moly rings in it.

Gaskets

Gaskets are available in sets and are a must for a rebuild. Gasket kits like those shown here will contain all of the gaskets needed to complete your engine. These two kits are manufactured by Victor Reinz (a division of Dana) and contain everything in the following list. When buying a gasket kit make sure of what you are getting ahead of time. Most kits will have a list of contents printed on the side of the box. Kits come sealed and, as a rule, are not returnable once the inner seal has been broken on the packaging.

	Quantity
Air pump	1
Air pump	3
Cylinder head	2
E.G.R. valve	1
E.G.R. valve	1
Exhaust manifold	2
Intake manifold	1
Intake manifold	1
O-ring	1
Valvecover	2
Valvestem seals	8
Valvestem seals	8
Water outlet	1
Crankshaft seal	1
Oil filter	1
Oil pan	1
Oil pan drain plug	1
Timing cover	1
Timing cover seal	1
Water pump	1

Oil Pumps

The oil pump is the heart of your engine. One of the fastest ways to burn up an engine is to run one with a faulty oil pump. We went with longtime oil-pump king Melling for our rebuild. As an experienced engine builder, David performs an internal inspection of the oil pump before installing it (covered in the next chapter). The vast majority of the time you will have no problem pulling the pump from the box and bolting it onto the engine, but remember, if there is a problem with the pump, it will be a major inconvenience if you notice it and a catastrophe if you do not.

MACHINING AND CHOOSING PARTS

Aftermarket Gauges

WORKBENCH TIP

There is no substitute for accurate engine information. I accept that what you are working on will determine your course. On a valuable vintage car, a set of aftermarket gauges will stand out like a sore thumb. On the other end of the spectrum, many late-model cars have a full set of factory gauges. But for all of the others, a good set of aftermarket gauges will complement your rebuild nicely.

Coolant-temperature gauge—A coolant-temperature gauge relies on a sensor in the manifold or block, with the probe directly in the coolant flow. Thus the device is really a simple thermometer. The nice thing about aftermarket gauges is that most have gradients marked with actual temperature readings. This allows the driver to know pretty much the exact temperature of the coolant, which is an improvement over the factory's blue/red unmarked bar gauge.

Oil-pressure gauge—There are two types of oil-pressure gauges—electrical and mechanical. An electrical gauge relies on a pressure sensor to read the pressure. This sensor turns the measurement into an electrical signal that is sent to the gauge and then turned back to mechanical form at the gauge needle. The mechanical gauge, on the other hand, needs no electricity to operate. It relies on a small tube that runs from the engine directly to the gauge. The tube is connected to an oil passage and becomes pressurized just like the rest of the oil system. The pressure in the tube presses against a diaphragm in the gauge. Thus when the pressure increases, the diaphragm pushes the needle more to the right. I have always been a fan of the mechanical oil-pressure gauge, operating according to the philosophy that accomplishing something without electricity is better than with it. As they are simpler, they are less likely to fail. The one drawback of the mechanical oil-pressure gauge is that it requires an active oil line in the cockpit. If the gauge leaks or if the tube has been improperly installed or kinked during installation, the result can be hot engine oil leaking from under the dash. If you buy a good gauge and properly install it this should not be an issue. I have run these gauges all my life and have never had a problem.

Ammeter/voltmeter—This is a matter of preference. An ammeter shows the electrical system's condition in terms of whether it is being drained or charged, while a voltmeter shows the electrical system's condition in terms of volts. I lean toward voltmeters, but I've had both and don't really have a problem with either.

This brings me to getting an accurate reading of the engine's oil pressure. I will cover this again in the start-up and break-in section, but it is worth discussing here as you make engine decisions. If your vehicle has an oil-pressure gauge, and you trust it, you should be fine. Just make sure someone who can read it is watching it when you first crank your rebuilt engine. If your car either has an untrustworthy oil-pressure gauge or relies on an "idiot light" to indicate an oil-pressure problem, I suggest adding an oil-pressure gauge.

Cylinder Heads

Like the other main stock components of the engine, stock cast-iron heads are fine for stock rebuilds. Bare replacement heads and assembled heads (with valves and springs installed) are available from a number of sources. To increase an engine's performance, the cylinder head is really the place to start. In order to dramatically increase an engine's power, it must have more fuel and more air to burn in the combustion chamber. A surefire way to get more in is to put the biggest intake valve you can in the cylinder head. Again, this will involve work beyond the scope of this text. Another type of cylinder head is made of aluminum, and is available from a number of aftermarket sources. The main advantage of an aluminum cylinder head is weight reduction. By replacing the stock cast-iron cylinder heads with aluminum cylinder heads, 50 lbs or so can be eliminated from

CHAPTER 4

the gross vehicle weight. Since aluminum heads are sold to the performance crowd, they will most likely have large intake and exhaust valves. The downside to aluminum heads is that they are not as durable as iron heads. That's not to say that a properly prepared and mounted set of aluminum heads won't be reliable. It's just that you are replacing iron with aluminum. The other downside of aluminum cylinder heads is price. You may spend as much for your bare, unmachined aluminum heads as you do on the rest of the rebuild.

Valvesprings

The stock valvesprings have around 85 to 115 pounds of resistance at their maximum compression. Springs are available with higher pressures of resistance at the same compression. The benefit of this additional pressure is that the valve will close faster and will be less likely to "float" off of the back of the cam lobe. The downside of this increased pressure is the valve is harder to open and thus more stress is added to the valvetrain from the rocker arm to the camshaft lobe.

Rocker Arms

As with other valve components, the choice of rocker arms is vast. The stock rockers are stamped steel and, like the other stock components, are adequate for everyday street use. The only reasons to go to an aftermarket rocker are a need to compensate for increased valvespring pressure or to eliminate weight. Magnum engines have rocker arms that are individually bolted on to the heads, and LA engines have rocker arms that mount on a rocker shaft on each head.

Worksheet 6

Calculating Compression

Cylinder at Bottom Dead Center (BDC)

Cylinder Volume
Bore _____ x Bore _____ x Stroke _____ x 0.7853982 = _____
Deck Clearance Volume
Bore _____ x Bore _____ x Deck Clearance _____ x 0.7853982 = +_____
Piston Compensation Volume
Manufacturer's Addition / Subtraction _____ = +_____
Head Gasket Volume
Bore _____ x Bore _____ x Compressed Gasket Thickness _____ x 0.7853982 = +_____
Chamber Volume
Combustion Chamber Cubic Centimeters _____ x 0.0610237 = +_____

    BDC Volume   = _____

Cylinder at Top Dead Center (TDC)

Deck Clearance Volume
Bore _____ x Bore _____ x Deck Clearance _____ x 0.7853982 = _____
Piston Compensation Volume
Manufacturer's Addition / Subtraction _____ = +_____
Head Gasket Volume
Bore _____ x Bore _____ x Compressed Gasket Thickness _____ x 0.7853982 = +_____
Chamber Volume
Combustion Chamber Cubic Centimeters _____ x 0.0610237 = +_____

    TDC Volume   = _____

    BDC Volume _____ Divided by TDC Volume _____ = _____ :1 Compression Ratio

MACHINING AND CHOOSING PARTS

Camshafts

There are a million cams out there. If you elect to stray from stock, you will be entering the world of lift, duration, and experimentation. In a nutshell, the profile of the cam lobes can be machined to open the valve higher (lift) and to keep it open longer (duration). Increasing either or both of these allows for one thing—to get more fuel in the combustion chamber and to get the exhaust out faster each time the valve opens. If you are seriously considering a cam change, work closely with a cam supplier, telling them exactly what you have and what you are trying to accomplish. Chances are their opinion will be much more educated than your best guess. Adding an aggressive high-performance camshaft to a stock engine is more likely to cause trouble than to increase power.

Painting Engine Parts

WORKBENCH TIP

Painting the exterior of your engine is a great way to prevent rust and keep it looking good. Some perfectly acceptable engine paints are available at just about any auto parts store. Although they cost a bit more than common spray paint, engine paints are tougher than the run-of-the-mill discount spray paint.

Color, of course, is a matter of choice. If you are going for factory authenticity, do a bit of research on your car or truck to find out the correct colors. Colors like Chrysler Industrial Red (our choice) are readily available. Later-model engines are most often black. Black is nice because it won't show dirt and grime as much as a bright, colorful engine, but it will also make any leaks more difficult to spot. Our project motor was black when it left the factory, but as I like more colorful powerplants (and it's my truck), it will return to the engine bay coated with Chrysler Industrial Red.

There are two main methods of engine painting. One is quick and easy, and the other is time consuming and laborious. The quick and easy method is to assemble the motor and paint the entire unit "tractor style." This will adequately protect the engine, but all of the bolts and gasket edges will also be painted. If this is your choice you can skip ahead and start building you engine.

The second method of painting is much more laborious but will result in an engine with much more detail. This is accomplished by painting all of the individual components before they are assembled. Using this method, all of the gasket edges give the engine detail and each bolt, with its contrasting finish, jumps right out at you. But be prepared. This process will probably take longer than you think. Machined surfaces must be taped off before painting. The oil pan and front engine cover can be bolted on the block, without gaskets, for painting. This will ensure that the visible surfaces of the block will be painted but not the areas that are covered or the gasket surfaces. Go through your bolt bins and find some appropriate sized bolts to run into the threaded holes like the motor mount points. The old freeze plugs can be set back into place in order to cover the freeze plug apertures in the block. Make sure you clean them well before setting them into place. You will have to have adequate room to spread everything out to paint and time to let everything dry. And remember, each clamp, bolt, and bracket must be refinished or replaced. Any obviously used piece on the otherwise freshly painted engine will stand out like a sore thumb.

Sandblast Finishes

External engine pieces can be media blasted and painted before being reinstalled. I advise that any piece that has an internal engine connection not be blasted. Cast engine parts are porous, and when you blast sand or other media into them, you will not get it all out, so you are essentially adding sand inside your engine. If you do blast internal pieces, they should go through a very thorough cleaning and blowout when you get it back. Media blasting is perfect for brackets and such if you want to dress them up before replacing them. On later-model engines, the aluminum mounts for the engine accessories can be lightly blasted to clean them and give them a uniform finish. They can be replaced as is or can be painted with a clear paint to help protect the finish. Clear paints can yellow a bit over time, but they will protect the part from fingerprints during installation and dirt and grime during operation.

CHAPTER 5

ASSEMBLY

Before you start bolting things together, there are a couple of "make sure" steps that must be taken. This chapter begins with the block fully machined and all of the parts purchased and on the workbench ready to go. The two questions that must be answered are (1) are all of the parts present, and (2) are all of the parts correct? It is prudent, if at all possible, to have all of the engine's components on hand at the beginning of the build. It's a pain when you get on an "assembly roll" and have to stop to wait for a part, or go to the store. But it's not enough just to have all of the new or reconditioned parts. Try to fight the desire to start bolting things together, and once again get out your measuring tools. Before anything is bolted together each part, diameter, bore, and length should be inspected just as the used parts were in Chapter Three. You can skip this step if you like, but if you do you are putting your rebuild completely in the hands of your machine shop and parts supplier. If both of these entities have done their job correctly and all of the machining and parts are in tolerance, then you will have no trouble. But if a mistake was made, you may not catch it, or if you do catch it you may be halfway through your rebuild and everything will come to a grinding halt. Parts are made and machined by humans and by machines controlled by humans, and mistakes are made. Since these steps are the same as the earlier inspection, it really won't take all that long and is worth the peace of mind.

Unless you are able to complete your rebuild in one session, cover it between work sessions to keep any foreign matter out of the inside of the engine. A large, clean plastic trash bag will work nicely.

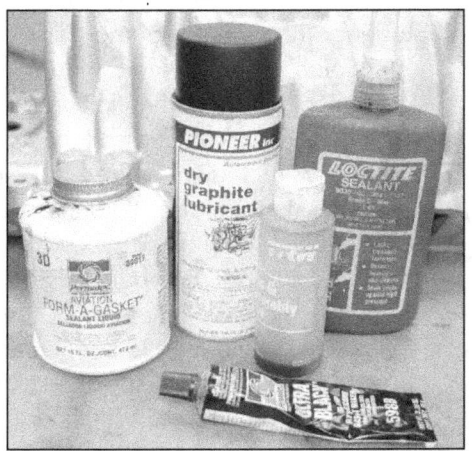

Gasket sealers and a couple of types of lubricants will be needed during assembly. Pioneer graphite lubricant is an excellent general-purpose lubricant, while TRW Cam and Lifter Lubricant should be used on camshafts and flat-tappet lifters. For additional gasket sealing I used Permatex Aviation Form-A-Gasket and Permatex Ultra Black Silicone Gasket. A small tub of grease (I used Kendall SHP) and a jar of petroleum jelly will also be needed. The last chemical required is Loctite, which offers two benefits. It gives extra hold to threaded fasteners when it dries, and it also acts as a lubricant when screwing the thread in.

ASSEMBLY

Cam Bearings

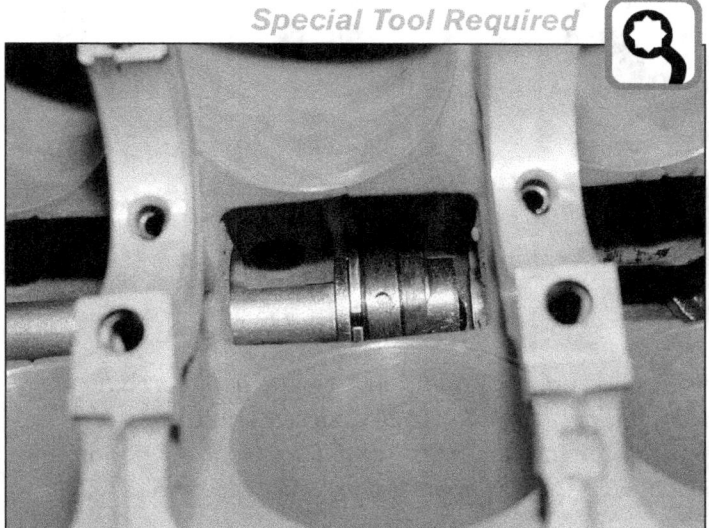

Special Tool Required

This is a job that requires special tooling and is probably best left to the machine shop. If you are determined to do it yourself, you must first buy a cam-bearing seating tool. This is basically a long, sturdy bar with inserts to fit to just under the outside diameter of the cam bearings. The one I used has adjustable heads so that it can be used on an almost infinite number of bearings of different diameters.

Notation Required

The bearings will come with a guide sheet giving the diameters and position of each bearing. Make sure that you use this information to determine which bearing goes into which bore. Chrysler used different-sized bearings in the engine, so they are not interchangeable.

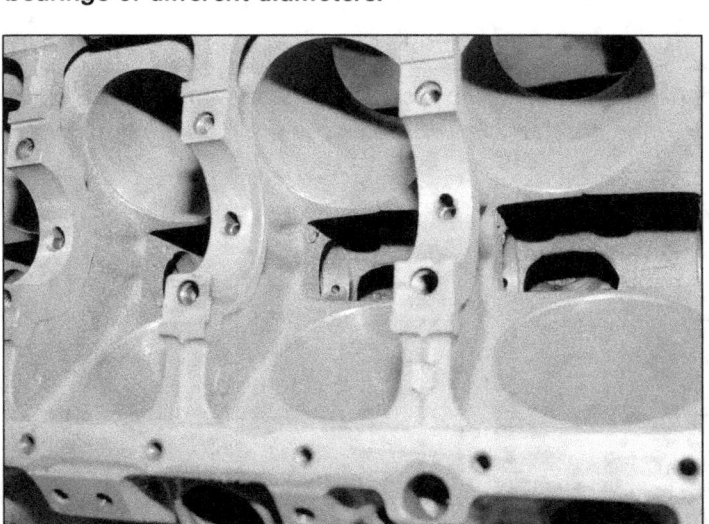

With the block cleaned, the new camshaft bearings can be installed. Each of the five bearings will be pressed (hammered) into its bore in the block. Before driving the bearings home, inspect and locate the oil passages in each bore and in each cam bearing. Use acetone and a clean rag to make sure the bores and bearings are completely clean.

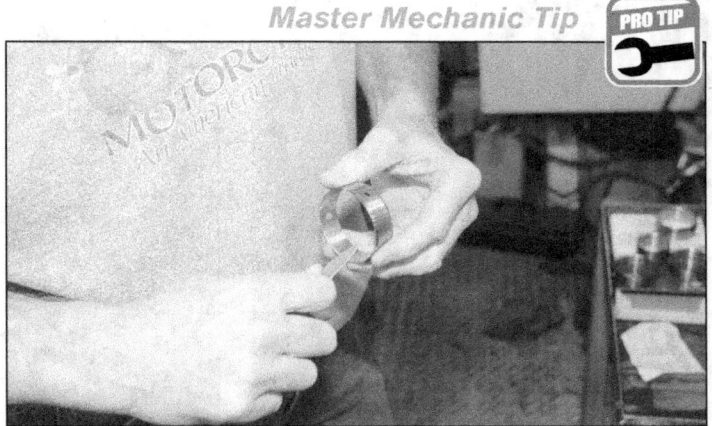

Master Mechanic Tip

Use a sharp pocketknife to take the edges off of the bearings. This eliminates a shape edge, allows for more accurate installation of the bearings and the camshaft, and will not hurt the performance of the bearing. It will prevent small burrs from being formed as the camshaft is installed, and the rounded edge will allow the oil to fall off of the edge of the bearing more efficiently.

Lubrication

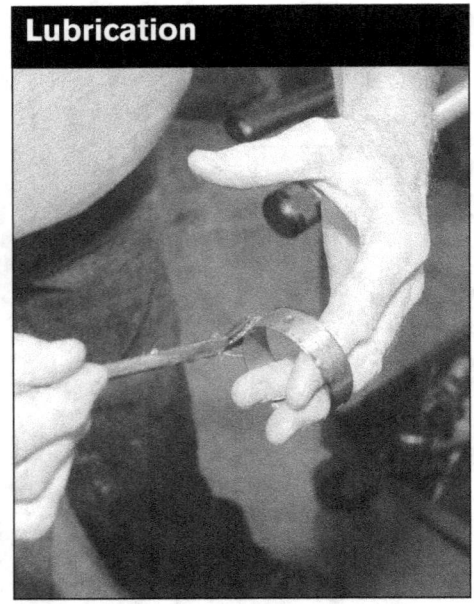

To begin installation, grease the outside of the bearing with quality grease. This grease will keep the bearing from binding as it is driven into position.

Lubrication

Once greased, fit the bearing onto the end of the bearing driver. Then position the bearing in front of its proper bore. When positioning the bearings, it is critical that all of the oil passages in the block and cam bearings line up. There is nothing guiding the bearing into the proper position in relation to the oil passages, so close attention must be paid.

With the bearing seated on the edge of the bore, it can be hammered home. The tool must be kept cylindrical in relation to the bore. If the bearing is kinked the camshaft may not fit into the bores, and if it does it will not rotate freely. This means friction, wear, and ultimately premature failure.

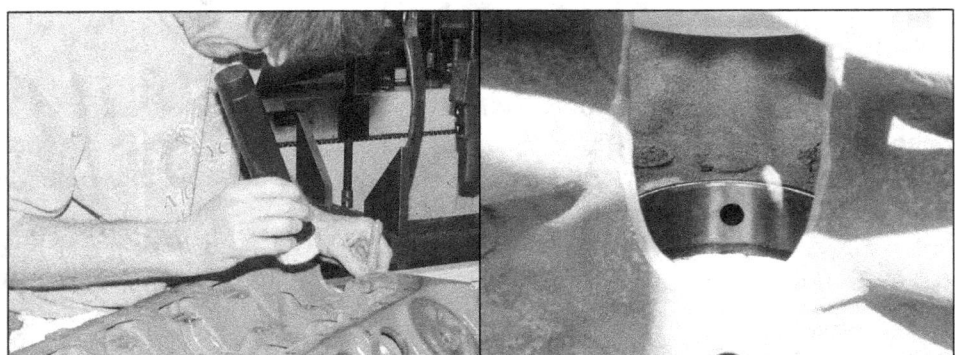

After driving each bearing home, stop and inspect your work. Make sure the bearing is fit flush in the bore and the oil passages are in alignment.

All of the bearings are put in through the front of the engine so you can start with the bearing located on the back of the block and then work towards the front. It will be necessary to thread the bearing and tool through the other cam bearing bores to hammer in the first bearings.

The front bearing will be the last and will require a shorter driving rod to hammer into place.

ASSEMBLY

When the bearings are in, the result should be a concentric cradle in which the camshaft can rotate. When the bearings are in it's worth a quick check.

Lube the camshaft with cam lube thoroughly and slide it in through the front of the engine. Once in place you can slide the timing gear on the camshaft and test the camshaft's rotation. You should be able to rotate the cam without too much effort. After checking the ease of rotation remove the cam.

Pistons and Pins

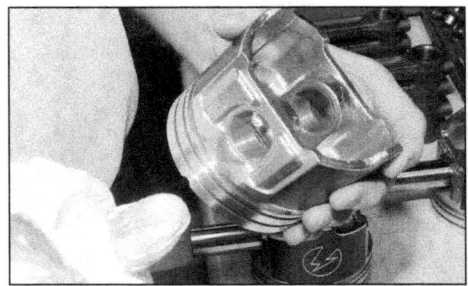

This is why you clean new parts. This out-of-the-box piston still had residue in the piston-pin bore, which would have inhibited the pressing process to come. Don't assume that new parts are clean—in fact, never assume anything.

Special Tool Required PRO TIP

PRO TIP The pin-pressing process will be beyond the scope of most home shops. The best way to attach the pistons and rods is with a special machine that is in every competent engine shop. To fit the rods to the piston, the small end of the rod is heated and as a result expands, making the bore in the rod's small end bigger.

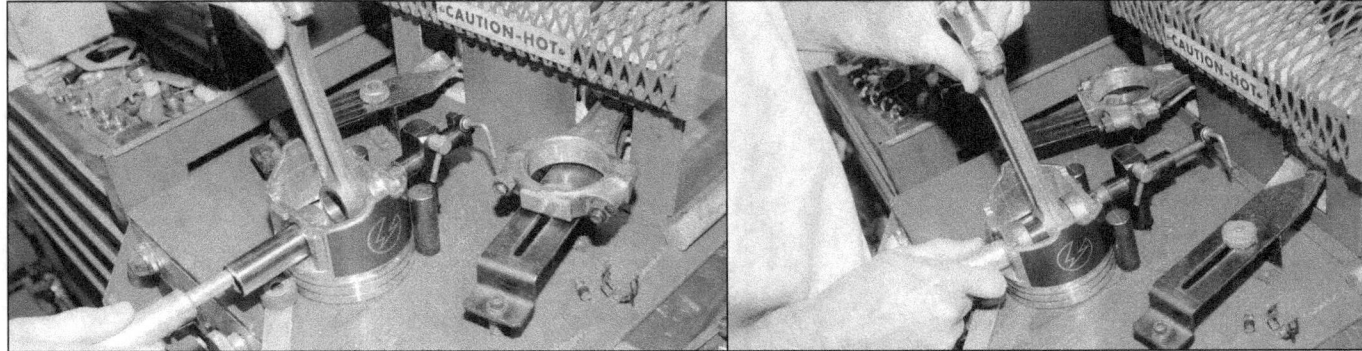

Then, while the small end of the rod is still very hot, the piston is put in position over the rod and the pin is pushed home. As the connecting rod cools it contracts and soundly attaches itself to the pin, locking the piston on. It is possible to do this operation without the machine, but it cannot be done as well and it's a pain. An engine shop's charge for this service is usually quite reasonable, so it's best to let them do it.

HOW TO REBUILD THE SMALL-BLOCK MOPAR

Set up for the rebuild in as roomy an area as possible. Have a table, cart, or workbench close by for parts and tools. Try not to set small tools, screws, bolts, or parts on the block while assembling. If you drop something in the block and don't retrieve it, then you will have a rude awakening when you start the engine. Try to have enough room to lay things out and not be crowded. Lastly, set your soft drink or coffee on the floor so that when you spill it, it won't be all over your clean, well-lubricated parts. I did a good bit of assembly outside, as the light is much more conducive to photography and I was enjoying some fine early spring weather. If you do elect to work outside, don't leave your block unattended, as bugs and bird droppings should be kept out of the inside of your engine. To begin assembly, put the block on a sturdy cart, workbench, or, if you have to, a clean floor. I prefer the cart as it is a bit more stable than many engine stands and allows access to the front, rear, and both sides. It takes a bit more effort to turn over, but the benefits outweigh the effort. If you do elect to use an engine stand you might want to skip ahead and install the freeze plugs and threaded plugs at the rear of the block, as they will be inaccessible while the engine is on the stand. If you don't do it now you will have to remove the engine from the stand to access the rear of the block.

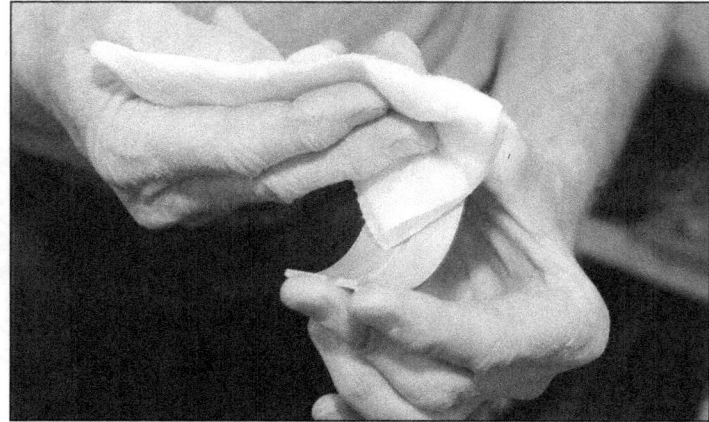

Then clean both sides of each of the bearing halves.

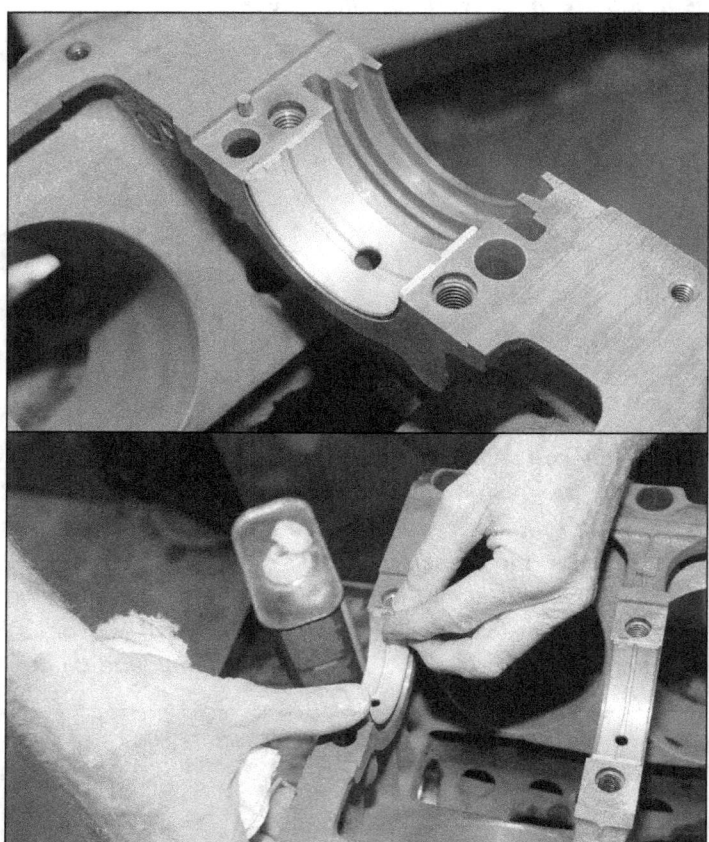

With the cleaning done, hand press the lower bearing halves into the block.

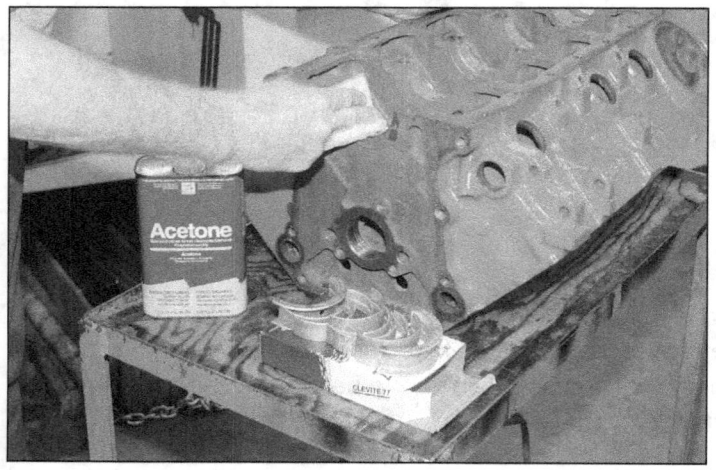

Using acetone and a clean rag, clean the bearing surfaces of the block and caps.

ASSEMBLY

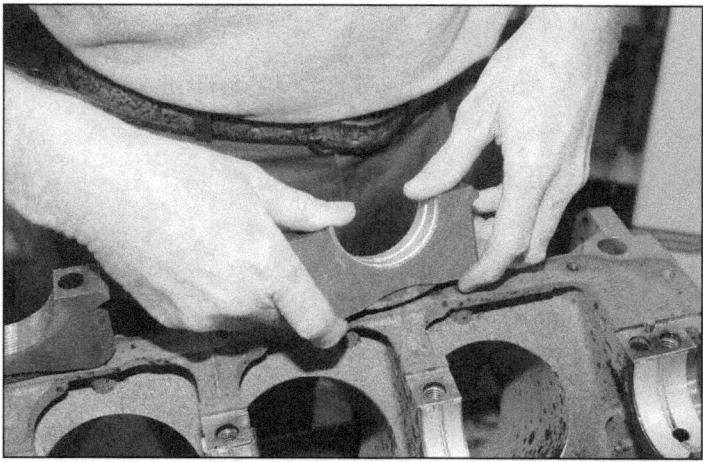

The remaining halves of the bearings should then be hand pressed into the main caps.

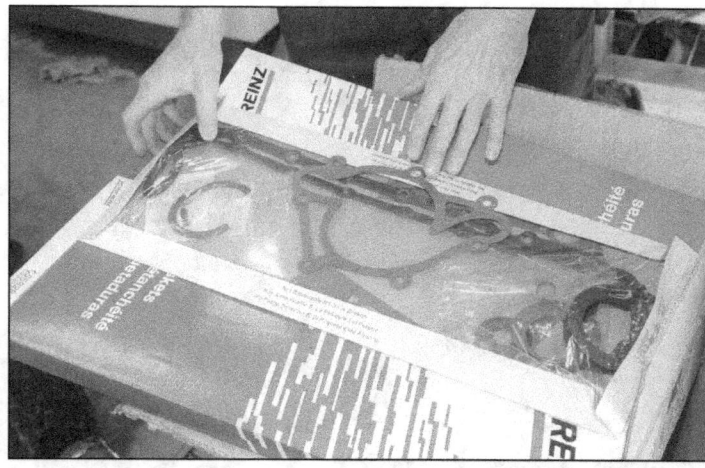

Break into the gasket kit for the rear main seals. Never re-use seals and gaskets. New ones are not expensive and will decrease your chance of leaks by 1,000 percent.

Lubrication

Once the bearings are in place in the block and caps, give them a good spray with graphite lubricant.

Now it's time to install the rear seal. Like the bearings, this seal comes in halves. First, install half of the rear seal into the block. The seal has a front and a rear, so make sure the half with the smaller lip on the inside diameter is facing out from the block. The seals will be installed a bit differently than the bearings. Allow a half of an inch of one side of the seal to extend past the surface of the block. This means the other side will be recessed by the same amount.

HOW TO REBUILD THE SMALL-BLOCK MOPAR

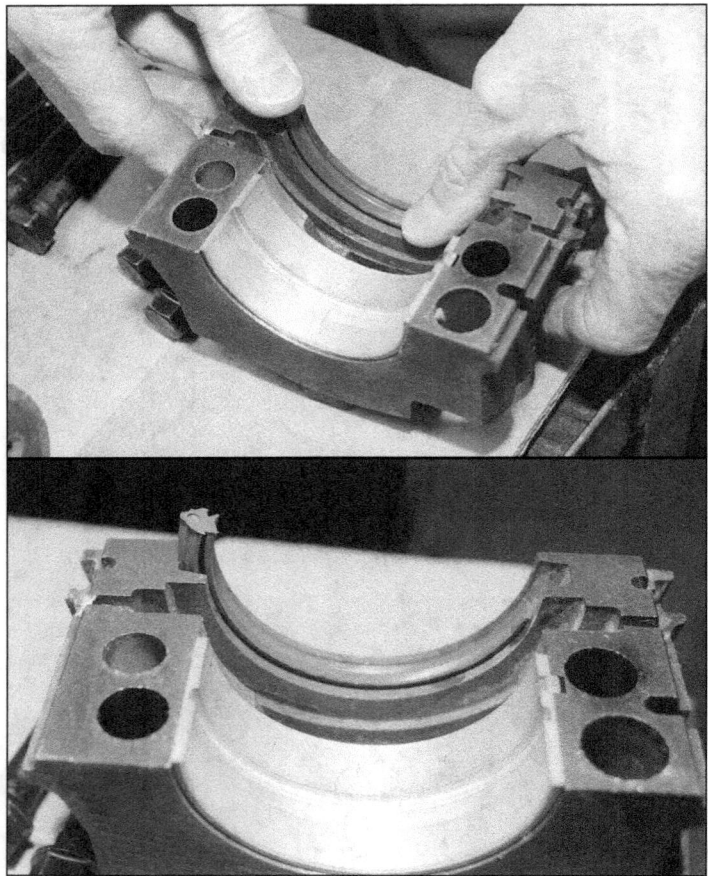

When the other side of the seal is installed on the front main cap, allow the seal to extend half an inch past the mating surface on the opposite side.

On the sides of the block outboard of the seal, put a dollop of silicone gasket material. This will help seal this metal-to-metal joining surface.

Once in place, give the seal halves a good coat of grease where they will meet the crankshaft.

Critical Inspection

It's now time to get the crankshaft out of its safe place. Give the journals a once-over with lacquer thinner and take a look at all of the oil passages to make sure there are no obstructions. Then carefully set the crankshaft into place. It can certainly be a one-man job, but if you have a competent friend around don't be afraid to make it a two-man job. You don't want to drop the crank and damage it or the bearings in the block.

ASSEMBLY

Once the crankshaft is in place, an extra squirt of graphite lube won't hurt anything. When the engine is first fired, the oil system will take a while to fill and begin working.

Work down the length of the block setting the caps in place, being careful not to let the bearing separate from the cap.

Once the crankshaft is in its cradle, the main caps can be installed. Make sure each of the bearings is still properly seated in the cap and that the surface is clean. Start with the rear main and carefully lower the cap in place, making sure that the extended ends of the seal halves slide into place.

It may be necessary to tap (not hit) the top of the caps with a polyurethane or rubber hammer to get them to seat properly in the block.

CHAPTER 5

Lube the bolt threads with oil and finger tighten them.

Use a speed wrench to snug the bolts down. Refer to the diagram for the order of tightening. At this point you want to take the bolts just past finger tight but no tighter.

With the main caps on the crankshaft, thrust can be set. The proper spec for this engine is .002 to .007, so I shot for .004 inch, measured with a feeler gauge between the thrust front of the thrust bearing (number 3) and the crankshaft.

At the rear of the block insert a screwdriver between the block and a crankshaft counterweight and pry the crankshaft toward the front of the engine. This will seat the crankshaft against the thrust bearing in the block and cap. Then torque the bolts down, first to 20 ft-lbs each, then to 30 ft-lbs. This will help seat the seat the bearings evenly.

When the bolts have been torqued to 30 ft-lbs, the screwdriver used to set thrust can be removed and the bolts torqued to their final specification. Continue torquing the bolts in 10-ft-lb increments until you reach the final torque specification of 85 ft-lbs.

Once complete, try to turn the crankshaft by hand. There should be some resistance, but the crankshaft should not require too much of an effort to rotate.

ASSEMBLY

Pistons, Rods and Rings

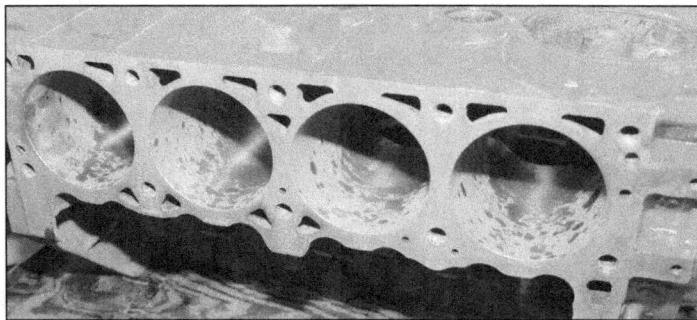

Roll the block on its side to check the ring end-gap. There may be some graphite-lube overspray in the cylinders from the crankshaft installation. Use a rag to wipe it down.

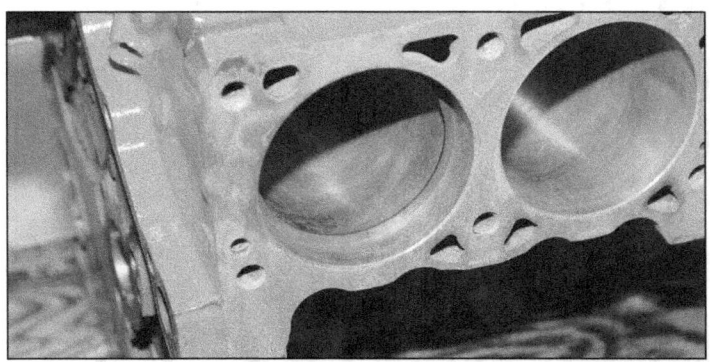

Before the rings can be installed onto the pistons, the end gap must be checked. Beginning with this process, the components for each cylinder should be isolated and kept separate from each other. Place the ring in the cylinder bore and put it in a position where it is as close to exactly perpendicular to the cylinder wall as you can get it.

Critical Measurement

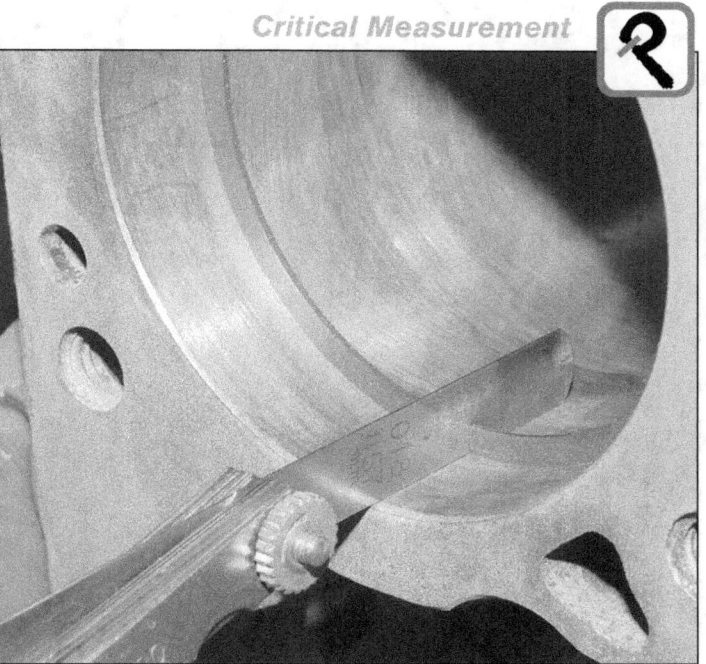

While holding the ring in place, insert a feeler gauge into the gap between the ends of the rings. The proper gaps are listed in the tolerance chart. If the ends of the rings touch, or the gap is too small or too large, something is wrong. In regular piston sets the rings come pre-sized to the bore, so you have either a bore or a ring out of specification. Some rings are ground, but these are for racing and high-performance applications. If you have properly inspected your cylinder bores and they are correct, then you have a bad ring.

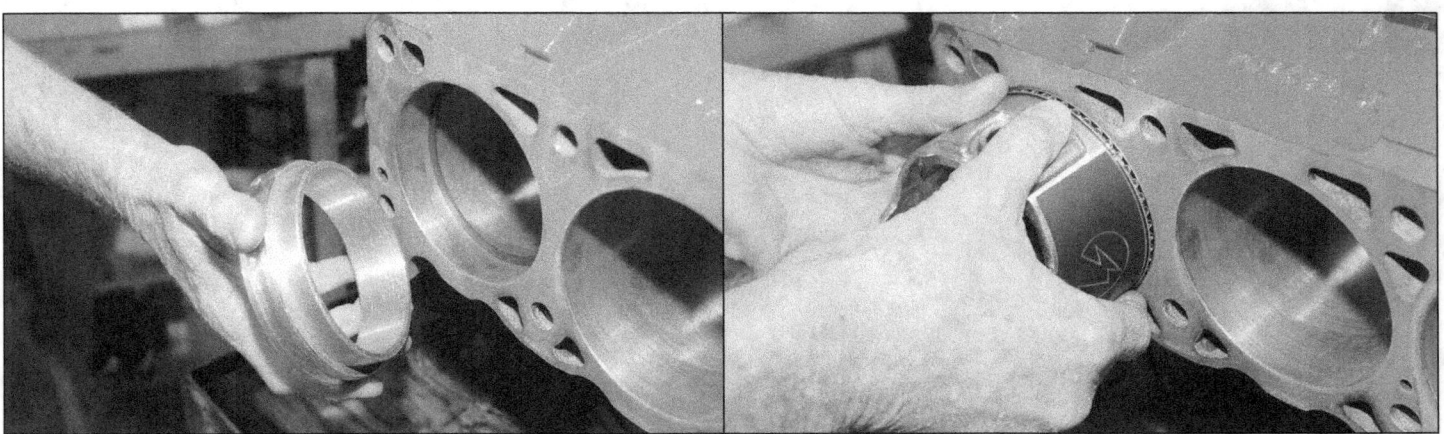

They make a special tool to locate the ring in the cylinder, but you can save a couple of bucks and use one of your new pistons to locate the ring. To get an accurate ring-gap measurement, it is essential for the ring to be perpendicular to the cylinder wall, so pay attention.

HOW TO REBUILD THE SMALL-BLOCK MOPAR

Most rings will come with instructions for proper installation. Make sure you read these and follow these directions, as the rings will have marks that cue their proper installation. The installation of the piston's rings can be done holding the piston in hand or by securing it in a soft-jawed vise. If you use a soft-jawed vise, do not clamp the piston too hard. A regular workbench vise can be used by attaching dense foam, rubber, or soft wood on the inside of the jaws where they will grip the piston.

The two flat oil-compression rings will be installed sandwiching the expansion ring. Install one of these below the expansion ring and then the other above it.

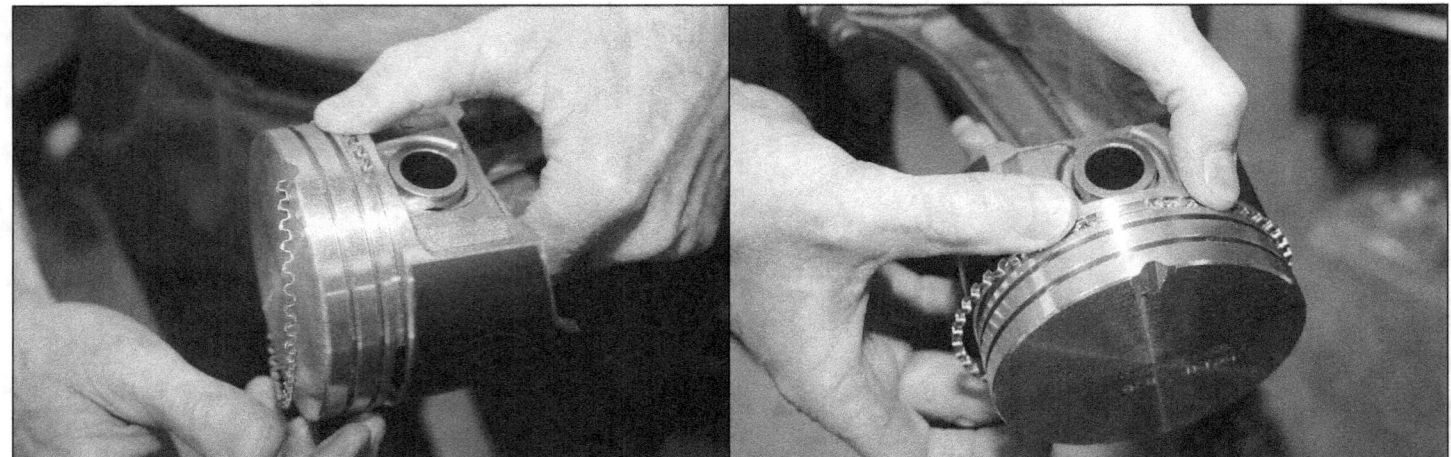

The top two rings are compression rings. The lowest groove on the piston is for the oil-control rings. This will consist of a wavy ring called an expansion ring, and two thin rings. Ring installation will begin at the bottom of the piston. Position the gap of the expansion ring over the piston pin.

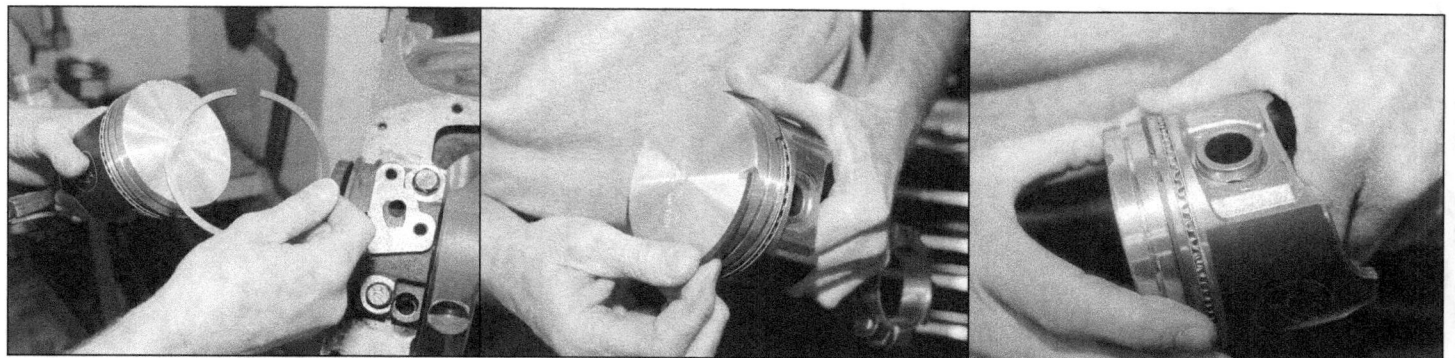

With the oil rings installed, the compression rings can be installed. These will be installed in the same manner as the previous rings. Most rings have a dot that should be positioned towards the top of the piston. Check the instructions carefully, as the two compression rings are color-coded.

Note: Some builders install rings by hand and some use a ring expander. I suggest you hand-install them. When an expander is used, and the ring is spread, all of the tension goes to the point directly opposite of where the ring is split. When hand installing, the ring can be manipulated in a manner that spreads the force more evenly through the ring as it can flex on two axis. You can use your old rings and pistons to practice a couple of times before starting with your new parts.

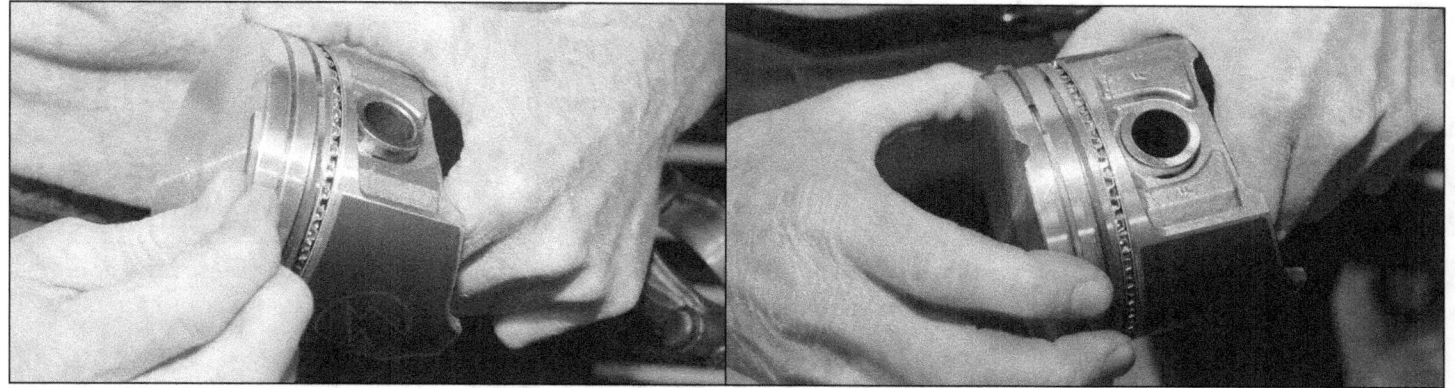

The last ring to be installed is the top compression ring. Don't worry too much about the gap location while putting the rings on the pistons. They can be set just before the piston is installed in the cylinder during the next step.

Clean the cylinder with a clean rag and acetone, and then give each cylinder a squirt of oil and wipe it down with a clean rag.

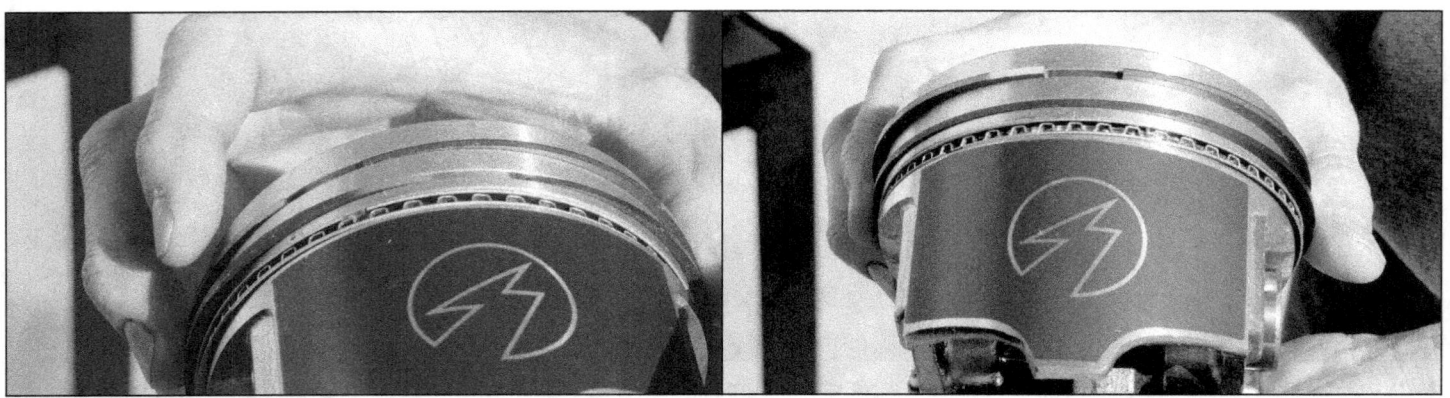

Just before installing the pistons, the ring gaps must be positioned properly. The gap in the top ring should be located toward the spark plug. The gap on the second ring should be located 180 degrees opposite, facing the inboard side of the engine. Likewise, the top oil ring gap should be toward the plug and the bottom toward the inside. The expansion ring can be positioned over either end of the piston pin.

Hand press the rod's bearing half into the connecting rod. Before the piston and rod are installed, give them a liberal coating of graphite lube. Spray the inside of the piston around the pin and the outside of the piston on both the rings and the skirt.

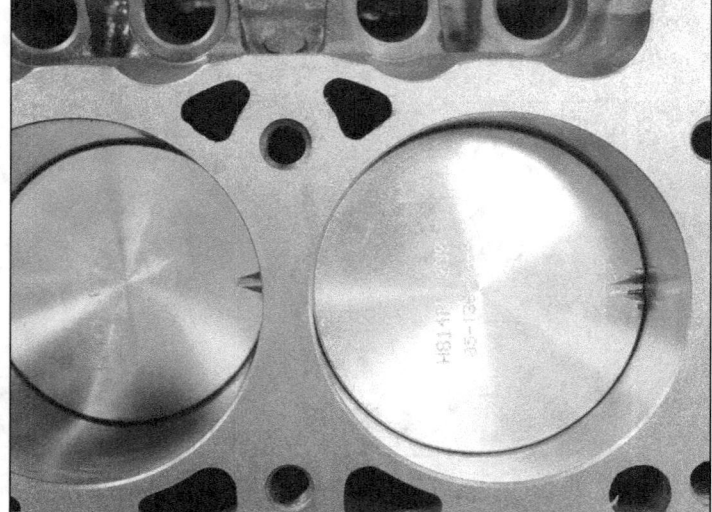

When installing pistons, the notches in the tops of the pistons should all face forward in the block.

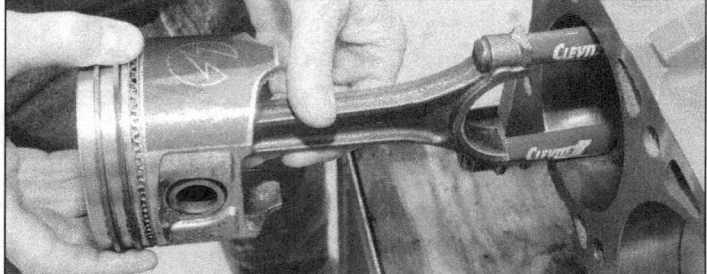

Attach protectors to the rod bolts on the big end of the rod. Protectors can be purchased from most engine shops, but a couple of pieces of 3/8-inch-diameter fuel or vacuum line cut to length will suffice. These keep the sharp edges of the bolts from scratching the polished surface of the crankshaft journals. If you cut the lines long like this they will help center the rod in the cylinder. Either type of bolt protector will help keep the bearing half in the rod if pressed all the way down the rod bolt.

ASSEMBLY

When the rings have been properly aligned, it's time to slide the rod and piston into the cylinder. Carefully lower the rod's big end into the cylinder, making sure it does not bang against the cylinder walls or against the crankshaft. It should take little force to push the piston into the cylinder. If the piston binds as it is being inserted into the cylinder, pull it back out and make sure that the bore is clear, the piston is clean, and that the rings are properly installed and undamaged. Then try again. It will be necessary to hold the piston in one hand, and with the other reach to the bottom of the cylinder to guide the end of the connecting rod. Slide the piston in until the rings are just above the block's deck.

Special Tool Required

To properly install the piston assemblies into the cylinders you will need to buy, beg, or borrow (or rent) a ring compressor. Fit the ring compressor around the top of the piston so that it covers the piston's rings. Using a wooden (or plastic) hammer handle, push the top of the piston into the block while compressing the rings. *Do not hammer on the top of the piston.* Place the end of the handle firmly on the top of the piston and push.

HOW TO REBUILD THE SMALL-BLOCK MOPAR

CHAPTER 5

Once the piston's rings have entered the top of the cylinder bore, the ring compressor can be removed.

Reach around to the bottom side of the block and grasp the big end of the rod so that you can guide it into position around its proper location on the crankshaft.

Once the rod bearing has been seated on the crankshaft, the cap can be put into place. Like the main bearings, make sure that the rod bearing half is properly seated in the cap and then slide the cap onto the rod bolts. Also, like the main caps, make sure that the bearing half does not fall out while it is being attached.

Once the cap is in place, squirt a bit of oil on the rod-bolt threads, put the nuts on the rod bolts, and finger tighten.

ASSEMBLY

Torquing Fasteners

When the first cylinder is complete, move to the next and repeat the process. When one side of the block is done, roll it over and install the pistons on the other side. When all of the piston/rod assemblies have been installed they can be torqued down.

Like the main caps, the rod bolts will be torqued down in increments. First, torque them to 10, then 20, then 30, and then to 45 ft-lbs—the final torque spec. This will help the rod caps to be pulled down to the crankshaft evenly.

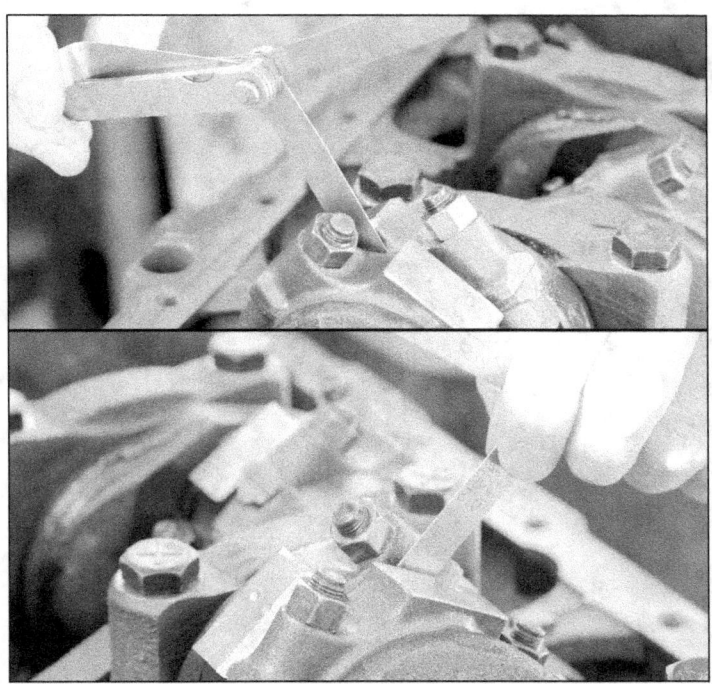

With the rods torqued, the rod gap can be checked. Insert a feeler gauge between each rod-to-rod gap. Proper rod gap tolerances are listed on the tolerance chart.

Freeze Plugs

Special Tool Required

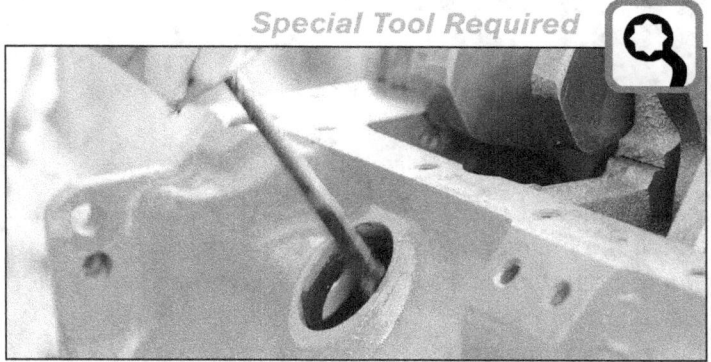

The next step is to drive new casting (or freeze) plugs back into the block. It's a good idea to do this with the block resting on a firm (and clean) surface so that it doesn't move while driving the plugs. Make sure that the surface of the hole where the plug fits is free of burrs. Coat the inside of the plug hole with a good sealer. Some folks use J-B Weld to secure the plugs.

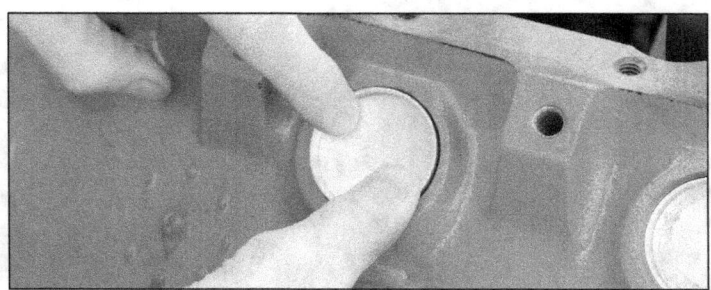

Fit the plug into place over the hole. Try to set it as evenly as possible.

Master Mechanic Tip

To drive the plugs you can use a special tool, but a large deep-well socket will do just as good a job. Drive the plug into the hole with steady blows.

HOW TO REBUILD THE SMALL-BLOCK MOPAR

Watch the position of the plug closely as you hammer it in and do not drive it too far. The proper position is with the top lip of the plug just below the top rim of the hole. There are plugs located on the back of the block as well. These cannot be driven home with the block on an engine stand, thus the reason for beginning assembly with the block on a cart.

I'm going to give the small plug on the front of the block a bit of special attention (this is an optional step). I drill a small 1/32-inch hole in the center of the plug.

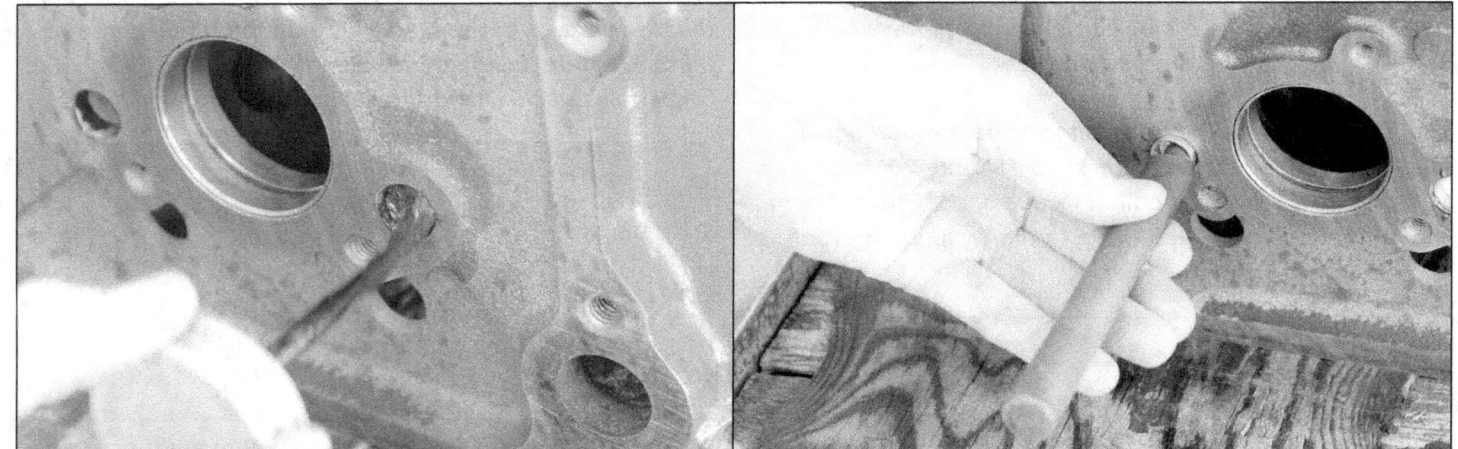

The plug will be installed like the larger plugs on the sides of the block. The hole is coated with sealer and the plug hammered home.

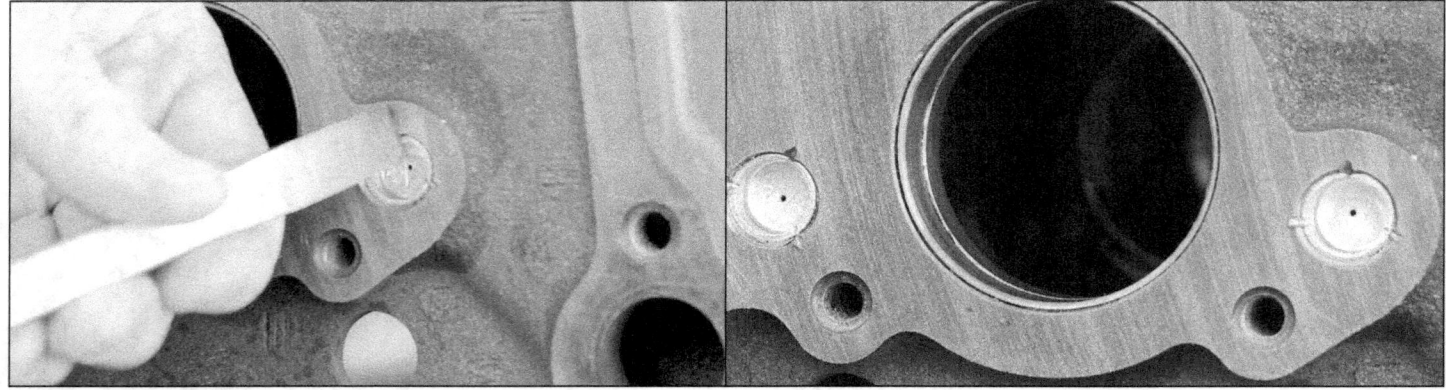

These plugs will be under the pressure of the oil system so they must not come loose. Using a chisel and a hammer can provide a little insurance. Position the chisel so that the edge of the plug and the edge of the block will be dinged. This will further secure the plug in the block. The little hole that I drilled earlier will allow a bit more oil to lubricate the timing chain, which will add to its lifespan.

ASSEMBLY

Screw-In Plugs

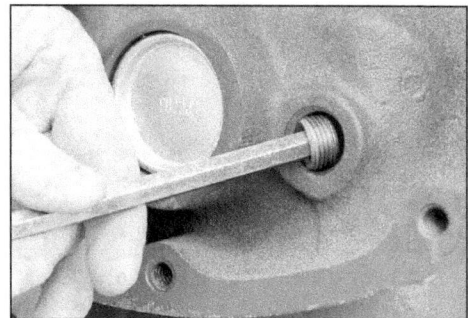

When all of the press-in plugs have been driven home, the screw-in oil plugs on the back of the block can be installed. The first plug to be screwed in will be the internal plug that closes the internal oil passages. If this plug is left out of the rebuild you are doomed as you will have no oil pressure, and this will most likely lead you to your second rebuild. Coat the threads with Loctite and mount the plug on the proper-sized hex wrench.

Once the internal plug is in place and tightened, the outer plugs can be installed. After these are screwed in, the engine can be bolted on the engine stand. Once the engine is on the stand, the rest of the oil-galley plugs can be screwed in.

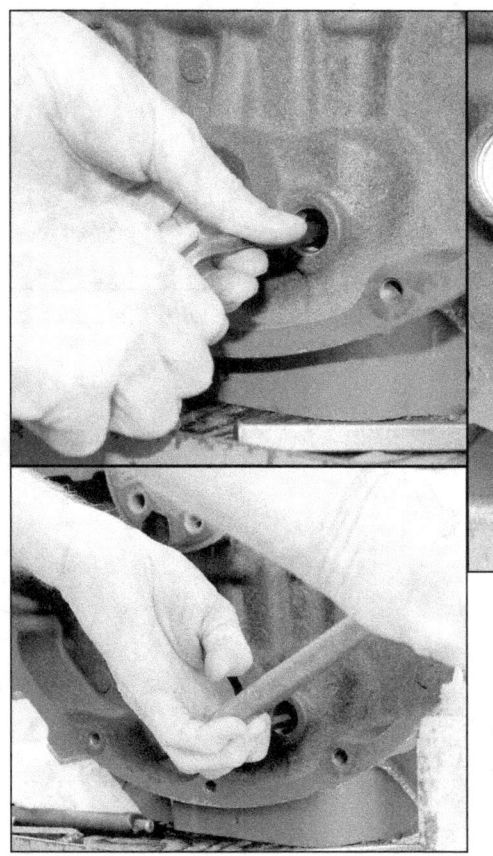

Insert the plug and wrench through the large hole in the back of the block and thread it into place. A small cheater bar can be used to tighten the plug to about 30 ft-lbs. Then withdraw the wrench, leaving the plug in place.

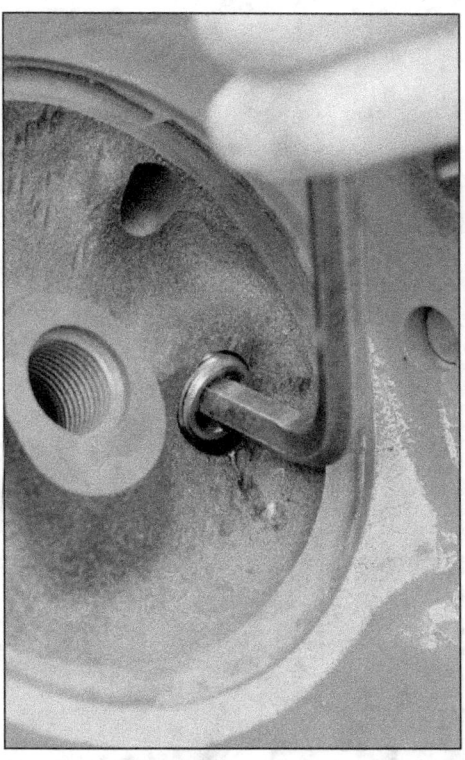

Don't forget the plug in the oil-filter mounting area.

Oil-Shaft Bushing

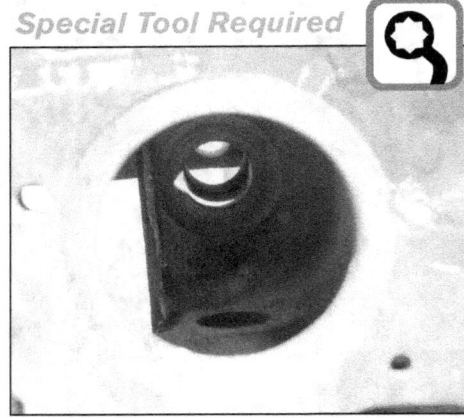

Special Tool Required

If you removed the oil pump shaft bushing (and you should have) it's time to put it back. Inspect the area in the block where it seats to make sure it is clean.

Coat the mounting area with grease to help the bushing drive home.

A rod with a shoulder will be needed to drive the bushing home. The intermediate shaft bushing should be installed with a special tool (Miller Special Tools number C-3053). This special tool expands the bushing into the bore and burnishes it to the proper size all in one step. When the tool is not used, sometimes the intermediate shaft won't fit into the bushing.

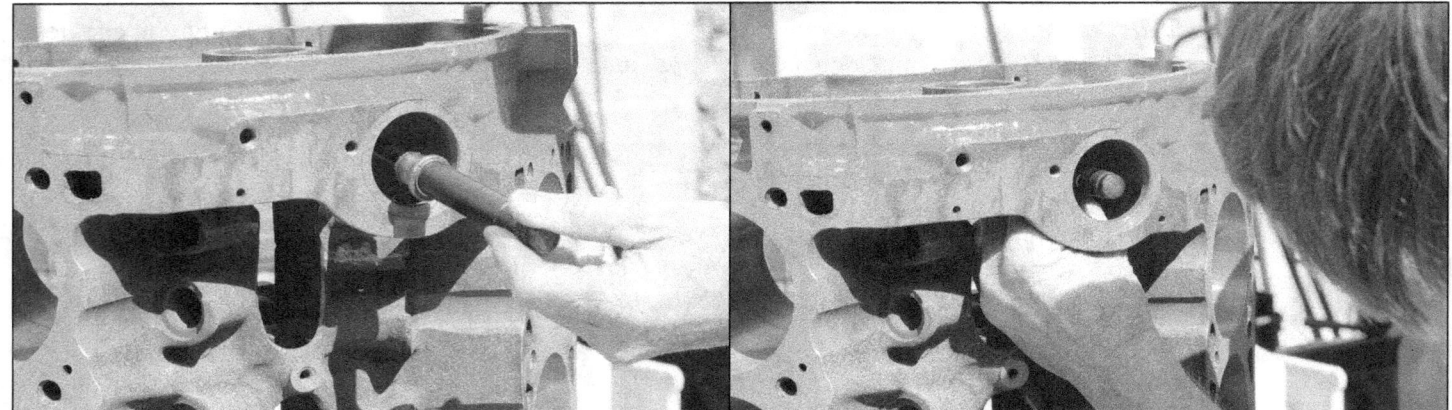

Put the bushing on the rod and position it over the bore. Make sure the bushing is level and concentric with the bore.

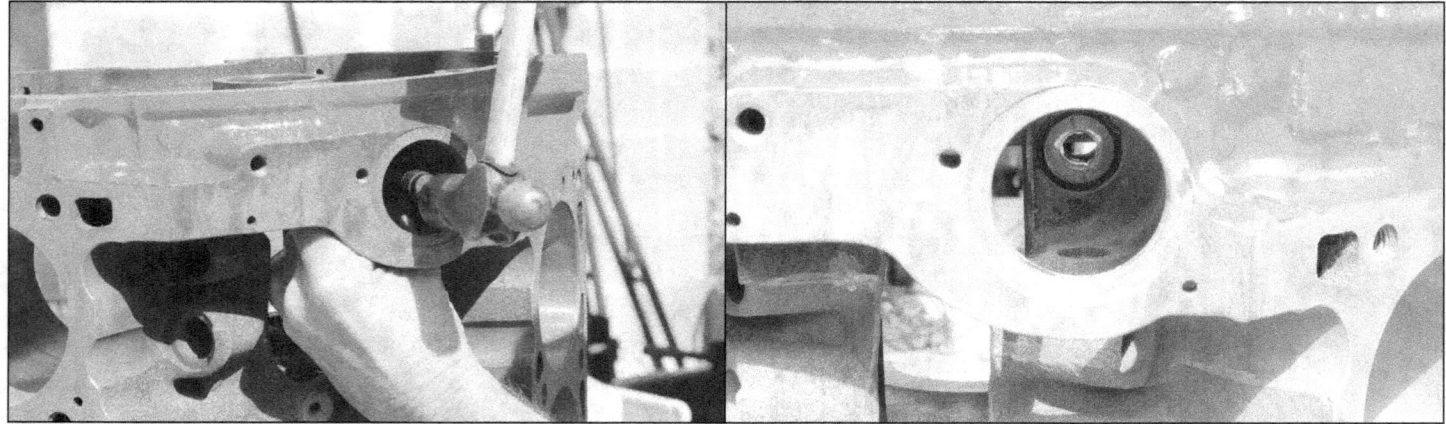

Use a medium hammer to drive the bearing in.

ASSEMBLY

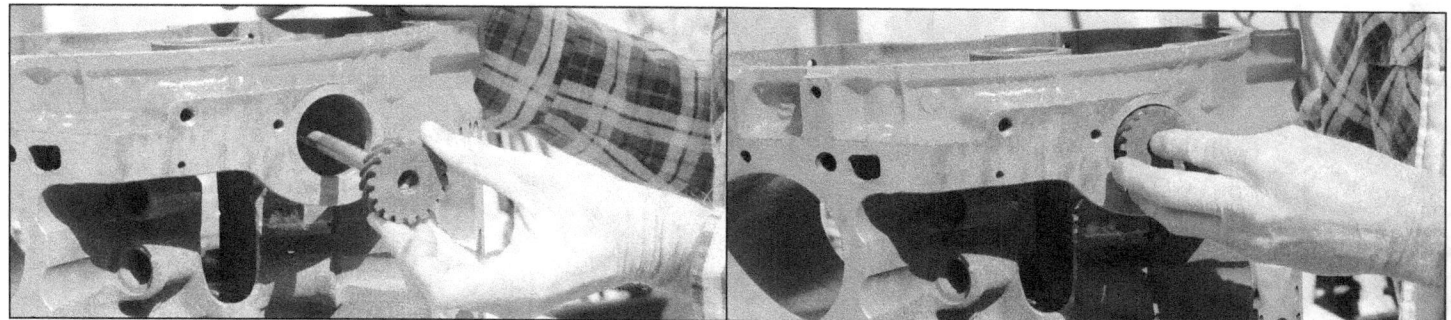

Once the bushing is in, lubricate and insert the oil-pump driveshaft to make sure it fits and will spin with little resistance. Check this now. It will be a while before the shaft is permanently installed, and you don't want a problem on down the line as it will be much more difficult to correct. After checking the bushing, remove the shaft and store it in a safe location.

Camshaft

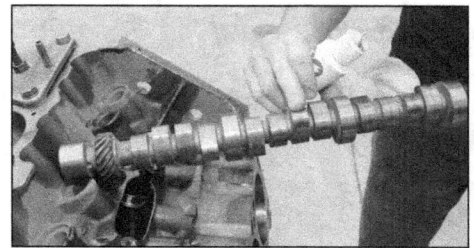

Make a last visual inspection of the camshaft, running your finger over each of the lobes to make sure that they are all smooth and undamaged.

Once the cam is completely coated with lubricant, carefully slide it into the bore. Try not to let it bang into the cam bearings any more than is necessary. A long bolt can be threaded into the front of the cam to help hold it while installing.

Begin the camshaft installation with a complete lubrication of the entire cam. Put a dollop of cam lube on each lobe and then massage it all over the cam.

When the camshaft has passed through the first camshaft bearing it will be possible to stick a finger or two through the oil-return holes in the block and guide the camshaft on the inside of the engine.

CHAPTER 5

Performance Tip

Once the camshaft is in place, secure it by bolting the camshaft thrust plate into position. Note: If you drilled holes in the small plugs that are behind the plate, then 3/8-inch holes must be drilled in the thrust plate in front of the plugs. If you elected not to drill the holes in the plugs, no holes will have to be drilled in the thrust plate. Make sure to install the drip guide on the lowest thrust-plate bolt.

Timing Gear

When the engine is at TDC, the gear can be slid onto the crankshaft. Its rotational position will be located by the keyway. The dimple on the gear should be mounted facing the front and oriented upward.

With the camshaft and crankshaft installed in the engine, the timing gear can be mounted. For the installation of the timing gear the bottom end of the engine must be put at top dead center (TDC). This means that the piston in the number-1 cylinder will be at the absolute top of its stroke (its highest position in the cylinder). Standing in front of the block, it will be the one closest to you on the right. You can put the bolt back in the front of the crank or use a large adjustable wrench to rotate the crank. If you use this method, be careful not to damage the front of the crankshaft.

Next, the cam gear can be mounted on the camshaft. Once the gear is on the cam (located by another keyway) the gear can be put on the cam and the cam rotated until the gear's dimple is on the bottom of the cycle.

ASSEMBLY

When both gears are mounted, the dimples should be aligned with the dimple on the crankshaft gear at the top, and the dimple on the camshaft gear at the bottom. In order to achieve the correct alignment, the crankshaft and camshaft must be indexed correctly.

Once both of the gears are in the correct rotational position, the gears and chain can be permanently mounted. Take the gears off of the crankshaft and camshaft, making sure not to change their positions. Then wrap the chain on the gears and slide them back on at the same time. If the chain had been properly installed, the little bit of slack in the chain will be equal on both sides. Install the bolt in the end of the cam to secure the gear and torque it to 30 ft-lbs.

Oil Pump

If you completely trust your parts supplier skip ahead to install the oil pump, but I suggest you take a few minutes and check your pump out. First, bolt the pump to the bottom of the block. Don't worry about installing the pickup tube at this point, as the pump will be coming back off.

Remove the bolts that secure the cover to the bottom of the pump and remove the cover.

HOW TO REBUILD THE SMALL-BLOCK MOPAR

This is the heart of your engine's lubrication center.

Run the tip of your finger all around the housing, checking for burrs or sharp edges.

Remove the pump rotor, which is permanently mounted to the driveshaft. Then lift the outer ring, with the pump's profile out of the pump housing.

Use a small screwdriver to push the bypass valve back and forth, making sure that it slides easily.

Reinstall the inner and outer rotors.

ASSEMBLY

Use a dial gauge, or a straight edge and feeler gauge, to check the distance between the top of the rotor and the top of the housing.

It's now time to do a final reassembly to the pump. Take the rotors back out and spray the housing with graphite lubricant. This will give the pump some lubrication during the first cranking.

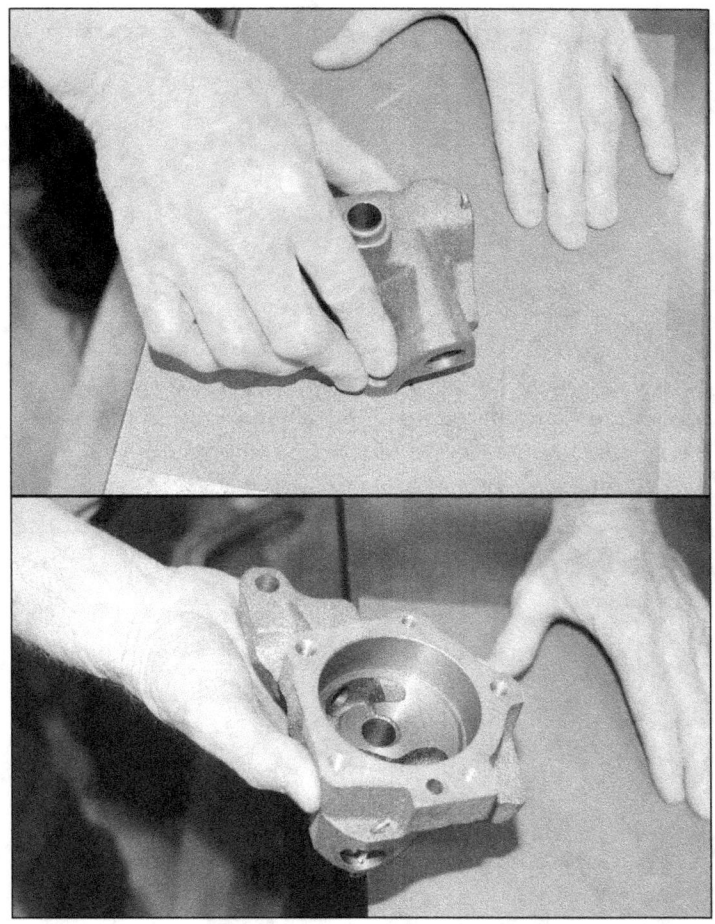

The distance between the rotor and the top of the housing was about .005 inch, which is common for new pumps. This is a little high for David's liking, as he prefers .002 to .003 inch. To tighten this tolerance he did a light sanding on a flat surface and rechecked the tolerance.

Reinstall the rotors and lubricate liberally again.

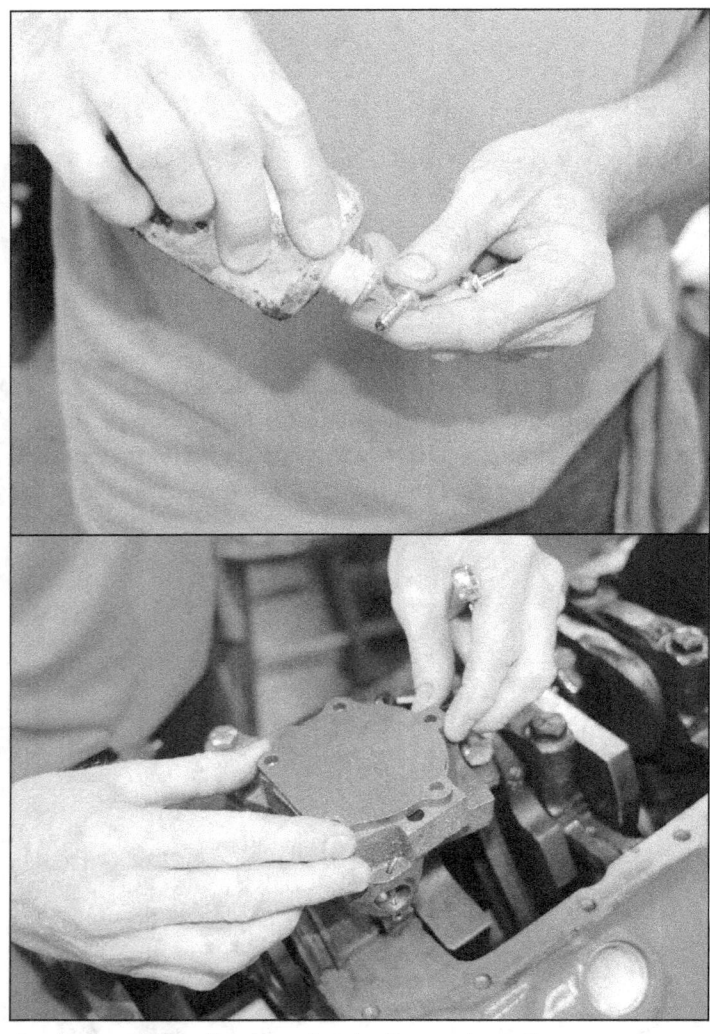

Before installing the oil pump, the pickup tube must be screwed into the pump. This will not be possible once the pump is bolted to the block. Coat the end of the pickup tube with Loctite and screw it in.

Apply Loctite to the housing bolts, replace the rear cover, and remove the pump from the block.

Make sure the pickup screen is clean and that the tube is clear of any obstructions.

The pump can then be bolted to the block. Coat the threads of the bolts with Loctite and hand tighten.

Use a straight edge and a measuring tape to measure the distance from the bottom of the inside of the pan to the surface where the pan meets the block. Then measure the distance from the surface where the block meets the oil pan to the bottom edge of the pickup screen. You should have at least 1/8 inch of clearance to get proper oil supply.

Assemble Cylinder Heads

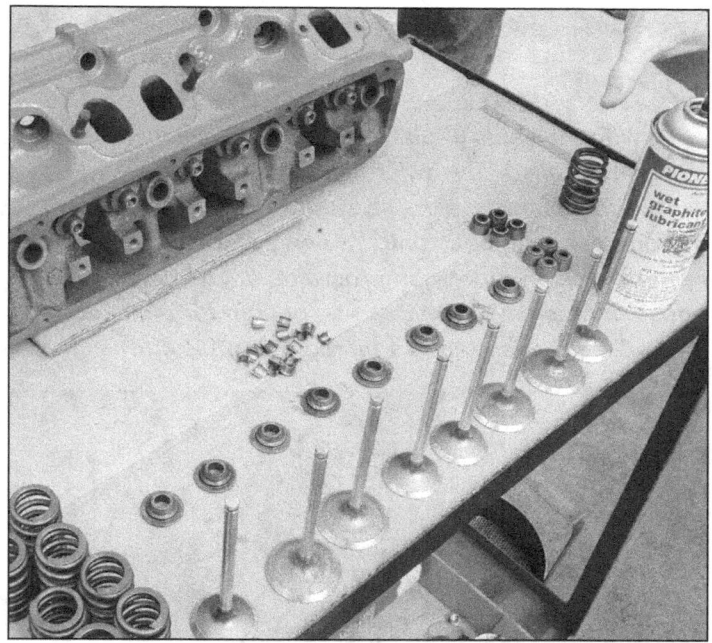

It's now time to let the block rest a while and get the cylinder heads ready to mount. Before the cylinder heads can be bolted to the block, the valves and valvesprings must be installed. Lay the head on your cart or workbench and get the valves, valvesprings, seals, keepers, and locks ready. You will also need your graphite lubricant.

Lay the cylinder head on its side with the intake side down and spray each valveguide with graphite lube.

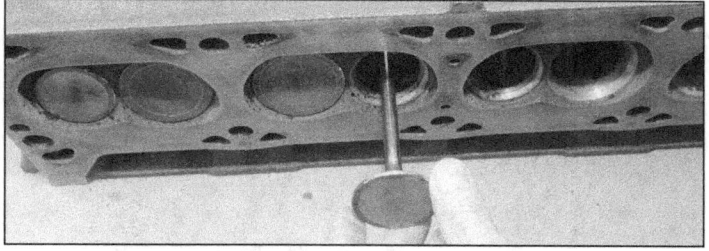

Beginning at the end of the head, insert each valve in its proper guide and slide it into the closed position. Work the valve in and out to make sure that the motion is fluid and not binding. A single metal shaving or grain of dirt can affect the valve's ability to slide, so make sure the bore has not been contaminated.

When the valves are all in the cylinder head, press the valveseals into place. The seals for the intake and exhaust valves will be different. The intake valves will usually be black while those for the exhaust valves will be red.

When properly installed, the seal's bottom will be snug against the block all the way around its perimeter. Do one valve at a time until all of the valves are in and the seals seated.

Carefully position the head on its end, making sure the valves don't drop out. Close the valve and slide the valveseal over the valvestem and press it as far down as you can.

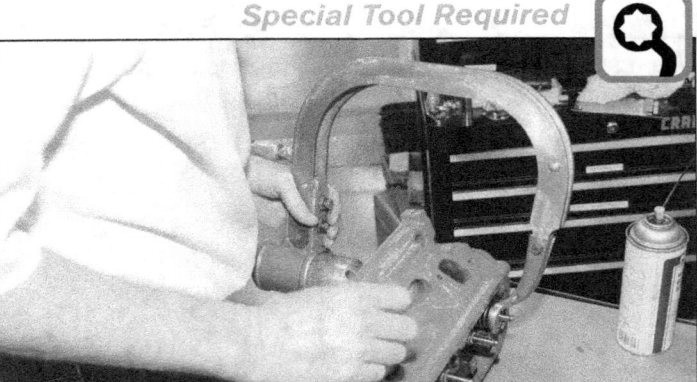

Special Tool Required

With the seals in place the valvesprings can be installed. This will require a special tool—a valvespring compressor. The best way to go is to buy or borrow a pneumatic unit. You may also check with rental shops and tool loan programs at your local parts house. A mechanical unit can be bought for about $20 and will do the job but is a bit more unwieldy.

Use a deep-well socket to drive the seal onto the boss in the cylinder head. Just make sure the bottom rim of the socket is the same diameter as the outer diameter of the seal. It may require a fair bit of pressure to set the seals.

Put the valvespring into position on the top of the cylinder head. Valvesprings have a top and a bottom, so make sure the smaller, tapered end is mounted upward.

ASSEMBLY

With the spring in place, position the retainer on the top of the spring. Then position the spring compressor with the back of the compressor centered on the valve and the front on the top of the valve retainer.

When the compressor is activated it will compress the spring and slide the retainer down the valvestem.

With the two keeper halves in place, release the pressure on the spring compressor.

Once the spring is compressed, the keepers can be positioned at the top of the valvestem. Position the keepers so that the taper is toward the head and the top of the keeper is just under the lip at the top of the valvestem.

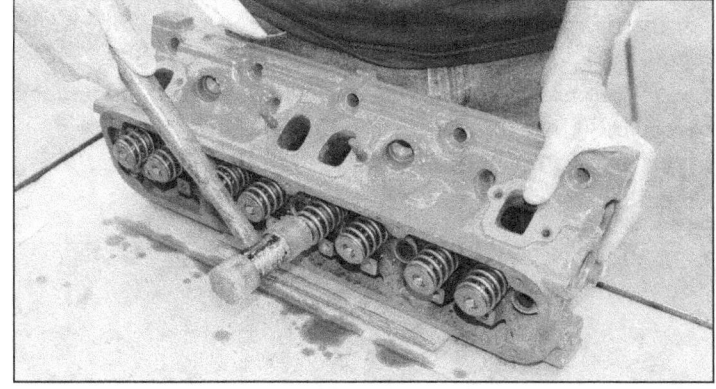

If you've done your job, the retainer will slide around the taper on the keepers and lock into place. When the first valve is complete, repeat this process all the way down the cylinder head until all of the valves and springs are secured. When all the springs are in, place the head on a workbench, combustion side down, and tap the top of each valve with a polyurethane hammer. This will take any binding tension off of the individual components and ensure that everything has fit together properly. When all of the valves and springs are finished, set the heads to the side and roll the block back out.

CHAPTER 5

Mounting Cylinder Heads

Head Pins

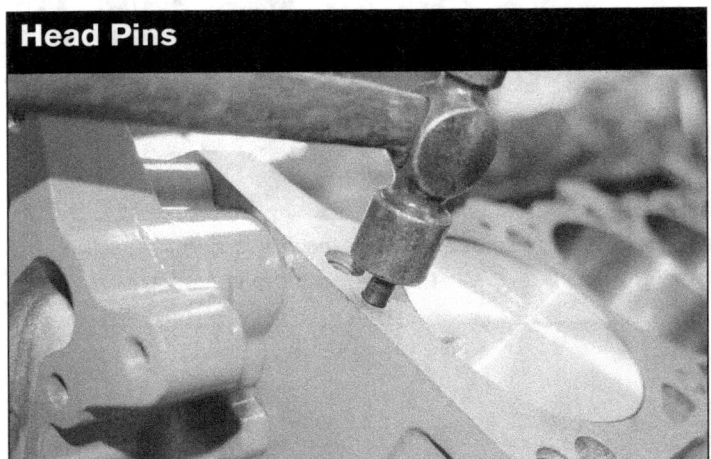

If the locating pins on the block's decks were removed to machine the block, and not replaced by the machine shop, then you'll have to put them in. Clean them, hold them in place over the proper hole, and tap (don't whack) them down into the hole. It should not require much force to drive them home.

Note: If you are working on an engine with flat-tappet lifters, you can wait until the heads have been bolted on before installing the lifters. You don't have to, but if you put them in and roll the block over on the stand they will fall out. If you are working on a later-model engine with a roller camshaft and lifters, they will need to be installed before the head gaskets and cylinder heads are mated to the block. The roller lifters are too tall to get into the lifter bores once the cylinder head is in place.

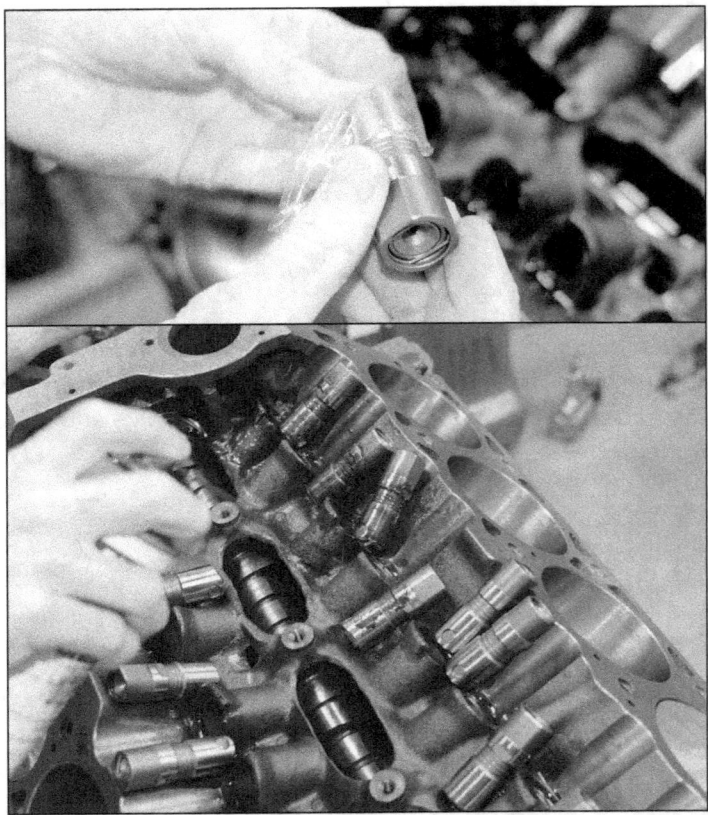

Take the lifters from their wrapper and lay them by their appropriate bore. If you are using new lifters it does not matter which lifter goes with which bore, but if you are re-using your cam and lifters then you need to put each lifter in the bore from which it was removed.

Spray the lifter bores with graphite lube.

Orient the lifter with the oil hole toward the inside and drop the lifter into the bore. Hold the lifter with your fingers and slide it up and down to make sure the lifter is moving freely. If it does not, remove it and check the lifter and bore for burrs or contamination. The paint mark on the Magnum lifters must go toward the center of the engine, or it will trap air in the lifter.

ASSEMBLY

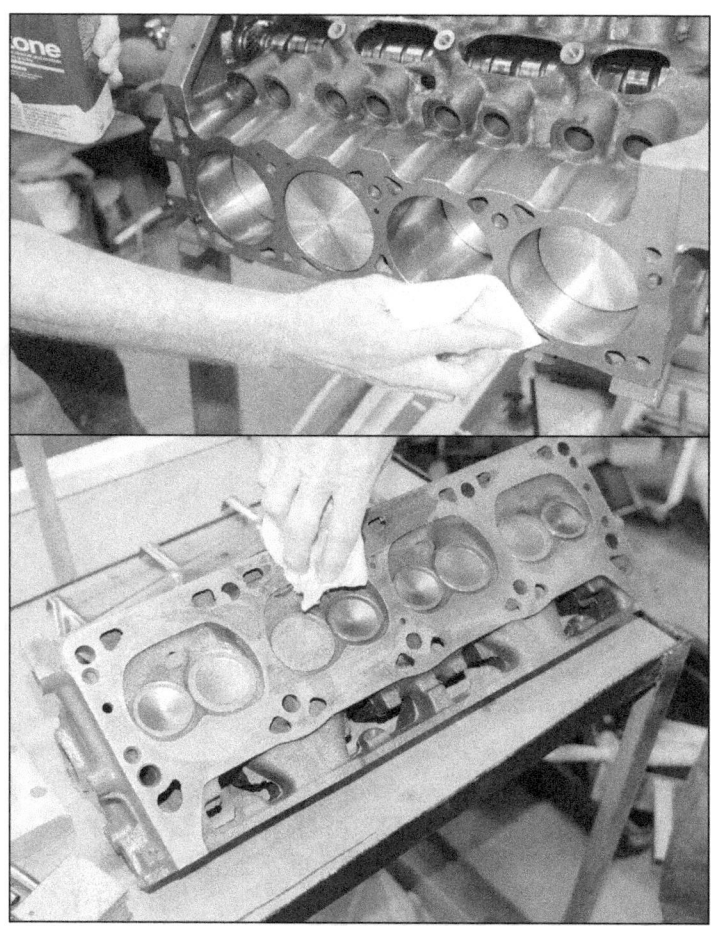

Using acetone and a clean rag, make sure that the mating surfaces of the block and head are both spotlessly clean.

Carefully lower the head onto the block, being careful not to move, or damage, the head gasket.

With the lifters installed, the cylinder heads can be mated to the block. Position the head gasket over the block, making sure all of the bolt holes and the cooling passages match up.

Rotate the block on the stand so that the bottom mating surface of the head is parallel to the floor. Be careful when rotating the engine. When a head is put on, the engine will become top-heavy and will have a mind of its own about how it will spin. If the head side spins downward before the head bolts are in, the head will come off and it's going to hit your foot if you're slow, and the floor if you're quick. Either way it will be bad, so pay attention.

HOW TO REBUILD THE SMALL-BLOCK MOPAR

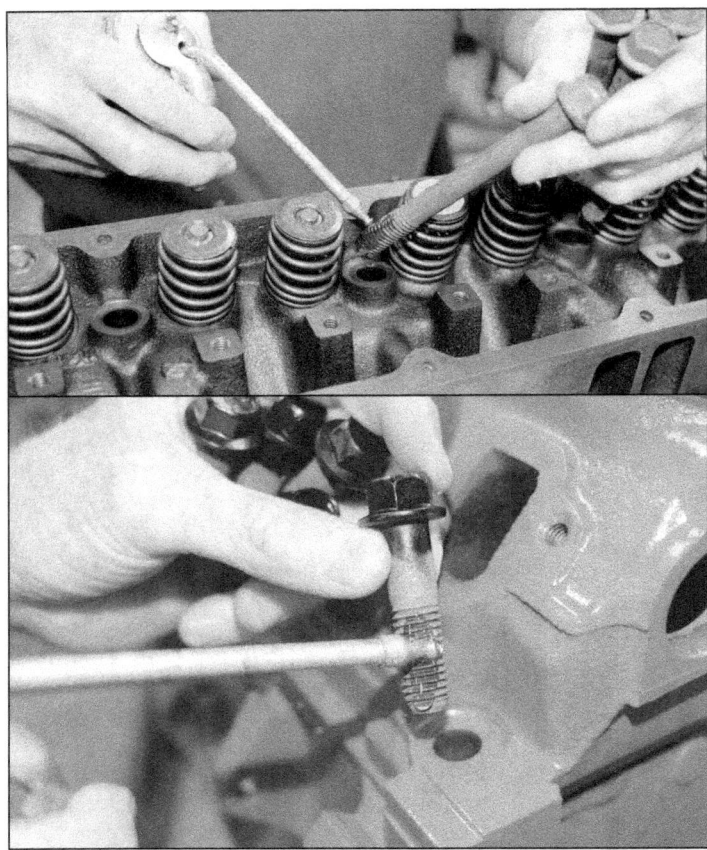

The long head bolts will be used in the holes located under the valvecover, and the short bolts for the holes on the outboard side of the head, outside of the valvecover. Before either is inserted coat their threads with oil.

Use a speed wrench to tighten the bolts just until they seat and become difficult to turn.

Set your torque wrench to 20 ft-lbs and start tightening, beginning with the bolts in the center and working your way outward from the center bolt (see diagram).

Torquing Fasteners

When all of the bolts have been taken to 20 ft-lbs, repeat the process, taking them to 30. Then repeat, each time gaining by increments of 10 ft-lbs until the bolts are at their final specification of 105 ft-lbs. It is critical that the bolts are tightened in the proper order. This allows the head and gasket to have the pressure. Begin in the center and move outwards. This allows the load to be applied in an outward motion, which helps eliminate buckling in the gasket or the cylinder head itself. Once one head is done, repeat the process on the other heads. Once again, *be careful* while rotating the engine on the stand.

The Valvetrain

Flat-Tappet Lifters

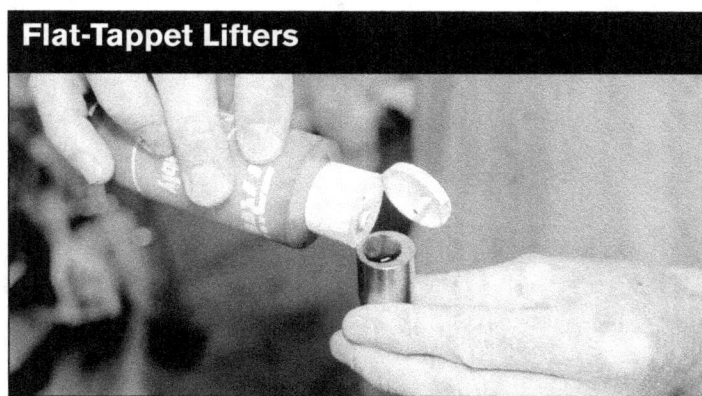

If you are working on a flat-tappet engine, now's the time to put them in. Flat-tappet lifters will be installed using the same process described earlier for roller lifters, with one exception. Flat-tappet lifters should have the crowned end that meets the cam well lubricated with cam lube before installing.

Lifter Retainers and Guideplates

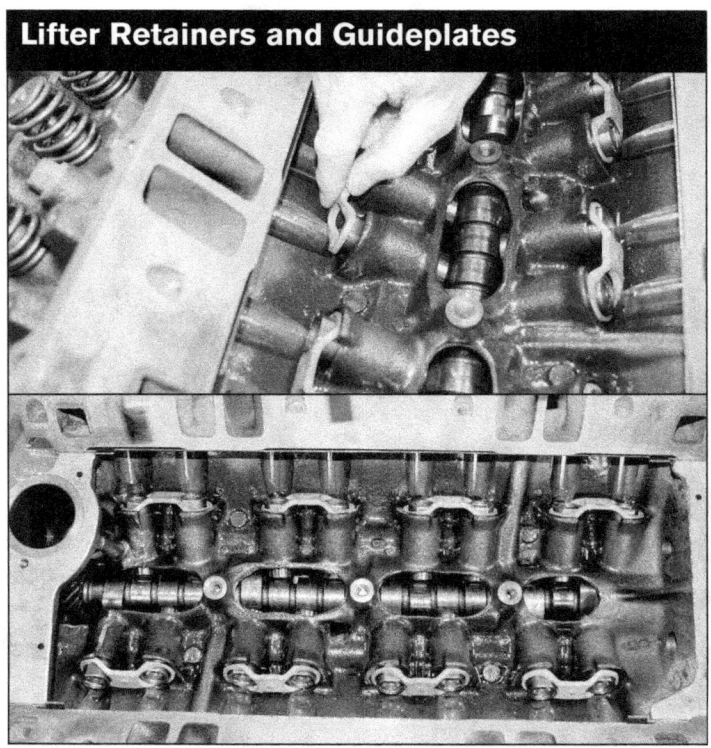

Late-model engines have a few components that their predecessors don't have. With roller lifters, retainers were used to keep the lifters in their bores. The lifter retainers can be placed by hand and will fit snugly inside the lip of the lifter bore. Place all of the retainers into position and check that they are all seated properly.

The hydraulic roller lifters are secured in place with a one-piece retainer bracket. Set the bracket into place making sure that each of the bracket's arms fits over the center of their appropriate retainer. Coat the threads of the three bolts that hold the bracket in place with Loctite and torque them to 20 ft-lbs.

Pushrods

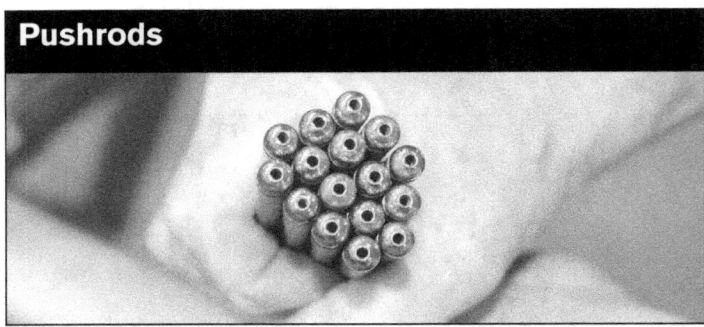

With the lifters properly installed in their bores, the pushrods can be dropped into place. Make sure that they are clean and the oil passages through the center are clear. Magnum engines will have hollow pushrods that allow oil to flow up to the head (shown above). LA engines will not have the holes in the pushrods, and oil flows to the heads through passages in the block, heads, and rocker shafts.

Once all of the pushrods are in place, the rest of the valvetrain can be assembled.

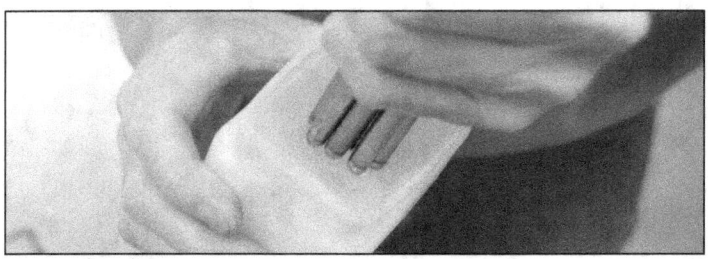

Dip both ends of the pushrods in petroleum jelly. This will provide good lubrication during the initial starting and will then dissolve in the engine's oil once the engine comes to temperature.

Drop the 16 pushrods into their proper locations. It is obvious where the bore is, so just make sure the bottom end of the pushrod fits onto the center of the top of the lifter.

Rocker Arms

Coat the top of the valve with grease to add lubrication during first cranking.

Place each of the guideplates in their appropriate position on the cylinder head.

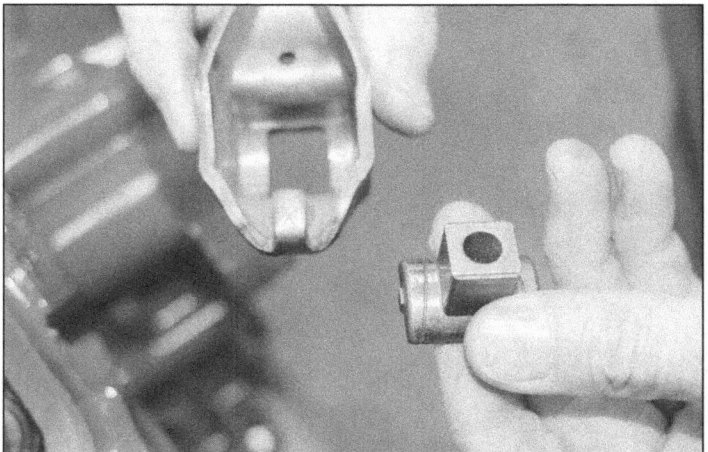
This is the Magnum rocker arm and pivot. LA engines have rocker arms that pivot on the rocker shaft.

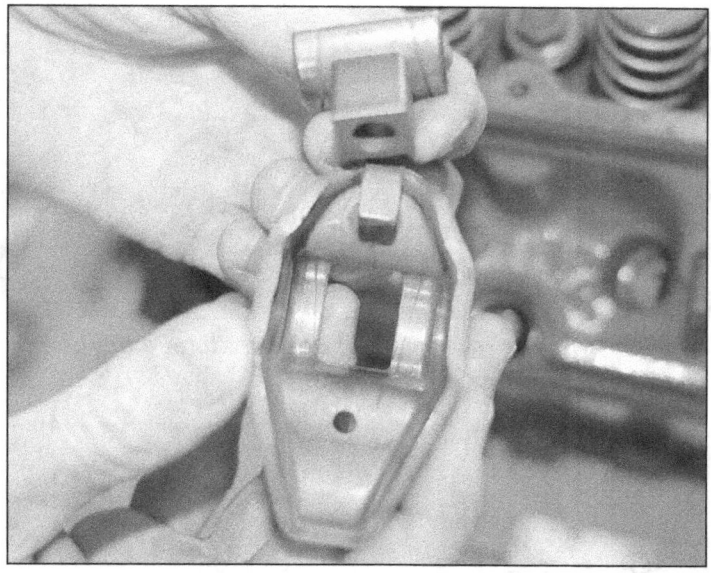
The rocker arm is made up of two pieces, the rocker arm and the fulcrum, the piece on which the rocker pivots. The fulcrum has channels to help facilitate oil distribution. Its pattern will be burnished in the top half, so put them together so they match if you are re-using your rocker arms.

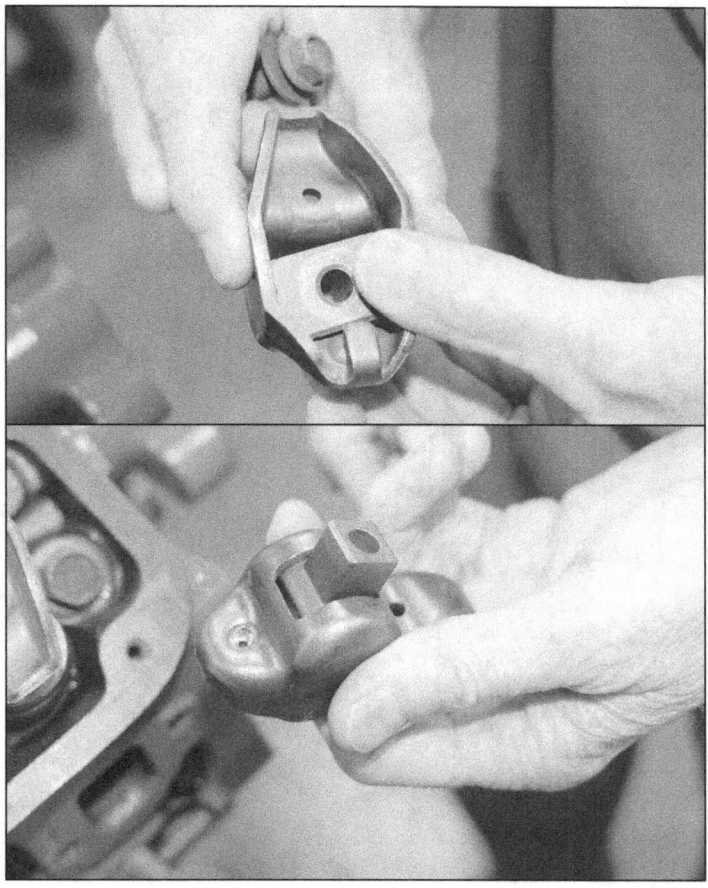
Once you have oriented the two pieces, fit them together.

While holding the guideplate in position, thread the bolt through the rocker arm and the hole in the guideplate and finger tighten.

When the rocker-arm bolts are tightened, the guideplate will be forced into its proper position.

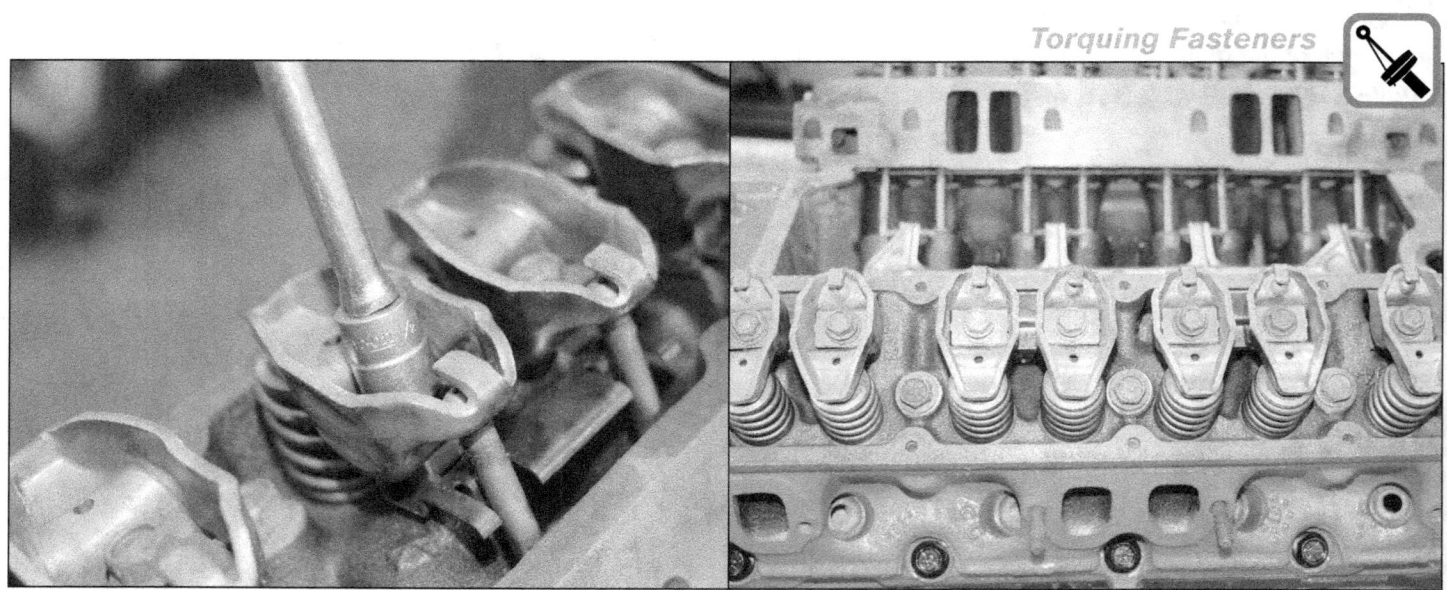

Torque the rocker arm bolts to 20 ft-lbs.

Front Engine Cover

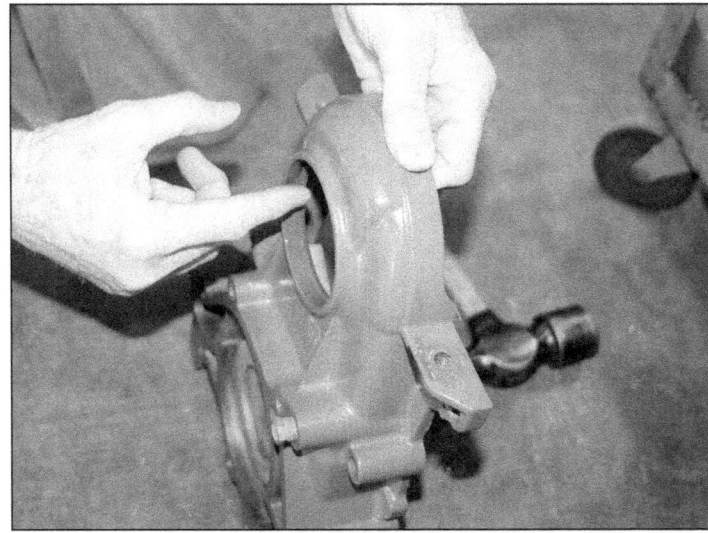

Before the front engine cover can be bolted on, the front crankshaft seal must be installed in the cover. This begins by coating the inside of the bore in the front engine cover with Loctite. Note: The surface of this bore is covered with paint. This cover was painted about a month before assembly with a quality engine paint. This gave the paint time to fully set. If you have painted your cover shortly before the rebuild, remove the paint from the inner bore.

Place the front engine cover on a sturdy (flat) workbench or the floor, and position the seal in the bore. You'll need a seal driver to drive the seal into the bore. Use a hammer to drive the seal into the bore.

Once the seal is firmly set in the bore, coat its inner diameter with grease.

Use your Permatex Aviation gasket material and paint the surface of the block and front cover where the two meet.

HOW TO REBUILD THE SMALL-BLOCK MOPAR

Harmonic Balancer

Lay the gasket on the front engine cover, making sure the holes match up. Fit the cover onto the block and thread the bolts home. Only the lower bolts can be put in at this time. The upper bolts pass through the water pump and front engine cover and will be installed shortly. Finger tighten the bolts only and roll the block over for the next step.

With the front engine cover on, the harmonic balancer can be mounted. Before putting it on the crankshaft, put a dollop of silicone gasket material on the end of the keyway. This is a possible leaking point of oil, and the silicone will help seal the connection.

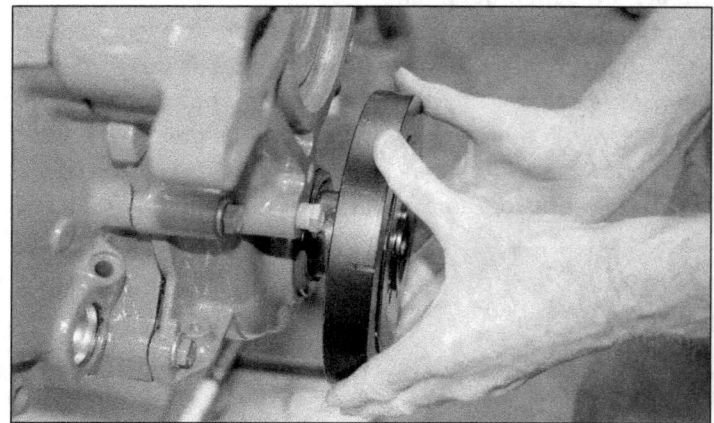

Grease the outside diameter of the balancer where it passes through the front seal.

With the block inverted, position the timing cover where the bottom of the cover and the bottom of the block are flush. The oil-pan gasket will travel across this surface, and if the two are not flush you will have an oil leak. Once the two surfaces meet evenly, the cover bolts can be tightened.

Slide the balancer evenly onto the front of the camshaft.

ASSEMBLY

The best way to go is with the puller/presser that I suggested in Chapter 1. This will be the most controlled way to mount the balancer. If you didn't buy one you can use good old Plan B and drive the balancer on with a hammer and a block of wood. Hold the block of wood against the front of the crankshaft and hammer the balancer. Never hit the front of the crankshaft directly with the hammer.

Oil Pan

Before mounting the oil pan, use your oil can to pump some oil onto the timing chain to help during the first start.

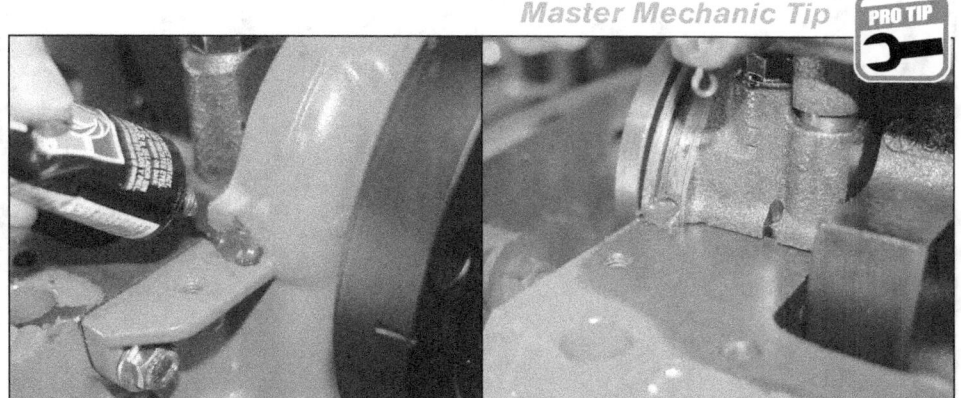

Master Mechanic Tip

Squeeze a dollop of silicone gasket material in the corners where the front engine cover meets the block and where the rear main meets the block. It is difficult for the gasket to seal here, and this will help eliminate small oil leaks.

Your gasket kit should contain a new oil-pan gasket. Press it into place, locating the bolt holes in the correct place.

HOW TO REBUILD THE SMALL-BLOCK MOPAR

Put another dollop of silicone gasket on the topside of the gasket in the same locations as you did under the gasket to reinforce the corner seals.

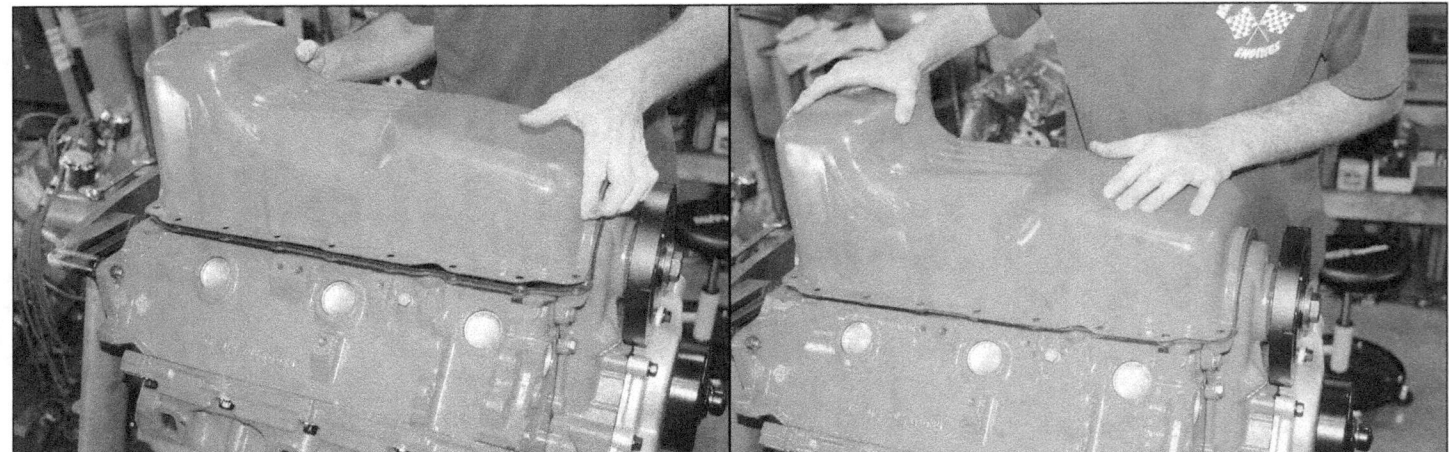

Mount the pan on the block. It may be necessary to wiggle the pan a bit while pressing to get it to properly seat on the thick gasket.

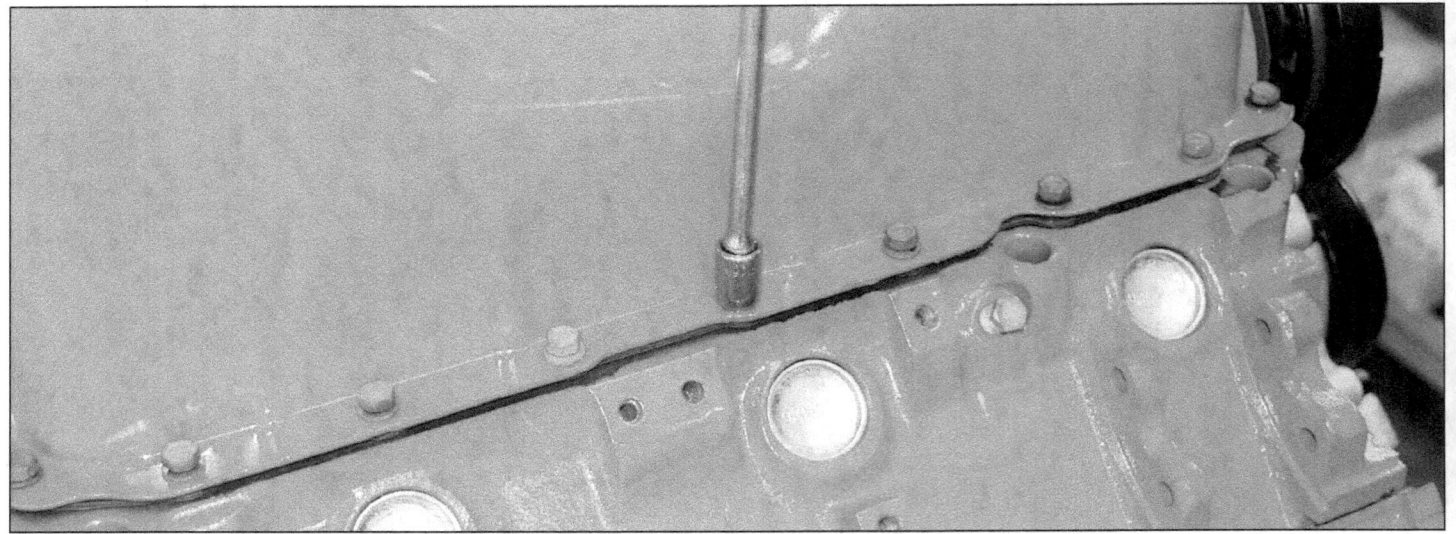

Reinstall and tighten the oil-pan bolts.

ASSEMBLY

Oil Filter Fitting

The oil-filter hardware must be remounted back on the block. Your gasket kit should contain a gasket that will fit under the filter mounting plate.

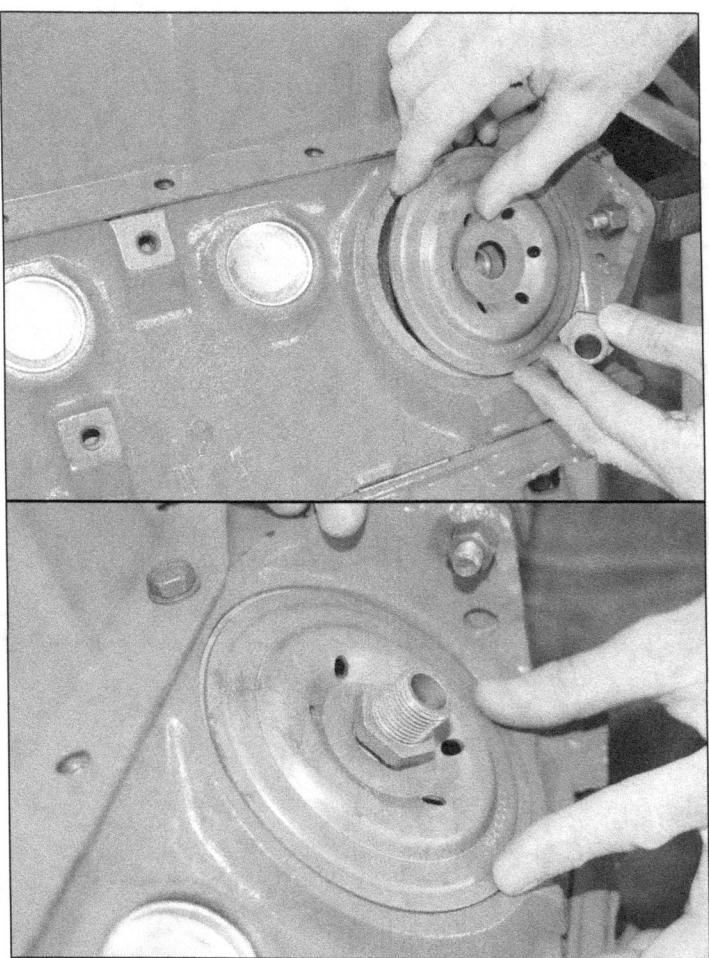

Place the plate over the gasket, making sure of a good seal, and then screw in the double-threaded fitting. Coat the threads that screw into the block with Loctite and then use a deep-well socket to torque the fitting to 30 ft-lbs.

Oil-Pump Shaft

Lubricate the oil-pump shaft with cam lube and lower it into the block. The hex shape on the bottom end of the shaft must fit into the hex receiver on the top of the oil pump, so check the orientation before installing the shaft.

When the shaft is properly installed, the tab will be in the oil pump and the gear will be meshed with the cam gear. The tab on the bottom of the distributor shaft will seat in the top of the gear on the oil-pump shaft. The orientation of the slot in the oil-shaft gear will determine the rotational position of the distributor shaft and thus the location of the rotor. If you are still at TDC on the number-1 cylinder, you can drop the distributor in and put the rotor on, and this will show you where number-1 is on the cap. If you like the position, proceed, and if you don't, take the oil shaft back out and rotate it to get the positioning that you desire.

HOW TO REBUILD THE SMALL-BLOCK MOPAR

CHAPTER 5

Valvecovers

Lay the valvecover gasket on the cylinder head, lining up the holes for the valvecover bolts.

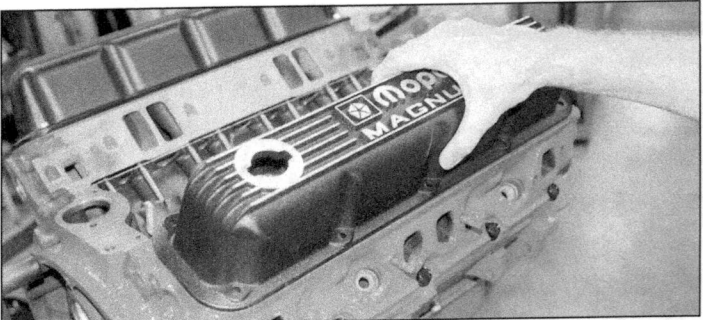

Mount the valvecover, install the bolts, and tighten the bolts just past snug. Do not over tighten the bolts, as it will deform the valve cover gasket and make an oil leak much more likely. Tighten the bolts as you did with the cylinder-head bolts, starting in the center and working outward equally in each direction.

Exhaust Manifolds

Depending on your vehicle, you may or may not elect to mount your exhaust manifolds before you drop your engine. Since I'm working on a truck with plenty of room in the engine well, and since I have a questionable back and hate to work leaning over, I elected to go ahead and put them on. First, mount the gasket onto the block, lining it up carefully with the exhaust ports.

Put the manifold in place, making sure that the gasket does not move and restrict a port.

Torquing Fasteners

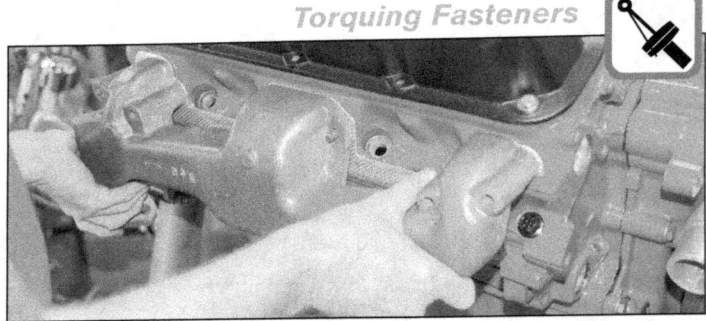

Torque the bolts to 20 ft-lbs and mount the other manifold in the same manner.

Your engine is now ready to come off of the stand and go back into the vehicle. The rest of the bolt-ons, and a few hints on engine installation, start-up, and break-in, will be covered in the next chapter.

ASSEMBLY

Plastigage

If you are not able or willing to shell out the money for a set of calipers and gauges, you can get some pretty accurate measurements with Plastigage. Plastigage is a plastic material that comes in the form of thin rods. You place it on the surface of a part, in this case the crankshaft, and then the mating part is assembled and torqued to specification. When this is complete, the parts are disassembled, revealing that the thin rod of Plastigage has been compressed. The width of the flattened Plastigage is then compared to the band widths that are printed on the packaging to determine the measurement. The advantage of Plastigage is that it is cheap. The disadvantage is that you have to assemble and disassemble parts and that the measurement will only be accurate for the spot on which the Plastigage was placed, in this case this one spot on the crankshaft. There could be a problem on the opposite side of the crankshaft that goes undetected.

Remove the bearing cap and wipe the oil from the bearing insert and crankshaft journal. Tear off a piece of Plastigage as long as the full bearing width. Lay the piece of Plastigage across the full width of the lower bearing shell about 1/4 inch off center.

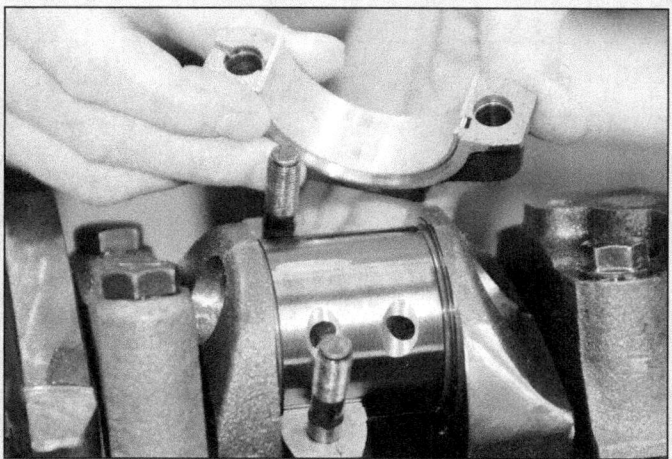

Install and tighten the bearing cap to the proper torque specifications. Do not rotate the crankshaft while making this check. Remove the bearing cap. The flattened Plastigage will adhere to either the bearing shell or the crankshaft.

Compare the width of the flattened Plastigage at the WIDEST point with the graduations. The number within the graduations, which matches the flattened Plastigage width, indicates the total bearing clearance in thousandths of an inch. If the width of the flattened Plastigage does not exactly match one of the envelope graduations, interpolation can be used to determine the fraction of a thousandth in the same manner as when using micrometers.

HOW TO REBUILD THE SMALL-BLOCK MOPAR

CHAPTER 6

START-UP AND BREAK-IN

Depending on hood clearance and personal preference, you can install your engine with the intake manifold off or on. I elected to keep it off, as my fuel-injection manifold is tall and is easier to preassemble and then put on once the engine is in the vehicle.

For those with late-model fuel-injection engines, make sure that you replace the gasket under the plate on the bottom side of the manifold. This area is notorious for leaking oil into the intake manifold, so you might want to reinforce your gasket with silicone.

I'm not going to spend a lot of time talking about putting your engine back in. You took it out, so you should be able to get it back in. Installation of your engine is the reverse of removal, and if you took the time to mark all of your connections and noted the order in which you took things off, your installation should go smoothly. The highly motivated can yank an engine one weekend and throw it back in the next. For the rest it may be weeks or months before the engine goes back in. If you did not document your removal process and don't have a photographic memory, you have my condolences.

START-UP AND BREAK-IN

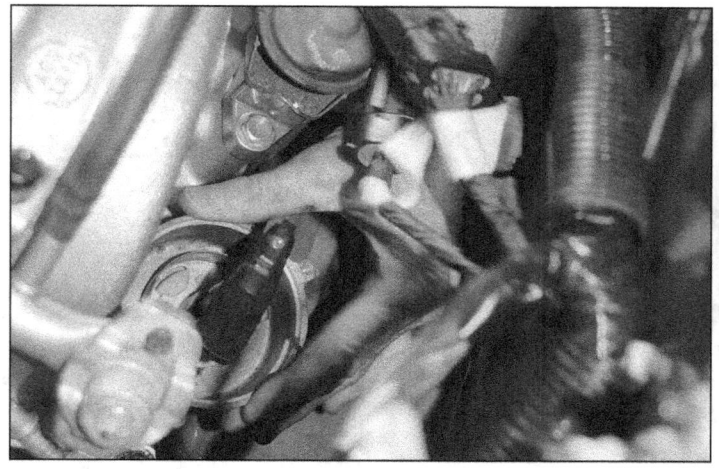

Before you install your engine, check your distributor shaft's rotational position with the rotor attached. With the number-1 cylinder at TDC, the rotor will point to the number-1 plug wire.

It may take some wiggling to get the engine to mate up with the bell housing. Do not get your fingers between the two, as a nasty pinch can be the result.

Before beginning I'll throw a few pieces of advice your way. First, don't get impatient. If this engine is the only thing keeping you from hopping in your ride and getting on down the road, the desire and impatience are understandable. But don't stumble in the stretch. Take a methodical approach, do one thing, do it well, and then move on. My second piece of advice is to have everything there and ready to complete the job. Endless trips to the store will grow tiring. My third piece of advice is to replace anything that remotely looks like it will give you trouble. When you calculate the cost of hoses, belts, power-steering lines, sending units, plug wires, and ignition parts, it can add up. But if you can afford it, then do it. If you replace these support items it will probably save a little trouble down the road. In our case it will mean you can take the old support pieces that still have a little life in them and assemble a fine box of backups just in case. My last piece of advice is to be very careful as you put the engine in. An engine hanging on a hoist is dangerous. If it drops it will maim or kill whatever is under it. Only use grade 8 bolts when attaching the hoist chain to the engine. As you position the engine, make sure to keep your fingers away from between the engine and the engine mounts and the block and bell housing, as you can get smashed before you know it.

Dropping an engine in a vehicle is a job that is more than twice as easy with double the help. One reasonably competent friend can make the job go much faster and, depending on the quality of your friends, much more smoothly. With one raising and lowering the engine and the other trying to wrestle it into place the job will be easier than trying to accomplish both of these tasks on your own. To attach the engine to the transmission, the engine will have to be quite accurately aligned. The pins that locate the bell housing to the block make it necessary to have the block level and square to be aligned. Once the engine is in place, install the block-to-bell-housing bolts and the engine-mount bolts. If your vehicle is equipped with an automatic, have someone turn the engine while you line up holes in the flexplate with the holes in the torque converter. Use some Loctite on the bolts before you put them in. If your vehicle is equipped with a manual transmission, it will be necessary to align the clutch. As soon as the engine is bolted to the engine mounts you can begin to install and connect all of its support systems. This is where your order list will come in handy. Make sure that whatever you are putting on will not keep you from putting something else on.

Once the bell-housing bolts and the engine-mount bolts are in you can remove the lift.

HOW TO REBUILD THE SMALL-BLOCK MOPAR

CHAPTER 6

When installing the intake manifold gaskets, back them up with some silicone gasket material around the cooling ports.

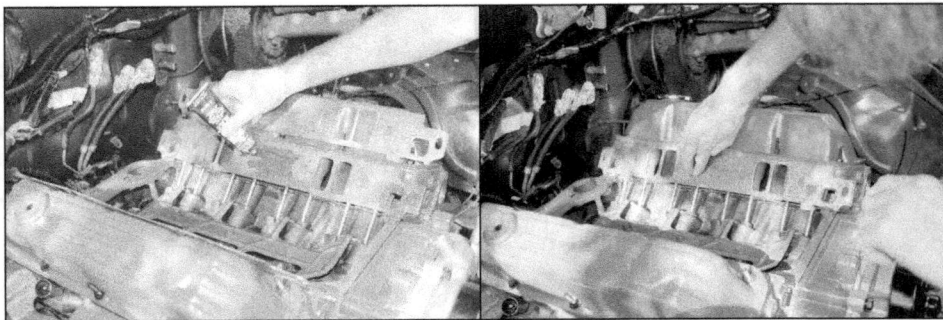

It's also advisable to spread a bit of silicone on the flat between the intake ports in the head. This will help hold the gaskets in place while you lower the intake manifold into position.

Once you drop the manifold, tighten the bolts and hook up whatever fuel-supply system that your vehicle has.

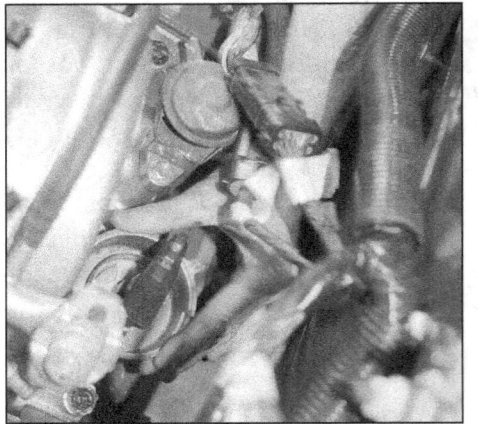

Our gasket kit came with cork gaskets to run under the front and rear of the manifold, so I elected to scrap them and build my own with a thick bead of silicone. If you elect to do the same, make sure that you run a thick enough bead to completely seal the manifold.

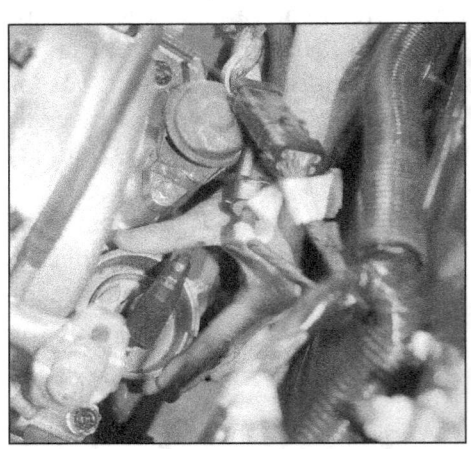

If you haven't done so, install your distributor and check the rotor's position with the number-1 cylinder at TDC.

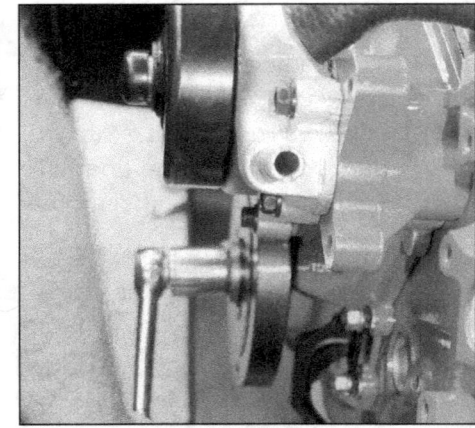

If you need to rotate the engine to hook up the flexplate or to put the engine in TDC, you can turn it with a socket on the balancer bolt.

Adding Fluids

I like to get the cooling system hooked up as early in the process as possible. This way you can go ahead and put coolant and oil in the engine. If you made a mistake big enough to cause a non-pressurized leak, it's better that all of the other systems are not hooked up. Granted, it's a small consolation if the engine has to come back out, but it is some. When you put the oil filter on, fill it with oil a little less than halfway. The filter will mount on an angle, so don't overfill it. If you do you will get a face full of oil when you screw the filter onto the engine. Once everything is hooked up and all of the fluids are in the engine, it's time for the last step—install the battery and hook it up.

HOW TO REBUILD THE SMALL-BLOCK MOPAR

START-UP AND BREAK-IN

If you leave your engine during assembly, seal everything up. Put the air cleaner on and stuff rags or plugs in any open orifices that might look like an appealing home for a colony of bugs.

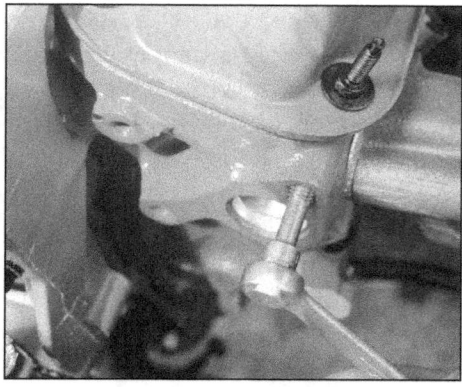

If you have difficulty bolting on an accessory, run a thread-chasing tool down it. It is a good idea to freshen up all of the threads while the engine is still on the stand.

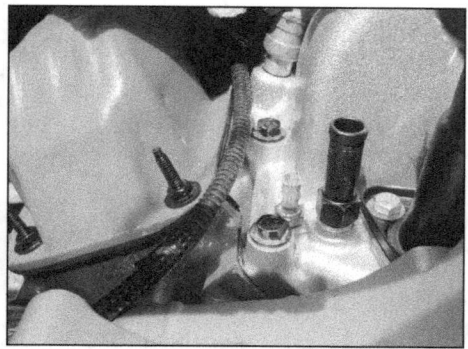

Sending units are fragile and often will not survive the disassembly. If you want your gauges and engine-information systems to operate properly you had better count on replacing them.

Fuel System

For cars equipped with throttle-body injection and those with fuel injection, the fuel system is supplied via an electric fuel pump that will pressurize the system and make it ready to crank pretty much immediately. For engines equipped with a carburetor and a mechanical fuel pump, a little priming is prudent for the first crank. When you turn a carbureted engine over after a rebuild, it will take the pump a while to pump the fuel up to the carburetor. When fuel is poured into the carb it allows the engine to fire sooner and will give the pump time to catch up while the oil pump is lubricating the engine.

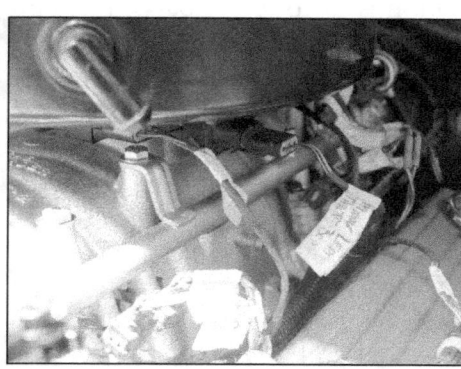

If you marked and tagged your connections, it will pay off during installation. If you lost a tag or did not mark one, hook up everything that you did mark to eliminate as many possibilities as you can. Then try to trace down any strays.

First Crank

Your initial cranking method will differ depending on the type of lifter in your engine. Regardless, it's best to have two people for the first cranking. Put someone on the ignition switch with the added responsibility of watching the oil-pressure gauge while

With the engine fully hooked up, crank it as described in the text. When breaking in a new engine, try to avoid short trips. Let it get to temperature and try to run it at least 15 or 20 minutes. Refrain from test-drives around the block and cranking it for your friends.

you watch the engine. If your parts are good and your assembly was done correctly, the engine should fire immediately. Watch it closely. Take a glance under it to make sure that nothing is leaking. If you see something leaking, turn the engine off immediately and start looking for the leak.

Flat-Tappet Lifter Engines

If you have an older engine with flat-tappet lifters, the first cranking should be executed as follows. First, disconnect the coil wire so that it will be impossible for the engine to start. Then turn the key to engage

HOW TO REBUILD THE SMALL-BLOCK MOPAR

the starter and turn the engine over. This is done to allow the oil system to begin operating. It is essential for a flat-tappet lifter system to get plenty of oil to keep from wiping a lobe off of the camshaft when starting for the first time. Don't grind on the starter for longer than about five seconds. Stop, wait about 10 seconds, and re-engage the starter. Continue this until you have oil pressure. If your car does not have an oil-pressure gauge, you have two options. The first is doing what was just described five or six times and hope you have oil pressure. The better option is to go to the parts store and buy a mechanical oil-pressure gauge. Even if you do not permanently mount it, you can hook it up for the start-up, and then, when you know your engine has started correctly, you can reconnect the factory sensor.

Once the engine has been spun a few times and you are sure that you have oil pressure, put the coil wire back on and fire it up. When the engine cranks, take it from 1,500 to 1,700 rpm and hold it there until the engine comes to operating temperature. Then shut it off, pack your desire to go for a ride away, and let it sit overnight to cool completely. When you do this you are actually doing a type of heat-treating that is aimed at hardening the camshaft and the lifters. The next day, crank it again and bring the car up to temperature. If everything checks out, you can begin driving your vehicle. The main thing in doing so is to break the engine in with longer trips. Don't crank the car and go around the block just to let your friends hear it.

I am not an oil expert, but I will pass along some information that has been discussed in some technical automotive circuits. According to some literature that I have come across, the rate of flat-tappet lifter failure has increased. While there is more than one theory as to why this is happening, one has to do with lubrication and is worth mentioning. The pushrod-type OEM engines being produced today by all manufacturers make use of roller lifters, making the flat-tappet lifter, as far as they are concerned, a thing of the past. This ultimately had an effect on the contents of today's engine oils. Lubricating the lifter/cam lobe contact area was always one of the most difficult things that engine oil had to accomplish. When the roller lifter was introduced it dramatically lowered the friction between the lifter and the cam thus making the oil's task simpler. Well, as luck would have it, some of the nastier additives in oil were to ensure good lifter lubrication, so they were slowly eliminated from the oil. This is why many feel that there are more lifter failures. By presenting this to you I am neither confirming nor eliminating this as a concern. But it concerns David, and I've found that when something concerns David mechanically it's best to listen. His proactive move for this has been to switch to Shell Oil's blend for diesel engines, which still has many of the additives in it. Consult your local speed shop and get their opinions and advice.

Roller-Lifter Engines

With roller-lifter engines, the concern around the lifter-cam surface pretty much disappears. Remove the coil wire and turn the engine over a few times to build some oil pressure. Again, don't continually grind on the starter, as this will harm it. Turn it over a few seconds and then let the starter cool for a few seconds. Once you have built a bit of oil pressure, replace the coil wire and attempt to crank the engine. Once it fires, run it up to 1,500 to 1,700 rpm. Look for leaks and listen for any sound that is out of the ordinary. Once you have determined that everything is running fine, take her for a spin. Don't romp on it for the first few trips, and change your oil after 500 miles.

Ignition Timing

Once the engine has cranked the timing should be dialed in accurately. Use a timing gun on the timing marks on the balancer and dial the timing in with the distributor. When the distributor is in the position that provides the correct timing, tighten the distributor clamp. It's a good idea to take a Sharpie marker and mark the distributor's position on the block. If the distributor's bracket bolt ever loosens and the distributor moves, you will be able to get it back in time on the side of the road.

Problems

If the engine fails to crank, the most likely cause will be either a wire left unconnected or improperly connected, or a timing issue. Double check all of your connections and make sure they are sound. Also recheck and make sure that the distributor is installed correctly with the rotor pointed at the number-1 plug-wire post with the number-1 cylinder at top dead center (TDC). Then recheck that each of your ignition wires runs to the proper spark plug. You may have a fuel-delivery issue if the car fires and then cuts out. Check and make sure you have fuel pressure, and try again.

APPENDIX A

Source Guide

Automotive Racing Products
(ARP)
1863 Eastman Ave.
Ventura, CA 93003
(805) 339-2200
www.arp-bolts.com

ACCEL Performance Products
Mr. Gasket Performance Group
10601 Memphis Ave. #12
Cleveland, OH 44144
(216) 688-8300
www.accel-ignition.com

Air Flow Research (AFR)
10490 Ilex Ave.
Pacoima, CA 91331-3137
(818) 890-0616
www.airflowresearch.com

Barry Grant Fuel Systems
1450 McDonald Rd.
Dahlonega, GA 30533
(706) 864-8544
www.barrygrant.com

Be Cool, Inc.
310 Woodside Ave.
Essexville, MI 48732
(800)691-2667
www.becool.com

Birmingham Piston Warehouse
112 39th Street North
Birmingham, AL 35222
(800) 221-3368
www.internalengineparts.com

Cloyes Gear and Products, Inc.
6101 Phoenix Avenue #2
Ft. Smith, AR 72903
(479) 484-5555
www.cloyes.com

Coast High Performance
2555 W. 237th St.
Torrance, CA 90505
(310) 784-1010
www.coasthigh.com

Comp Cams
3406 Democrat Rd.
Memphis, TN 38118
(901) 795-2400
www.compcams.com

Crane Cams
530 Fentress Ave
Daytona Beach, FL 32114
(386) 252-1151
www.cranecams.com

Edelbrock Corporation
2700 California St.
Torrance, CA 90503
(310) 781-2222
www.edelbrock.com

Engine Parts Center Atlanta
260 Maxham Road
Austell, GA 30168
(800) 690-4334

Engine Parts Warehouse
1809 Vanderhorn Drive
Memphis, TN 38134
(800) 238-2508

Federal-Mogul
26555 Northwestern Highway
Southfield, MI 48033
(248) 354-7700
www.federal-mogul.com

Flowmaster Mufflers
100 Stony Point Rd., #125
Santa Rosa, CA 95401
(800) 544-4761
www.flowmastermufflers.com

APPENDIX A

Holley Performance Products
1801 Russellville Rd.
Bowling Green, KY 42102-7360
(270) 782-2900
www.holley.com

Hooker/FlowTech
704 Highway 25 South
Aberdeen, MS 39730
(270) 781-9741
www.holley.com

HyLift Johnson
1185 East Keating Avenue
Muskegon, MI 49442
www.toplineauto.com

Ignitioneering
2216 E. Mineral King
Visalia, CA 93292
(559) 739-1515
www.ignitioneering.com

JBA
7149 Mission Gorge Rd., Suite D
San Diego, CA 92120
(800) 830-3377
www.jbaheaders.com

JC Whitney
761 Progress Parkway
LaSalle, IL 61301
(800) 603-4383
www.jcwhitney.com

Jeg's High Performance
101 Jeg's Place
Delaware, OH 43015
(800) 345-4545
www.jegs.com

K&N Performance
P.O. Box 1329
Riverside, CA 92502
(888) 949-1832
www.knfilters.com

Lunati Cams
11126 Willow Ridge Drive
Olive Branch, MS 38654
(662) 892-1500
www.holley.com

Mallory Ignition
Mr. Gasket Performance Group
10601 Memphis Ave.
Cleveland, OH 44144
(216) 688-8300
www.mrgasket.com

Miller Special Tools
(800) 801-5420
www.miller.spx.com

MSD Ignition
1490 Henry Brennan Dr.
El Paso, TX 79936
(915) 857-5200
www.msdignition.com

Perfect Circle, Cleavite 77,
and Mahle
www.engineparts.com

Performance Distributors
2899 Barris Dr.
Memphis, TN 38132
(901) 396-5782
www.performancedistributors.com

Qualcast
1854 Air Lane Drive
Unit 10
Nashville, TN 37210
(888) 432-4552
www.qualcast.net

Summit Racing
P.O. Box 909
Akron, OH 44398-6177
(800) 230-3030
www.summitracing.com

Victor Reinz
Dana Automotive
www.victorreinz.com

APPENDIX B

TOLERANCES FOR THE MAGNUM 5.2L

General
Compression pressure 100 psi minimum
Maximum variation between cylinders 25 percent
Oil pressure At idle 6 psi
              At 3,000 rpm 30 to 80 psi

Engine block
Bore diameter 3.910 to 3.912 in
Taper limit 0.010 in
Out-of-round wear limit 0.005 in

Cylinder Heads and Valvetrain
Warpage 0.009 in per 12 in
Maximum valve margin 3/64 in
Valvestem-to-guide clearance
     Intake valve 0.001 to 0.003 in
     Exhaust valve 0.002 to 0.004 in

Valvespring free length
Intake 2.00 in   Exhaust 1.81 in

Valvespring installed height
Intake 1-5/8 to 1-11/16 in
Exhaust 1-29/64 to 1-33/64 in

Crankshaft and connecting rods
Main journal diameter 2.4995 to 2.5005 in
Main journal taper limit 0.001 in
Main journal out-of-round limit 0.001 in
Main-bearing oil clearance
     1 (standard) 0.0005 to 0.0015 in
     1 (limit) 0.0015 in
     2, 3, and 4 (standard) 0.0005 to 0.0020 in
     2, 3, and 4 (limit) 0.0025 in

Connecting rod journal
     Diameter 2.124 to 2.125 in
     Taper limit 0.001 in
     Out-of-round limit 0.001 in

Connecting-rod bearing oil clearance
Standard 0.0005 to 0.0022 in
Limit 0.0022 in
Connecting rod endplay 0.006 to 0.014 in

Crankshaft endplay
Standard 0.002 to 0.007 in
Limit 0.0010 in

Pistons and Rings
Piston-to-bore clearance (measured at top of skirt)
     .0005 to .0015 in
Compression ring gap (84-89 hp engine) .001 to .002 in
Oil ring gap .015 to .055 in
Compression ring side clearance .0015 to .0030 in
Oil ring side clearance .002 to .005 in

Torque Specifications
Connecting-rod cap nuts 45 ft-lbs
Man-bearing cap bolts 85 ft-lbs

APPENDIX C

WORKBENCH WORK-A-LONG SHEET

DISASSEMBLY

Project Statistics
Your Name _____ Today's Date_____
Vehicle Engine Removed From _____ Engine Year _____
CI _____ Block Casting _____ ❏ 2 barrel ❏ 4 barrel ❏ Fuel Injection

Accessories Attached to Used Engine
❏ A/C Pump ❏ AIR Pump ❏ AIR Distributor Lines and Hoses ❏ Water Pump ❏ Flywheel
❏ Clutch ❏ Flexplate ❏ Transmission ❏ Starter ❏ Fuel Pump ❏ Exhaust Manifolds
❏ All Pulleys; Except _____ ❏ Alternator ❏ Distributor ❏ Coil ❏ Carburetor
❏ Motor Mounts ❏ Motor Mount Attaching Brackets ❏ Spark Plug Heat Shields
❏ EGR Valve ❏ Dipstick Tube ❏ All Bolts; except _____ ❏ _____ ❏ _____

Operational Notes
Oil consumption _____ Compression check pressure variation _____ psi
Leak-down percent _____ Other observations _____

Disassembly Notations
Crank uses centerbolt ❏ Yes ❏ No
Heat riser restricted on ❏ Left ❏ Right ❏ Both
Head gaskets ❏ Steel shim ❏ Composition
Worn/damaged lifters ❏ No ❏ Yes; where _____
Vibration damper pulley screws ❏ 3/8-NC ❏ 3/8-NF
Location of timing-pointer attaching points: _____
Oil filter adapter type: ❏ Spin-on ❏ Long cartridge (late) ❏ Short cartridge (early)
Type of rear main seal: ❏ Rubber—two piece ❏ Rubber—one piece (late) ❏ Rope (early)

INSPECTION

Initial Parts Inspection Observations
Block OK ❏ Yes ❏ No; describe problem _____
Heads OK ❏ Yes ❏ No; describe problem _____
Crank OK ❏ Yes ❏ No; describe problem _____

WORKBENCH WORK-A-LONG SHEET®

Bearings OK	❏ Yes	❏ No; describe problem _____
Pistons OK	❏ Yes	❏ No; describe problem _____
Cam/lifters OK	❏ Yes	❏ No; describe problem _____
Damper OK	❏ Yes	❏ No; describe problem _____
Intake manifold OK	❏ Yes	❏ No; describe problem _____
Exhaust manifold OK	❏ Yes	❏ No; describe problem _____
Oil pump OK	❏ Yes	❏ No; describe problem _____

Oil pump/rear main cap mating surfaces damage/abnormalities ❏ No ❏ Yes
Identifying mark you placed on all parts: _____

AT THE MACHINE SHOP

Parts Delivered to the Machine Shop
- ❏ Block
- ❏ Main Caps
- ❏ Crankshaft
- ❏ Oil Pump
- ❏ Oil Pump Pickup
- ❏ Connecting Rods
- ❏ Pistons
- ❏ Piston Rings
- ❏ Camshaft
- ❏ Lifters
- ❏ Vibration Damper
- ❏ Main Bearings
- ❏ Rod Bearings
- ❏ Cam Bearings
- ❏ Rod Bolts
- ❏ Gasket Set
- ❏ Push Rods
- ❏ Rockerarms
- ❏ Head Bolts
- ❏ Main Bolts/Studs
- ❏ Miscellaneous Nuts/Bolts/Brackets for Cleaning
- ❏ Water Pump
- ❏ Timing Cover
- ❏ Oil Pan
- ❏ Flywheel/Flexplate
- ❏ Clutch
- ❏ Exhaust Manifolds
- ❏ Motor Mounts
- ❏ Motor Mount Attaching Brackets
- ❏ Assembled Heads
- ❏ Disassembled Heads with: ❏ Valves ❏ Springs ❏ Retainers ❏ Keepers
- ❏ Rocker Balls and Nuts ❏ Intake Manifold ❏ With Heat Riser Shield ❏ Installed ❏ Not Installed
- ❏ _____ ❏ _____ ❏ _____ ❏ _____ ❏ _____
- ❏ _____ ❏ _____ ❏ _____ ❏ _____ ❏ _____

Special Instructions for Machine Shop
- ❏ Bore block ❏ Use torque plates ❏ Desired piston-to-wall clearance: 0._____-inch ❏ Grind crank
- ❏ Rod bearing clearance: 0._____-inch ❏ Main bearing clearance: 0._____-inch ❏ Deck to clean
- ❏ Surface heads ❏ Install cam bearings ❏ _____ ❏ _____

Is pilot bushing to be installed in crankshaft (required for manual transmission)? ❏ Yes ❏ No
Are intake manifold heat shield holes to be tapped for 8-32 screws? ❏ Yes ❏ No

After You Pick Up Your Parts
- ❏ Yes ❏ No Threaded holes reconditioned/chased
- ❏ Yes ❏ No Head/block dowels properly installed
- ❏ Yes ❏ No Galleries tapped for screw-in plugs
- ❏ Yes ❏ No Add 0.030-inch hole in thrust face
- ❏ Yes ❏ No Retaining straps on core plugs
- ❏ Yes ❏ No Manifold heat-shield holes tapped for 8-32 screws
- ❏ Yes ❏ No Drilled holes and edges chamfered
- ❏ Yes ❏ No Are cam bearings properly installed
- ❏ Yes ❏ No Add 0.030-inch hole in gallery plug
- ❏ Yes ❏ No Core plugs properly installed
- ❏ Yes ❏ No Crank keys properly installed

PRE-ASSEMBLY FITTING

Measured and Recorded During Pre-Assembly Fitting
- ❏ Yes ❏ No Do all valveguides have proper clearance? If no, which are correct
- ❏ Yes ❏ No Do all valveseats meet dimensional specs? If no, which are faulty
- ❏ Yes ❏ No Do all valveseats hold solvent? If no, which leak
- ❏ Yes ❏ No Have all valveguides been machined concentric for press-on seals?

Retainer to Valveguide clearance 0._____-inch; adequate on all valves? ❏ Yes ❏ No
If no, which valves have insufficient clearance? _____
Recommended valvespring seat pressure _____ psi at _____ -inches installed height.

APPENDIX C

Measured valvespring installed height:
1 _____ 3 _____ 5 _____ 7 _____
2 _____ 4 _____ 6 _____ 8 _____
Spring shims used to obtain correct installed height:
1 _____ 3 _____ 5 _____ 7 _____
2 _____ 4 _____ 6 _____ 8 _____
Measured valvespring solid height _____ -inches
Calculated compressed spring clearance:
1 _____ 3 _____ 5 _____ 7 _____
2 _____ 4 _____ 6 _____ 8 _____

Connecting rod bore OK?   ❏ Yes ❏ No; Which rods are defective
_____
Crank straightness OK?   ❏ Yes ❏ No   Runout on center main of 0. _____ -inch
Main bearing clearance OK?   ❏ Yes ❏ No   Measured clearance 0. _____ -inch
Crank thrust OK?   ❏ Yes ❏ No   Measured clearance 0. _____ -inch
Main bearing clearance OK?   ❏ Yes ❏ No   Measured clearance 0. _____ -inch
Camshaft bearing fit OK?   ❏ Yes ❏ No; Describe problem _____
Block required clearance grinding for upper sprocket?   ❏ Yes ❏ No
Pin end clearance OK?   ❏ Yes ❏ No   Measured clearance 0. _____ -inch
Piston–to-wall clearance OK?   ❏ Yes ❏ No   Measured clearance 0. _____ -inch
                                Pistons with incorrect clearance _____

Measured ring end gap:
1 Top _____ 2nd _____   3 Top _____ 2nd _____   5 Top _____ 2nd _____   7 Top _____ 2nd _____
2 Top _____ 2nd _____   4 Top _____ 2nd _____   6 Top _____ 2nd _____   8 Top _____ 2nd _____

Rod bearing clearance OK?   ❏ Yes ❏ No   Measured clearance 0. _____ -inch
Rod side clearance OK?   ❏ Yes ❏ No   Measured clearance 0. _____ -inch
Piston-to-head clearance OK?   ❏ Yes ❏ No   Measured clearance 0. _____ -inch
                                Cylinders with incorrect clearance _____
Offset bushings/key used: ❏ + – 2   ❏ + – 4   ❏ + – 6   ❏ + – 8   ❏ + – 10   ❏ + – 12
Rotating assembly clearance OK?   ❏ Yes ❏ No;   Cause of interference
Crank index OK?   ❏ Yes ❏ No   Maximum _____ out of index on journal no.
Cylinder-to-cylinder deck height accurate?   ❏ Yes ❏ No   Maximum 0. _____ -inch variation
Rocker geometry OK?   ❏ Yes ❏ No; Describe problem _____
Rocker-to-stud clearance OK?   ❏ Yes ❏ No   Maximum 0. _____ -inch (Intake); 0. _____ -inch (Exhaust)
Piston-to-valve clearance OK?   ❏ Yes ❏ No   Maximum 0. _____ -inch (Intake); 0. _____ -inch (Exhaust)
Oil pump drive clearance OK?   ❏ Yes ❏ No   Measured clearance 0. _____ -inch
Intake manifold end-rail clearance OK? ❏ Yes ❏ No   Measured clearance 0. _____ -inch
Manifold surface parallel with head?   ❏ Yes ❏ No; Describe problem _____
Pulleys/accessories aligned?   ❏ Yes ❏ No; Describe problem _____

Additional Notes: _____
_____
_____
_____
_____

MORE GREAT TITLES AVAILABLE FROM CARTECH®

CHEVROLET

How To Rebuild the Small-Block Chevrolet* *(SA26)*
Chevrolet Small-Block Parts Interchange Manual *(SA55)*
How To Build Max Perf Chevy Small-Blocks on a Budget *(SA57)*
How To Build High-Perf Chevy LS1/LS6 Engines *(SA86)*
How To Build Big-Inch Chevy Small-Blocks *(SA87)*
How to Build High-Performance Chevy Small-Block Cams/Valvetrains *SA105*
Rebuilding the Small-Block Chevy: Step-by-Step Videobook *(SA116)*
High-Performance Chevy Small-Block Cylinder Heads *(SA125P)*
High Performance C5 Corvette Builder's Guide *(SA127)*
How to Rebuild the Big-Block Chevrolet* *(SA142P)*
How to Build Max-Performance Chevy Big Block on a Budget *(SA198)*
How to Restore Your Camaro 1967–1969 *(SA178)*
How to Build Killer Big-Block Chevy Engines *(SA190)*
How to Build Max-Performance Chevy LT1/LT4 Engines *(SA206)*
Small-Block Chevy Performance: 1955-1996 *(SA110P)*
How to Build Small-Block Chevy Circle-Track Racing Engines *(SA121P)*
High-Performance C5 Corvette Builder's Guide *(SA127P)*
Chevrolet Big Block Parts Interchange Manual *(SA31P)*
Chevy TPI Fuel Injection Swapper's Guide *(SA53P)*

FORD

High-Performance Ford Engine Parts Interchange *(SA56)*
How To Build Max Performance Ford V-8s on a Budget *(SA69)*
How To Build Max Perf 4.6 Liter Ford Engines *(SA82)*
How To Build Big-Inch Ford Small-Blocks *(SA85)*
How to Rebuild the Small-Block Ford* *(SA102)*
How to Rebuild Big-Block Ford Engines* *(SA162)*
Full-Size Fords 1955–1970 *(SA176)*
How to Build Max-Performance Ford FE Engines *(SA183)*
How to Restore Your Mustang 1964 1/2–1973 *(SA165)*
How to Build Ford RestoMod Street Machines *(SA101P)*
Building 4.6/5.4L Ford Horsepower on the Dyno *(SA115P)*
How to Rebuild 4.6/5.4-Liter Ford Engines *(SA155P)*
Building High-Performance Fox-Body Mustangs on a Budget *(SA75P)*
How to Build Supercharged & Turbocharged Small-Block Fords *(SA95P)*

GENERAL MOTORS

GM Automatic Overdrive Transmission Builder's and Swapper's Guide *(SA140)*
How to Rebuild GM LS-Series Engines* *(SA147)*
How to Swap GM LS-Series Engines Into Almost Anything *(SA156)*
How to Supercharge & Turbocharge GM LS-Series Engines *(SA180)*
How to Build Big-Inch GM LS-Series Engines *(SA203)*
How to Rebuild & Modify GM Turbo 400 Transmissions *(SA186)*
How to Build GM Pro-Touring Street Machines *(SA81P)*

MOPAR

How to Rebuild the Big-Block Mopar *(SA197)*
How to Rebuild the Small-Block Mopar* *(SA143P)*
How to Build Max-Performance Hemi Engines *(SA164)*
How To Build Max-Performance Mopar Big Blocks *(SA171)*
Mopar B-Body Performance Upgrades 1962-1979 *(SA191)*
How to Build Big-Inch Mopar Small-Blocks *(SA104P)*
High-Performance New Hemi Builder's Guide 2003-Present *(SA132P)*

OLDSMOBILE/ PONTIAC/ BUICK

How to Build Max-Performance Oldsmobile V-8s *(SA172)*
How To Build Max-Perf Pontiac V8s *SA78)*
How to Rebuild Pontiac V-8s* *(SA200)*
How to Build Max-Performance Buick Engines *(SA146P)*

SPORT COMPACTS

Honda Engine Swaps *(SA93)*
Building Honda K-Series Engine Performance *(SA134)*
High-Performance Subaru Builder's Guide *(SA141)*
How to Build Max-Performance Mitsubishi 4G63t Engines *(SA148)*
How to Rebuild Honda B-Series Engines* *(SA154)*
The New Mini Performance Handbook *(SA182P)*
High Performance Dodge Neon Builder's Handbook *(SA100P)*
High-Performance Honda Builder's Handbook Volume 1 *(SA49P)*

Workbench® Series books featuring step-by-step instruction with hundreds of color photos for stock rebuilds and automotive repair.

ENGINE

Engine Blueprinting *(SA21)*
Automotive Diagnostic Systems: Understanding OBD-I & OBD II *(SA174)*

INDUCTION & IGNITION

Super Tuning & Modifying Holley Carburetors *(SA08)*
Street Supercharging, A Complete Guide to *(SA17)*
How To Build High-Performance Ignition Systems *(SA79)*
How to Build and Modify Rochester Quadrajet Carburetors *(SA113)*
Turbo: Real World High-Performance Turbocharger Systems *(SA123)*
How to Rebuild & Modify Carter/Edelbrock Carbs *(SA130)*
Engine Management: Advanced Tuning *(SA135)*
Designing & Tuning High-Performance Fuel Injection Systems *(SA161)*
Demon Carburetion *(SA68P)*

DRIVING

How to Drift: The Art of Oversteer *(SA118)*
How to Drag Race *(SA136)*
How to Autocross *(SA158P)*
How to Hook and Launch *(SA195)*

HIGH-PERFORMANCE & RESTORATION HOW-TO

How To Install and Tune Nitrous Oxide Systems *(SA194)*
Custom Painting *(SA10)*
David Vizard's How to Build Horsepower *(SA24)*
How to Rebuild & Modify High-Performance Manual Transmissions* *(SA103)*
High-Performance Jeep Cherokee XJ Builder's Guide 1984–2001 *(SA109)*
How to Paint Your Car on a Budget *(SA117)*
High Performance Brake Systems *(SA126P)*
High Performance Diesel Builder's Guide *(SA129)*
4x4 Suspension Handbook *(SA137)*
How to Rebuild Any Automotive Engine* *(SA151)*
Automotive Welding: A Practical Guide* *(SA159)*
Automotive Wiring and Electrical Systems* *(SA160)*
Design & Install In Car Entertainment Systems *(SA163)*
Automotive Bodywork & Rust Repair* *(SA166)*
High-Performance Differentials, Axles, & Drivelines *(SA170)*
How to Make Your Muscle Car Handle *(SA175)*
Rebuilding Any Automotive Engine: Step-by-Step Videobook *(SA179)*
Builder's Guide to Hot Rod Chassis & Suspension *(SA185)*
How To Rebuild & Modify GM Turbo 400 Transmissions* *(SA186)*
How to Build Altered Wheelbase Cars *(SA189)*
How to Build Period Correct Hot Rods *(SA192)*
Automotive Sheet Metal Forming & Fabrication *(SA196)*
Performance Automotive Engine Math *(SA204)*
How to Design, Build & Equip Your Automotive Workshop on a Budget *(SA207)*
Automotive Electrical Performance Projects *(SA209)*
How to Port Cylinder Heads *(SA215)*
Muscle Car Interior Restoration Guide *(SA167)*
High Performance Jeep Wrangler TJ Builder's Guide: 1997-2006 *(SA120P)*
Dyno Testing & Tuning *(SA138P)*
How to Rebuild Any Automotive Engine *(SA151P)*
Muscle Car Interior Restoration Guide *(SA167P)*
How to Build Horsepower - Volume 2 *(SA52P)*
Bolt-Together Street Rods *(SA72P)*

HISTORIES & PERSONALITIES

Fuelies: Fuel Injected Corvettes 1957–1965 *(CT452)*
Yenko *(CT485)*
Lost Hot Rods *(CT487)*
Grumpy's Toys *(CT489)*
Rusted Muscle — A collection of junkyard muscle cars. *(CT492)*
America's Coolest Station Wagons *(CT493)*
Super Stock — A paperback version of a classic best seller. *(CT495)*
Rusty Pickups: American Workhorses Put to Pasture *(CT496)*
Jerry Heasley's Rare Finds — Great collection of Heasley's best finds. *(CT497)*
Street Sleepers: The Art of the Deceptively Fast Car *(CT498)*
Ed 'Big Daddy' Roth — Paperback reprint of a classic best seller. *(CT500)*
Rat Rods: Rodding's Imperfect Stepchildren *(CT486)*
East vs. West: Rods, Customs Rails *(CT501)*
Car Spy: Secret Cars Exposed by the Industry's Most Notorious Photographer *CT502*

CarTech®, Inc. 39966 Grand Ave., North Branch, MN 55056. Ph: 800-551-4754 or 651-277-1200 • Fax: 651-277-1203
Brooklands Books Ltd., PO Box 146 Cobham, Surrey KT11 1LG, England. Ph: 01932 865051 • Fax 01932 868803
Brooklands Books Aus., 3/37-39 Green Streeet, Banksmeadow, NSW 2019, Australia. Ph: 2 9695 7055 • Fax 2 9695 7355

Visit us online at
www.cartechbooks.com *for more info!*

Additional books that may interest you...

HOW TO REBUILD THE BIG-BLOCK MOPAR by Arvid Svendsen The Chrysler R and RB engines—360, 383, 400, 413, and 440 built from 1958 to 1976—have powered millions of muscle cars and typical passenger cars. But there comes a time in every engine's life when a rebuild is required for reliability, fuel efficiency, and improved performance. Author Arvid Svendsen takes you through each crucial step of the rebuild process, so you can rebuild your big-block Mopar with confidence and attain professional results. He also takes the rebuild process one step further by providing balancing, blueprinting, and upgraded parts selection, so you can build a high-performance big-block for race or street. Softbound, 8.5 x 11 inches, 144 pages, 400 color photos. *Item # SA197*

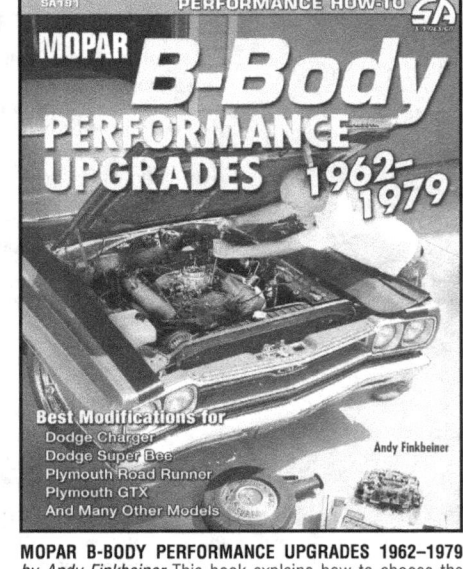

MOPAR B-BODY PERFORMANCE UPGRADES 1962–1979 by Andy Finkbeiner This book explains how to choose the ideal heads, cams, intake, and carb for a complete top-end performance package. In addition, the author discusses and explains the building of a stroker engine as well as considerations for engine swaps. Manual and automatic transmissions swaps are also discussed. When going fast, you must be able to stop, so substantial brake upgrades are a necessity. All the stock disc upgrades and aftermarket offerings are included, including Baer and Wilwood systems. Author Andrew Finkbeiner explains how to fabricate, as well as install, subframe connectors and upgrade K-frame members. Softbound, 8.5 x 11 inches, 144 pages, 400 color photos. *Item # SA191*

HOW TO BUILD MAX-PERFORMANCE MOPAR BIG-BLOCKS by Andy Finkbeiner Naturally aspirated Mopar Wedge big-blocks are quite capable of producing between 600 and 900 hp. This book covers how to build Mopar 383-, 400-, 413-, and 440-ci engines to reach these power levels. Detailed engine builds at 600-, 700-, 800-, and 900-hp levels provide insight and reveal what can be done with real-world component packages. In addition, the book explains how to optimize fresh and spent fuel, discussing single- and dual-plane intake manifolds, as well as the exhaust-system design to optimize scavenging. With this book, time, proper tools, and the right components, you can transform a stock Mopar Wedge big-block into a standout street or strip warrior. Softbound, 8.5 x 11 inches, 144 pages, 400 color photos. *Item # SA171*

HOW TO BUILD BIG-INCH MOPAR SMALL BLOCKS by Jim Szilagyi The small-block Mopar is one of the easiest engines in which to increase displacement without extensive modifications or specialized machine work—the engine was practically designed for more cubes! This book shows you how to get that big-cube power, and then it shows you how to optimize the small-block's other systems—induction, heads, valvetrain, ignition, exhaust, and more—to make the most of the extra cubic inches. Author Jim Szilagyi is a Performance Specialist for Dodge Motorsports and Mopar Performance Parts. He covers building big-inchers from Mopar 318/340/360-ci LA or Magnum 5.2-/5.9-liter engines, using both factory and aftermarket parts. The photos in this edition are black & white. Softbound, 8.5 x 11 inches, 144 pages, 350 b/w photos. *Item # SA104P*

CHECK OUT CARTECH'S NEW, IMPROVED WEB SITE!

- Find helpful tech tips & articles
- Get bonus material from our books
- Browse expanded e-book selection
- Join the discussion on our blog
- Look inside books before you buy
- Rate & review your CarTech collection
- Easy, user-friendly navigation
- Sign up to get e-mails with special offers
- Lightning fast, spot-on search results
- Secure online ordering
- 24/7 access

- Check out our Featured Weekly Ride
- Reader's Rides – Show off your car!

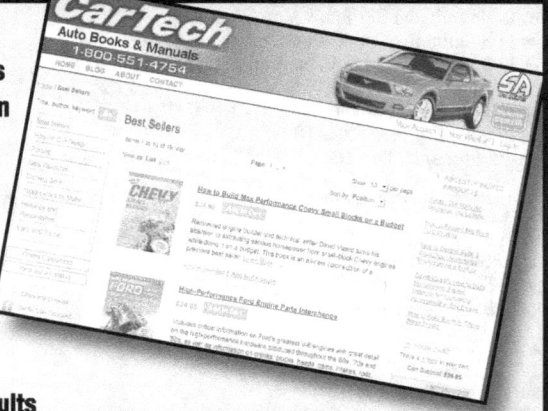

www.cartechbooks.com

www.cartechbooks.com or 1-800-551-4754

www.ingramcontent.com/pod-product-compliance
Lightning Source LLC
Chambersburg PA
CBHW051412070526

44584CB00023B/3402